LIVING *the* WORD

Scripture Reflections and Commentaries
for Sundays and Holy Days

**Laurie Brink, O.P., and
Deacon Frederick Bauerschmidt**

DECEMBER 1, 2013 THROUGH NOVEMBER 27, 2014   YEAR A

LIVING *the* WORD

Scripture Reflections and Commentaries
for Sundays and Holy Days

Vol. 29   December 1, 2013–November 27, 2014

Published annually

Individual copy: $14.95
2-9 copies: $10.95 per copy;
10-24 copies: $9.95 per copy;
25-99 copies: $8.95 per copy;
100 or more copies: $6.95 per copy

Editor: Alan J. Hommerding
Copy and Production Editor: Marcia T. Lucey
Cover Design and Typesetting: Tejal Patel
Cover Image: Matthew/winged man (angel) by Nicholas T. Markell
       www.markellstudios.com/1.651.204.5113
Director of Publications: Mary Beth Kunde-Anderson

In accordance with c. 827, with the material having been found free from any doctrinal or moral error, permission to publish is granted on August 12, 2013, by the Very Reverend John F. Canary, Vicar General of the Archdiocese of Chicago.

World Library Publications,
the music and liturgy division of J. S. Paluch Company, Inc.
3708 River Road, Suite 400, Franklin Park, IL 60131-2158
800 566-6150 • fax 888 957-3291
wlpcs@jspaluch.com • www.wlpmusic.com

Printed in the United States of America
WLP 006772 • (ISSN) 1079-4670 • (ISBN) 978-1-58459-668-4

Our liturgy presumes that those who gather for Eucharist, as members of the body of Christ, are already familiar with the word that they hear proclaimed every Sunday. *Living the Word* is designed to assist individuals, homilists, catechumens, candidates, discussion groups, religious education classes, and similar gatherings to deepen that familiarity with the Sunday scriptures.

Inside this book you will find the readings for each Sunday, holy day, and major celebration from December 2013 through November 2014, Year A of the liturgical cycle. Each day's readings are preceded by a brief passage intended to suggest a focus or approach to consider while reading these particular scriptures. The readings are followed by a commentary that provides a context for understanding them, making use of biblical scholarship and the Church's longstanding traditions. Then a reflection is offered that expands upon the initial focus and incorporates the fuller understanding from the commentary section. The discussion questions and suggestions for responses that follow are provided as helps to move from reflection to action, since the word of God always invites us to respond not only with our hearts but with our hands and lives as well.

When reflecting on the scriptures in a group setting or individually, it is best to do so in the context of prayer. Users of this book are encouraged to create an atmosphere that will foster prayerful reflection: in a quiet space, perhaps with lit candle and simple seasonal decoration (incense or soft music may also be appropriate), begin with a prayer and reading of the scriptures aloud for that day, even if you are alone. In a group, encourage members to focus on one word or idea that especially strikes them. Continue with each reading the same way, perhaps taking time to share these ideas with one another.

After you have sat quietly with the readings, ask yourself how they have changed you, enlightened you, moved you. Move on to the commentary, reflection, and response. Allow the discussion questions to shape your conversation, and try the "response" on for size. Will you rise to its challenge? Does it give you an idea of something to try in your own life? Share your ideas with someone else, even if you have been preparing alone.

Once you have spent a suitable time in reflection or discussion, you may wish to make a prayerful response to the readings by means of a song or a blessing of someone or something. Pray spontaneously as you think about the texts' meaning for you, or invite people in the group to offer prayers informally.

Finally, challenge yourself, or each other in your group, to take action this week based on your understanding of the readings. You may propose your own prayer for help to undertake this mission or simply stand in a circle and pray the Lord's Prayer. If you are in a group, offer one another a sign of peace before departing. If alone, surprise someone with a sign of peace, either in person, by making a phone call, or offering a simple prayer.

As you repeat this pattern over time, your prayerful reflection can deepen your appreciation of God's word and enable you to live it more fully every day.

Table of Contents

Prayers Before Reading Scripture

Lord Jesus,
we give you praise.
Speak to us as we read your word,
and send your Spirit into our hearts.
Guide us today and each day in your service,
for you are our way, our truth, our life.

Lord Jesus, we love you:
keep us in your love for ever and ever. Amen!

or

Blessed are you, Lord God,
king of all creation:
you have taught us by your word.
Open our hearts to your Spirit,
and lead us on the paths of Christ your Son.

All praise and glory be yours for ever. Amen!

or

Lord, open our hearts:
let your Spirit speak to us
as we read your word. Amen!

or

Lord Jesus,
to whom shall we go?
You have the words of eternal life.

Speak, Lord,
your servants are listening:
here we are, Lord,
ready to do your will. Amen!

Prayers After Reading Scripture

Blessed are you, Lord God,
maker of heaven and earth,
ruler of the universe:
you have sent your Holy Spirit
to teach your truth to your holy people.
We praise you for letting us read your word today.

Grant that we may continue to think and pray
over the words we have read,
and to share your thoughts with others
throughout this day.

Loving God, we praise you
and thank you in Jesus' name. Amen!

or

God of all graciousness, we thank you
for speaking to us today
through your holy word. Amen!

The spiritual and religious significance of Advent and Christmas are often overshadowed by the commercialism of the season. But the expectation and excitement over the holidays are found in equal measure in these two liturgical seasons. A brief introduction to each season's meaning, time frame, and general themes demonstrates that our Sunday readings are guiding the faithful to experience the ultimate holiday gift: the coming of the Messiah in the person of a tiny baby.

Advent is a celebration of awaiting the birth of Jesus and also anticipating his second coming (*parousia*). "Advent" comes from the Latin word *adventus*, which can refer to "the state of having arrived" or "being present at the arrival." It can also mean "a coming" or "an approach." We know that Jesus has already been born ("having arrived"), but we live in anxious anticipation of his "coming" again in the last days.

The themes of the Advent readings reflect a sense of expectancy. In the beginning of Advent, the focus is on eschatological and messianic expectations. Eschatology is a theology of the end-times. This thinking held that God would send a messiah who would initiate a new period in human history. Wrongs would be made right and justice would reign. On the Day of Judgment, the Lord would separate the good from the bad. As the Gospel reading for the First Sunday of Advent warns: "You also must be prepared, for at an hour you do not expect, the Son of Man will come." As Advent progresses, the focus turns to John the Baptist, who prepares the way for Jesus. Quoting the prophet Isaiah, John announces, "Prepare the way of the Lord, make straight his paths." In the final week of Advent, December 17–24, the readings describe the events that immediately precede the birth of Jesus.

During the Advent/Christmas season, while we are gathering with our families, the liturgy also focuses on the family of Jesus. This year on December 9, we will celebrate the Immaculate Conception, commemorating the mother of Jesus, born without sin so as to be the fitting bearer of the Christ. On December 29, the harrowing flight into Egypt and the slaughter of the Innocents recall the dangers endured by the Holy Family under the guidance and protection of St. Joseph.

Originally referred to as Christ's Mass in Old English, Christmas was traditionally celebrated for twelve days leading up to Epiphany. Today the liturgical season concludes with the feast of the Baptism of the Lord, celebrated on January 12. The Gospel readings for the Christmas season focus on the early life of Jesus. The Christmas day liturgy commemorates the Nativity, and Epiphany recalls the visit of the three magi from the East. After the baptism of Jesus, the Lectionary cycle returns to Ordinary Time, and the Gospel readings focus on the ministry of Jesus and his proclamation of the Reign of God.

December 1, 2013

FIRST SUNDAY OF ADVENT

Today's Focus: Wake Up—It's Advent!

As the Church's calendar turns over to a new year, we get new opportunities to re-visit our spiritual lives, and ask if we are truly ready for the Lord to come into our lives.

FIRST READING
Isaiah 2:1–5

This is what Isaiah, son of Amoz,
saw concerning Judah and Jerusalem.
    In days to come,
the mountain of the LORD's house
    shall be established as the highest mountain
    and raised above the hills.
All nations shall stream toward it;
    many peoples shall come and say:
"Come, let us climb the LORD's mountain,
    to the house of the God of Jacob,
that he may instruct us in his ways,
    and we may walk in his paths."
For from Zion shall go forth instruction,
    and the word of the LORD from Jerusalem.
He shall judge between the nations,
    and impose terms on many peoples.
They shall beat their swords into plowshares
    and their spears into pruning hooks;
one nation shall not raise the sword against another,
    nor shall they train for war again.
O house of Jacob, come,
    let us walk in the light of the LORD!

PSALM RESPONSE
Psalm 122:1

Let us go rejoicing to the house of the Lord.

SECOND READING
Romans 13: 11–14

Brothers and sisters: You know the time; it is the hour now for you to awake from sleep. For our salvation is nearer now than when we first believed; the night is advanced, the day is at hand. Let us then throw off the works of darkness and put on the armor of light; let us conduct ourselves properly as in the day, not in orgies and drunkenness, not in promiscuity and lust, not in rivalry and jealousy. But put on the Lord Jesus Christ, and make no provision for the desires of the flesh.

Rome – not a holy place

8

GOSPEL
Matthew 24:
37–44

Jesus said to his disciples: "As it was in the days of Noah, so it will be at the coming of the Son of Man. In those days before the flood, they were eating and drinking, marrying and giving in marriage, up to the day that Noah entered the ark. They did not know until the flood came and carried them all away. So will it be also at the coming of the Son of Man. Two men will be out in the field; one will be taken, and one will be left. Two women will be grinding at the mill; one will be taken, and one will be left. Therefore, stay awake! For you do not know on which day your Lord will come. Be sure of this: if the master of the house had known the hour of night when the thief was coming, he would have stayed awake and not let his house be broken into. So too, you also must be prepared, for at an hour you do not expect, the Son of Man will come."

❖ *Understanding the Word*

Today's first reading introduces the vision of God for Jerusalem as recounted by the prophet Isaiah. During the eighth century BCE (before the common era), Isaiah, a court prophet serving under the kings of Judah, announced numerous oracles indicting Jerusalem for its moral decline. The nation is filled with "people laden with wickedness/evil offspring, corrupt children!/They have forsaken the Lord/spurned the Holy One of Israel/apostatized" (Isaiah 1:4). But God anticipates a better future, a time when the house of Jacob will walk in the light of the Lord and nations will stream to the city of Jerusalem. The once unfaithful people will beat their swords into plowshares and peace will reign (Isaiah 2:4).

Nearly eight centuries after Isaiah's oracles, the apostle Paul echoes a similar plea, encouraging the Christians of Rome to put on the armor of light and to behave in a manner befitting a believer. The Roman Christians were to avoid orgies and drunkenness, sexual promiscuity, rivalry and jealousy. Paul had not visited the Roman churches. His list of vices are stereotypical behaviors associated with pagan practices, and not indicative of the Roman Christians' actual activities. Paul awaits the same just judgment that Isaiah anticipated, "For our salvation is nearer now than when we first believed" (Romans 13:11).

Many Jews in the first century believed that the coming of the Son of Man would herald the in-breaking of God, the beginning of the end-times. The Son of Man would sit as judge, dividing the good from the bad. The good would experience justice, and the bad, divine punishment. Isaiah's oracles anticipate an act of divine justice, but Matthew locates that divine justice in the person of Jesus. The early disciples of Jesus believed his return would be immediate. Paul, writing the Letter to the Romans about thirty years after the resurrection of Jesus, shared this sense of immediacy. By the time Matthew is writing in the late 80s, the urgency has lessened. In today's Gospel, the evangelist counters that complacency by reminding his community that Jesus urged believers to be ever vigilant and prepared.

Though Advent is a time of joyful expectation and not a "mini-Lent" in which we focus on repentance and reform, it is natural for us to use the closing of the calendar year and the opening of the liturgical year as an opportunity for taking stock. How do I prepare to recall in faith Christ's birth in Bethlehem, to welcome in love his daily arrival in my life, and to anticipate in hope his future coming in judgment? Though not a season of self-denial, Advent does invite us to self-scrutiny and preparation.

This Sunday's second reading suggests that perhaps the main thing we need to do is to wake up: "it is the hour now for you to awake from sleep." The twentieth-century Protestant theologian Karl Barth suggested that sin, rather than always being a "heroic" act of pride, often takes "the quite unheroic and trivial form of sloth." Many times we stumble into our sins; we acquire patterns of bad behavior through inattention and carelessness; we follow the allure of what seems to be the easier path. If we think of Lent as the season in which we turn away from the actions that keep us from God, perhaps Advent is the season in which we stir ourselves out of our spiritual lethargy and begin, as the first reading says, "to walk in the light of the LORD."

In our newly awakened state, we are not simply alert to the return of Jesus in the future; we are also attentive to the tasks to which he calls us in the here and now: the task of listening to the word of instruction that comes forth from God, the task of turning weapons of war into instruments of cultivation, the task of casting off the works of darkness and donning the armor of light.

✤ Consider/Discuss

- What are my "sins of sloth"—the things that I leave undone, or the things that I do because it seems the easier path?

- What opportunities does Advent present for me to walk in the light of the Lord? How are these sorts of activities different from the hustle and bustle of the secular "Christmas season"?

✤ Responding to the Word

Lord God, wake us up in this Advent season. Poke and prod us out of our sloth. Make us awake and aware of all of the ways in which you are present now in our world, and keep us waiting in joy-filled hope for the return of your Son Jesus. Amen.

December 8, 2013

SECOND SUNDAY OF ADVENT

Today's Focus: John the Baptist and
Jesus Fulfill Isaiah's Prophecy

Throughout Advent we are given stern warnings and hopeful promises: Advent is a both/and season: both warnings and promises, preparing us for the coming of Christ both at Christmas and the end of time.

FIRST READING
Isaiah 11:1–10

On that day, a shoot shall sprout from the stump of Jesse,
    and from his roots a bud shall blossom.
The spirit of the Lord shall rest upon him:
    a spirit of wisdom and of understanding,
    a spirit of counsel and of strength,
        a spirit of knowledge and of fear of the LORD,
        and his delight shall be the fear of the LORD.
Not by appearance shall he judge,
    nor by hearsay shall he decide,
but he shall judge the poor with justice,
    and decide aright for the land's afflicted.
He shall strike the ruthless with the rod of his mouth,
    and with the breath of his lips he shall slay the wicked.
Justice shall be the band around his waist,
    and faithfulness a belt upon his hips.
Then the wolf shall be a guest of the lamb,
    and the leopard shall lie down with the kid;
the calf and the young lion shall browse together,
    with a little child to guide them.
The cow and the bear shall be neighbors,
    together their young shall rest;
    the lion shall eat hay like the ox.
The baby shall play by the cobra's den,
    and the child lay his hand on the adder's lair.
There shall be no harm or ruin on all my holy mountain;
    for the earth shall be filled with knowledge of the LORD,
    as water covers the sea.
On that day, the root of Jesse,
    set up as a signal for the nations,
the Gentiles shall seek out,
    for his dwelling shall be glorious.

PSALM RESPONSE
Psalm 72:7

Justice shall flourish in his time, and fullness of peace for ever.

SECOND READING
Romans 15: 4–9

Brothers and sisters: Whatever was written previously was written for our instruction, that by endurance and by the encouragement of the Scriptures we might have hope. May the God of endurance and encouragement grant you to think in harmony with one another, in keeping with Christ Jesus, that with one accord you may with one voice glorify the God and Father of our Lord Jesus Christ.

Welcome one another, then, as Christ welcomed you, for the glory of God. For I say that Christ became a minister of the circumcised to show God's truthfulness, to confirm the promises to the patriarchs, but so that the Gentiles might glorify God for his mercy. As it is written:

> Therefore, I will praise you among the Gentiles
> and sing praises to your name.

GOSPEL
Matthew 3: 1–12

John the Baptist appeared, preaching in the desert of Judea and saying, "Repent, for the kingdom of heaven is at hand!" It was of him that the prophet Isaiah had spoken when he said:

A *voice of one crying out in the desert,*
Prepare the way of the Lord,
make straight his paths.

John wore clothing made of camel's hair and had a leather belt around his waist. His food was locusts and wild honey. At that time Jerusalem, all Judea, and the whole region around the Jordan were going out to him and were being baptized by him in the Jordan River as they acknowledged their sins.

When he saw many of the Pharisees and Sadducees coming to his baptism, he said to them, "You brood of vipers! Who warned you to flee from the coming wrath? Produce good fruit as evidence of your repentance. And do not presume to say to yourselves, 'We have Abraham as our father.' For I tell you, God can raise up children to Abraham from these stones. Even now the ax lies at the root of the trees. Therefore every tree that does not bear good fruit will be cut down and thrown into the fire. I am baptizing you with water, for repentance, but the one who is coming after me is mightier than I. I am not worthy to carry his sandals. He will baptize you with the Holy Spirit and fire. His winnowing fan is in his hand. He will clear his threshing floor and gather his wheat into his barn, but the chaff he will burn with unquenchable fire."

❖ Understanding the Word

Against the warnings of the prophet Samuel (1 Samuel 8), Israel desired a king, one who would protect the people from mightier nations. Samuel had warned them of the costs. He would commandeer their sons and use their daughters. He would take their best fields and tithe their flocks. But in today's reading, Isaiah describes a very different ruler. He will embody the ancient ideals of a good and just king, one upon whom God's spirit will rest. He will be a shoot from the stump of Jesse, that is, a king of the line of David. Though likely not speaking of any specific historical king of his day, Isaiah's oracle of the coming of a just and holy king becomes associated with Jesus.

The book of the prophet Isaiah became an important lens through which the Apostle Paul and later evangelists come to understand Jesus' life and ministry. Paul acknowledges, "For whatever was written previously was written for our instruction" (Romans 15:4). In his letter to the Christians in Rome, Paul associates Jesus with the lineage of Jesse, the father of David. Encouraging the Gentile believers in the Roman church, Paul reminds them that Christ ministered to the circumcised in order to confirm God's promises to the patriarchs. Quoting Isaiah, Paul also notes that the Gentile believers have a role to play. They are to glorify God for God's mercy.

In today's Gospel reading, the prophet Isaiah is invoked again. John the Baptist is "the voice of one crying out in the desert, Prepare the way of the Lord" of whom Isaiah had prophesied. John is blunt in his critique of the Pharisees and Sadducees coming for his baptism of repentance. They are "a brood of vipers" who are to produce good fruit as evidence of their repentance. John is preparing the way for "one mightier than he," whose baptism of the Holy Spirit and fire will separate the wheat from the chaff. Matthew makes several references to separating the good from the bad, which likely refers to his community's concern for rooting out those who were not appropriate members. As John the Baptist recognizes, it is only the one who is mightier—Jesus—who will make those judgments.

❖ Reflecting on the Word

In the prophet Isaiah we read of the blossoming forth of King David's lineage in the one who is endowed with God's Spirit. We also hear of all the good things that will come from this blossoming forth: righteous judgment, the restoration of the peace and integrity of creation, the restoration of true knowledge of God to all the world's peoples. It is passages such as this that Paul probably has in mind when he speaks of the encouragement provided by scripture that allows our hope to endure. Having some vision of the goal of one's journey is necessary to sustain us as we endure the hardships of the journey. It is because we trust in God's promise of a glorious future for all creation that we can continue our journey toward God's kingdom.

13

But John the Baptist, in our Gospel reading, takes a somewhat different approach. It is as if he wants to warn his listeners that hope in the promise of a glorious future is not sufficient if we want to be a part of God's kingdom. It seems that some of his listeners, having heard the encouragement of scripture, were presuming that simply being descendants of Abraham was sufficient to ensure them a place in God's kingdom. Rather than being sustained by the promises of scripture, they had become over-stuffed and self-satisfied. To them, John issues a stern warning, and it is one that we ought hear as well. We must repent so that our lives might be like trees bearing good fruit.

Along with this stern warning, however, John also issues a promise, the promise of a mighty one who will baptize us with the Holy Spirit and fire. This promise might sound at first like a threat, since fire can be destructive. But fire is also purifying, and the promise John makes is that the fire of God's Spirit will purify our hope, free us from self-satisfaction and complacency, and endow us with the gifts Isaiah speaks about: wisdom and understanding, counsel and strength, knowledge and reverence and fear of the Lord. Guided by the Spirit, we seek to walk that fine line between confidence and complacency, trusting in the promise of Christ while also heeding the demands of the gospel.

❖ Consider/Discuss

- What is the vision of God's kingdom that sustains my hope? How do I imagine the fulfillment of God's promise to creation?
- How do I distinguish between appropriate self-esteem and harmful self-satisfaction?

❖ Responding to the Word

Spirit of God, sustain us by the vision of God's kingdom, where there will be fullness of peace forever. Give us the gifts we need to bear good fruit as we await the coming in glory of our savior, Jesus Christ. Amen.

December 9, 2013

IMMACULATE CONCEPTION OF THE BLESSED VIRGIN MARY

Today's Focus: The Immaculate Conception
Reveals Our Life in Christ

In so many ways, Mary shows us how to be ready to welcome Christ into our lives. Freed from the ultimate power of original sin in our baptism, we still must strive to free ourselves from the effects of sin day by day.

FIRST READING
Genesis 3: 9–15, 20

After the man, Adam, had eaten of the tree, the LORD God called to the man and asked him, "Where are you?" He answered, "I heard you in the garden; but I was afraid, because I was naked, so I hid myself." Then he asked, "Who told you that you were naked? You have eaten, then, from the tree of which I had forbidden you to eat!" The man replied, "The woman whom you put here with me—she gave me fruit from the tree, and so I ate it." The LORD God then asked the woman, "Why did you do such a thing?" The woman answered, "The serpent tricked me into it, so I ate it."

Then the LORD God said to the serpent:
"Because you have done this, you shall be banned
    from all the animals
    and from all the wild creatures;
on your belly shall you crawl,
    and dirt shall you eat
    all the days of your life.
I will put enmity between you and the woman,
    and between your offspring and hers;
he will strike at your head,
    while you strike at his heel."
The man called his wife Eve, because she became the mother of all the living.

PSALM RESPONSE
Psalm 98:1a

Sing to the Lord a new song, for he has done marvelous deeds.

SECOND READING
Ephesians 1: 3–6, 11–12

Brothers and sisters: Blessed be the God and Father of our Lord Jesus Christ, who has blessed us in Christ with every spiritual blessing in the heavens, as he chose us in him, before the foundation of the world, to be holy and without blemish before him. In love he destined us for adoption to himself through Jesus Christ, in accord with the favor of his will, for the praise of the glory of his grace that he granted us in the beloved.

In him we were also chosen, destined in accord with the purpose of the One who accomplishes all things according to the intention of his will, so that we might exist for the praise of his glory, we who first hoped in Christ.

GOSPEL
Luke 1:26–38

The angel Gabriel was sent from God to a town of Galilee called Nazareth, to a virgin betrothed to a man named Joseph, of the house of David, and the virgin's name was Mary. And coming to her, he said, "Hail, full of grace! The Lord is with you." But she was greatly troubled at what was said and pondered what sort of greeting this might be. Then the angel said to her, "Do not be afraid, Mary, for you have found favor with God. Behold, you will conceive in your womb and bear a son, and you shall name him Jesus. He will be great and will be called Son of the Most High, and the Lord God will give him the throne of David his father, and he will rule over the house of Jacob forever, and of his kingdom there will be no end." But Mary said to the angel, "How can this be, since I have no relations with a man?" And the angel said to her in reply, "The Holy Spirit will come upon you, and the power of the Most High will overshadow you. Therefore the child to be born will be called holy, the Son of God. And behold, Elizabeth, your relative, has also conceived a son in her old age, and this is the sixth month for her who was called barren; for nothing will be impossible for God." Mary said, "Behold, I am the handmaid of the Lord. May it be done to me according to your word." Then the angel departed from her.

❖ Understanding the Word

Many of the narratives in Genesis 1—11 are etiological—they explain the origins of certain practices, rules, and behaviors. Why do humans wear clothes? Why does child-bearing cause pain? Why do we have to work so hard? But these first eleven chapters also depict the introduction of evil into the created realm. Genesis 3 describes God's discovery that the man and woman have disobeyed. Having eaten of the tree of the knowledge of good and evil, the first couple recognizes that they are naked, and when they hear God's voice they try to hide. The story becomes the foundation of the later theology of original sin. But despite their disobedience and God's punishment, today's reading ends with a note of hope. The experience has earned the woman a new name: Eve. She is the mother of all of living (Genesis 3:20). This profound misstep has not ended human potential, and as today's feast of the Immaculate Conception celebrates, God can enter into human existence through divine grace and wipe the slate clean.

As the second reading confirms, despite our sin, God's grace is lavished upon humanity. Through Christ, we have been chosen "before the foundation of the world, to be holy and without blemish before God" (Ephesians 1:4). Christ redeems humanity from its transgressions, and the Holy Spirit stands as proof of our redemption.

16

But in order for Christ to effect our salvation, Jesus himself needed be free of the stain of original sin. The dogma of the Immaculate Conception holds that Mary, the mother of Jesus, was a human being conceived without sin, making her the fitting vessel for the sinless Son of God. The idea isn't found in in today's Gospel, which describes Mary's encounter with the angel Gabriel. What is reported is that a young woman is invited to become the bearer of a holy child, conceived in an extraordinary way by the Holy Spirit of the Most High. Our readings bring us full circle. The disobedience of the first human couple stands in stark comparison with the obedience of the young woman, whose Magnificat sets in motion the process of redemption—"for nothing will be impossible for God" (Luke 1:37).

✢ Reflecting on the Word

A certain sort of knowledgeable Catholic can be a bit disdainful of those—including a number of Roman Catholics—who get confused concerning the Immaculate Conception, thinking that is refers to the virginal conception of Jesus without a human father rather than to the conception of Mary without original sin. Such condescension is probably not warranted; after all, the feast does fall during Advent, when we are focused on the incarnation of God in Christ. Moreover, Mary's immaculate conception is intimately related to the mystery of the Incarnation, since it is in order that she might be a fitting mother for the God-made-flesh that Mary is preserved from original sin. So while the Immaculate Conception is something we believe about Mary, it is also closely related to our beliefs about Jesus as God incarnate.

This feast also tells us something about our own life in Christ. If we are going to be able to say "yes" to God, to follow where God calls us to go, we must, like Mary, let God free us from the bonds of sin that hold us back. Mary's capacity to receive God's gift by saying, "May it be done to me according to your word" was itself a gift that she received from God. We speak of Mary as "full of grace" because her life was one that from the beginning was saturated by God's gift of love, a love that enabled her yes. We must come to see that our yes to God is similarly soaked in the gift of divine love. Our trust in this love is the source of our hope in this Advent season.

✢ Consider/Discuss

- When have I found myself free to say yes to God? When have I felt hindered in saying yes?
- How is Mary a model for us in our lives as followers of Jesus?

✢ Responding to the Word

Lord God, you kept Mary from being touched by sin from the moment of her conception, and in our baptism you free us from that same sin. Make us free to say yes to your call and—like her—to follow the way of your Son, Jesus Christ. Amen.

December 15, 2013

THIRD SUNDAY OF ADVENT

Today's Focus: "Rejoice!" God Continues to Bless Us

We must continually seek for what brings us true joy. Not mere happiness about the way things are going, but a deeper joy that sustains us through all our days, as we wait for the coming of Christ.

FIRST READING
Isaiah 35: 1–6a, 10

The desert and the parched land will exult;
   the steppe will rejoice and bloom.
They will bloom with abundant flowers,
   and rejoice with joyful song.
The glory of Lebanon will be given to them,
   the splendor of Carmel and Sharon;
they will see the glory of the LORD,
   the splendor of our God.
Strengthen the hands that are feeble,
   make firm the knees that are weak,
say to those whose hearts are frightened:
   Be strong, fear not!
Here is your God,
   he comes with vindication;
with divine recompense
   he comes to save you.
Then will the eyes of the blind be opened,
   the ears of the deaf be cleared;
then will the lame leap like a stag,
   then the tongue of the mute will sing.

Those whom the LORD has ransomed will return
   and enter Zion singing,
   crowned with everlasting joy;
they will meet with joy and gladness,
   sorrow and mourning will flee.

PSALM RESPONSE
Isaiah 35:4

Lord, come and save us.

SECOND READING
James 5:7–10

Be patient, brothers and sisters, until the coming of the Lord. See how the farmer waits for the precious fruit of the earth, being patient with it until it receives the early and the late rains. You too must be patient. Make your hearts firm, because the coming of the Lord is at hand. Do not complain, brothers and sisters, about one another, that you may not be judged. Behold, the Judge is standing before the gates. Take as an example of hardship and patience, brothers and sisters, the prophets who spoke in the name of the Lord.

GOSPEL
Matthew 11:
2–11

When John the Baptist heard in prison of the works of the Christ, he sent his disciples to Jesus with this question, "Are you the one who is to come, or should we look for another?" Jesus said to them in reply, "Go and tell John what you hear and see: the blind regain their sight, the lame walk, lepers are cleansed, the deaf hear, the dead are raised, and the poor have the good news proclaimed to them. And blessed is the one who takes no offense at me."

As they were going off, Jesus began to speak to the crowds about John, "What did you go out to the desert to see? A reed swayed by the wind? Then what did you go out to see? Someone dressed in fine clothing? Those who wear fine clothing are in royal palaces. Then why did you go out? To see a prophet? Yes, I tell you, and more than a prophet. This is the one about whom it is written:

> Behold, I am sending my messenger ahead of you;
> he will prepare your way before you.

Amen, I say to you, among those born of women there has been none greater than John the Baptist; yet the least in the kingdom of heaven is greater than he."

❖ Understanding the Word

The coming of the glory of God transforms everything, announces the prophet Isaiah. The wilderness and dry land will exult and the desert of Arabia will bloom. Those who have grown weak and fearful will be renewed. No intermediaries are mentioned. The living God will appear and bring salvation. This appearance of God will bring sight to the blind, hearing to the deaf, and mobility to the lame. Both land and people will be renewed and transformed.

In today's second reading from the Letter of James, the author is encouraging his community to be patient, despite the delay of the *Parousia*, the second coming of Christ. The Letter of James is a collection of sayings and admonitions likely directed at a community that had grown lax in its moral and ethical response to the gospel. James charges them not to complain or to judge one another, but rather to endure patiently and await the coming of the Lord.

Though Luke's Gospel presents John the Baptist and Jesus as relatives, Mark is probably more accurate when he reports that John the Baptist made inquiries as to Jesus' identity. "Are you the one who is to come, or should we look for another?" Jesus doesn't disparage John for his question. Instead he acknowledges his greatness. John has prepared the way for Jesus, just as scripture had foretold.

All three of our readings today focus on the divine one who is to come. In Isaiah, it is the manifestation of God whose coming will renew and heal. For James, it is the return of Jesus, who as Messiah will be the just judge. And Mark's Gospel shows that the exact identity of that Messiah—the one who is to come—is not certain. Jesus' answer to John's question is simply to point out what he has accomplished: the blind see, the lame walk, lepers are cleansed, the deaf hear, the dead are raised, and the poor have good news proclaimed to them. John the Baptist could hardly miss the parallel: the actions of Jesus are the same as the manifestations of the divine presence in Isaiah.

The traditional name of this Sunday, *Gaudete*, derives from the text of the official entrance chant for this day: "Rejoice in the Lord always." This theme is also reflected in the first reading, which speaks of the earth itself rejoicing as the desert blooms forth. But this reading also speaks of the earth waiting to rejoice. The redemption of God, which is the cause of our rejoicing, lies still in the future: the eyes of the blind will be opened, the tongue of the mute will sing, sorrow and mourning will flee. We do rejoice, but it is the particular kind of joy that is to be found in waiting for the source of our joy.

One of the tensions we experience in celebrating the season of Advent today is the tendency of the modern secular world to turn it into Christmas, with decorations going up the day after Thanksgiving—if not well before—and a busy round of Christmas parties. I have even seen an advertisement for an "after Christmas" sale that began on December 23! Rather than a season of joyful waiting, Advent becomes the season of immediate Christmas gratification. Those of us who want to keep Advent as a season of expectation might be tempted to adopt a "Bah! Humbug!" attitude toward the festivities of December. But perhaps we should be more forgiving of those who tend to rush the Christmas season. After all, the joy-in-waiting of Advent is rooted in our faith that Jesus is the one who is to come; we do not have to wait for another. The Lord is at hand; indeed, in Jesus Christ our redeemer is already here. While it is important that Advent be a season of waiting, it is also a season of joy, and when we encounter Christmas decorations in the midst of Advent, we should probably recall the words of James in the second reading: "Do not complain, brothers and sisters, about one another."

✦ *Consider/Discuss*

- What has brought me joy thus far in this Advent season?
- How do I try to keep Advent a season of waiting? How do I react to those who do not make the same choices that I do?

✦ *Responding to the Word*

God our redeemer, may our hearts rejoice and bloom with joyful song this Advent. May we recognize in Christ the one whom we await, the one who has come to heal and save. Amen.

December 22, 2013

FOURTH SUNDAY OF ADVENT

Today's Focus: Remain Open to God—
You Might Be Surprised

Sometimes we need to re-evaluate and reconsider our actions as the Spirit continues to work in our lives. On occasion we, like Joseph, have to put aside expectations and plans to do the will of God.

FIRST READING
Isaiah 7:10–14

The LORD spoke to Ahaz, saying: Ask for a sign from the LORD, your God; let it be deep as the netherworld, or high as the sky! But Ahaz answered, "I will not ask! I will not tempt the LORD!" Then Isaiah said: Listen, O house of David! Is it not enough for you to weary people, must you also weary my God? Therefore the LORD himself will give you this sign: the virgin shall conceive, and bear a son, and shall name him Emmanuel.

PSALM RESPONSE
Psalm 24:7c, 10b

Let the Lord enter; he is king of glory.

SECOND READING
Romans 1:1–7

Paul, a slave of Christ Jesus, called to be an apostle and set apart for the gospel of God, which he promised previously through his prophets in the holy Scriptures, the gospel about his Son, descended from David according to the flesh, but established as Son of God in power according to the Spirit of holiness through resurrection from the dead, Jesus Christ our Lord. Through him we have received the grace of apostleship, to bring about the obedience of faith, for the sake of his name, among all the Gentiles, among whom are you also, who are called to belong to Jesus Christ; to all the beloved of God in Rome, called to be holy. Grace to you and peace from God our Father and the Lord Jesus Christ.

GOSPEL
Matthew 1:
18–24

This is how the birth of Jesus Christ came about. When his mother Mary was betrothed to Joseph, but before they lived together, she was found with child through the Holy Spirit. Joseph her husband, since he was a righteous man, yet unwilling to expose her to shame, decided to divorce her quietly. Such was his intention when, behold, the angel of the Lord appeared to him in a dream and said, "Joseph, son of David, do not be afraid to take Mary your wife into your home. For it is through the Holy Spirit that this child has been conceived in her. She will bear a son and you are to name him Jesus, because he will save his people from their sins." All this took place to fulfill what the Lord had said through the prophet:

> *Behold, the virgin shall conceive and bear a son,*
> *and they shall name him Emmanuel,*
> which means "God is with us."

When Joseph awoke, he did as the angel of the Lord had commanded him and took his wife into his home.

✦ Understanding the Word

The reading from the prophet Isaiah announces hope for the beleaguered king and people of Judah. Having refused to revolt with Israel and Aram against the Assyrian overlords, Ahaz and the kingdom of Judah are now under attack by their very neighbors. God offers Ahaz a sign: a maiden shall be with child and will bear a son who shall be named Immanuel. The prophecy of Isaiah likely referred to the birth of Ahaz's heir, indicating that the rule of a Davidic king would not end. The evangelist Matthew understood the prophecy as heralding the coming of Jesus.

Paul also saw the coming of Christ as revealed in the Old Testament. He begins his Letter to the Romans by acknowledging that the gospel, the good news, about Christ Jesus is announced by the prophets (Romans 1:2), but is only fully realized in his resurrection from the dead.

This Sunday's Gospel reading introduces the story of Jesus' conception and birth through the eyes of Joseph. As the main character, Joseph is privileged with angelic encounters. An angel appears in a dream and tells him not to divorce Mary. Later the angel of the Lord will appear to Joseph in a dream to warn that he must take his family to Egypt (Matthew 2:13) and again when it is safe to return to Israel (Matthew 2:19). Finally, Joseph will be told in a dream to go to Galilee rather than Judea.

Joseph is called a righteous man and is concerned about Mary's reputation when he discovers she is pregnant. He plans a quiet divorce, until an angel appears to him in a dream and explains the situation. Matthew's understanding of who Jesus is—his Christology—is evident in the naming of the baby. The angel tells Joseph to call him Jesus, "because he will save his people from their sins." The name Jesus is derived from the Hebrew *Yehoshua*, meaning "the Lord is salvation," which is a longer version of Joshua. The baby will fulfill the prophecy of Isaiah: This Jesus will also be known as Immanuel, "God with us." So in Matthew's account of the naming of Jesus, he is both God's salvation and God incarnate.

22

We tend to think that with careful planning we can know ahead of time what the right—the "proper"—course of action is. We have some idea of what situations might arise and what good people do in a given situation. But sometimes we do not fully understand what the true situation is, and how our ideas about what is proper might or might not apply. This seems to be particularly the case when God enters into the equation.

In today's Gospel reading, Joseph is faced with a situation that he thinks he understands: his fiancée has become pregnant by another man. He prepares to do the proper thing and quietly break off the betrothal. This is not only "proper" but, given the situation as he understands it, it is even merciful, since it will spare Mary some measure of shame. But the situation is not what he thinks it is, and when the angel of the Lord appears to him in a dream and tells him that Mary has not been unfaithful, but rather has conceived her child through the Holy Spirit, Joseph has to rethink what the proper course of action is. He realizes that he has been playing according to the wrong rulebook. Part of what makes Joseph a truly honorable man is his willingness to rethink how an honorable man acts once God enters the picture in an unexpected way.

Our faith tells us that God is always entering the picture, and not only when angels appear to us in dreams. In every situation we have to be open to rethinking our notions of what is proper. It is of course a good thing to develop a sense of what is the fitting thing to do in a given situation, but as Advent moves toward Christmas we are reminded of God's capacity to surprise us, forcing us in turn to act in surprising ways.

✤✤ *Consider/Discuss*

- Have there been occasions when I was sure of the proper course of action and been forced to rethink things when I have come to a new understanding of the situation?
- How do situations look different once I put God into the equation?

✤✤ *Responding to the Word*

Lord God, help us always to remember that you are at work in our lives and in the lives of those around us. Deliver us from the presumption of thinking we know ahead of time the proper response to your surprising presence in our world. Amen.

December 25, 2013

CHRISTMAS: MASS DURING THE DAY

Today's Focus: The Heart of Christmas:
Christ Comes to Dwell Among Us

To get at the heart of Christmas we need to look past the surface details of the Christmas narratives and of our own celebrations. We must probe deeper to find the mystery of God-among-us in Jesus Christ.

FIRST READING
Isaiah 52:7–10

How beautiful upon the mountains
  are the feet of him who brings glad tidings,
announcing peace, bearing good news,
  announcing salvation, and saying to Zion,
"Your God is King!"

Hark! Your sentinels raise a cry,
  together they shout for joy,
for they see directly, before their eyes,
  the LORD restoring Zion.
Break out together in song,
  O ruins of Jerusalem!
For the LORD comforts his people,
  he redeems Jerusalem.
The LORD has bared his holy arm
  in the sight of all the nations;
all the ends of the earth will behold
  the salvation of our God.

PSALM RESPONSE
Psalm 98:3c

All the ends of the earth have seen the saving power of God.

SECOND READING
Hebrews 1:1–6

Brothers and sisters: In times past, God spoke in partial and various ways to our ancestors through the prophets; in these last days, he has spoken to us through the Son, whom he made heir of all things and through whom he created the universe, who is the refulgence of his glory, the very imprint of his being, and who sustains all things by his mighty word. When he had accomplished purification from sins, he took his seat at the right hand of the Majesty on high, as far superior to the angels as the name he has inherited is more excellent than theirs.

For to which of the angels did God ever say:
  You are my son; this day I have begotten you?
Or again:
  I will be a father to him, and he shall be a son to me?
And again, when he leads the firstborn into the world, he says:
  Let all the angels of God worship him.

In the shorter form of the reading, the passages in brackets are omitted.

GOSPEL
John 1:1–18
or 1:1–5, 9–14

In the beginning was the Word,
   and the Word was with God,
   and the Word was God.
He was in the beginning with God.
All things came to be through him,
   and without him nothing came to be.
What came to be through him was life,
   and this life was the light of the human race;
the light shines in the darkness,
   and the darkness has not overcome it.

[A man named John was sent from God. He came for testimony, to testify to the light, so that all might believe through him. He was not the light, but came to testify to the light.] The true light, which enlightens everyone, was coming into the world.
He was in the world,
   and the world came to be through him,
   but the world did not know him.
He came to what was his own,
   but his own people did not accept him.

But to those who did accept him he gave power to become children of God, to those who believe in his name, who were born not by natural generation nor by human choice nor by a man's decision but of God.

And the Word became flesh
   and made his dwelling among us,
   and we saw his glory,
   the glory as of the Father's only Son,
   full of grace and truth.

[John testified to him and cried out, saying, "This was he of whom I said, 'The one who is coming after me ranks ahead of me because he existed before me.' " From his fullness we have all received, grace in place of grace, because while the law was given through Moses, grace and truth came through Jesus Christ. No one has ever seen God. The only Son, God, who is at the Father's side, has revealed him.]

The book of Isaiah is a compilation of oracles and poems composed over hundreds of years by at least three different writers. Chapters 1–39 are the work of Isaiah of Jerusalem, who lived in the eighth century BCE, shortly after Assyria had destroyed the northern kingdom. Chapters 40–55 were composed by "Second" Isaiah, an unnamed prophet writing in the late sixth century, on the cusp of the exiles' return to Jerusalem. The focus in Second Isaiah is on hope and restoration. Chapters 56–66 are from another anonymous prophet writing in the name of Isaiah. Today's first reading demonstrates the joy and expectancy characteristic of much of Second Isaiah. The glad tidings and good news is that God is King and comes to restore Zion.

The reading from Hebrews seems to pick up from Second Isaiah. This redeemer whom Isaiah foretold is in reality God's Son. Originally part of a hymn, verses 3–4 describe this Son as pre-existent heir, in terms reminiscent of Wisdom in the Old Testament. Once he had accomplished the "purification of sin" he returned to the right hand of God. Since he is begotten of God, this Son ranks even higher than angels. The Letter to the Hebrews is actually a sermon in letter format, and at one time had been ascribed to Paul. It reflects on the death of Jesus as a saving act and finds support and direction from Old Testament texts.

John's Gospel does not begin with the nativity of Jesus. Rather, it reaches further back to the moment before creation. In the beginning, God and the Word existed and through the Word all things came to be. This Word stands as a beacon to human beings. John the Baptist testified to the coming of this light, and acknowledges that Jesus ranks ahead of him. This exalted, pre-existent Word became incarnate and lived among human beings. Like the reading from Hebrews, John is describing Jesus through a particular philosophical lens. Luke and Matthew tell a story of the birth, but John the Evangelist interprets Jesus' birth as the profound act of humility: the Word taking on flesh in order to reveal God to us—the ultimate Christmas gift.

Some people love the "making of" video that often accompanies movies on DVD, which takes viewers behind the scenes and gives them a different way of thinking about the film they have enjoyed. The Christmas Mass during the Night, commonly known as Midnight Mass, offers us the familiar Christmas story from Luke, but the Mass During the Day presents us with the beginning of John's Gospel and a different way of thinking about the mystery of the Incarnation. We might think of it as a "peek behind the scenes" of the beloved story of Mary and Joseph and Jesus.

John tells us that the Word who becomes flesh and dwells among us in Jesus Christ is the same Word through whom God created the universe. In Jesus, God's Word is in our midst to restore creation by shining the light of God's glory in a world grown dark through sin. The Gospel of Christmas Day reminds us that the true focus of our celebration is not the birthday of Jesus many centuries ago, but the mystery of God's continuing presence with us through Christ, the source of all grace and truth, the one through whom all things were made and in whom all things will be restored.

We can sometimes sentimentalize Christmas, with rustic crèches and chubby infants in mangers. John reminds us that behind this charming scene, Christmas is about the awesome mystery of God becoming human so that we might gaze upon the glory of God and become sharers in God's own life. Amid the hallowed traditions and images of Christmas, it is good to focus on the heart of what we are celebrating: God's dwelling among us in Christ.

✥ Consider/Discuss

- What elements of the beginning of John's Gospel connect to the traditional Christmas story?
- How can I make Christmas a celebration not simply of the birthday of Jesus, but of the Incarnation as the mystery of our salvation in Christ?

✥ *Responding to the Word*

O God, you have created us through your Word, and restored us to life through that same Word made flesh. Help us to see your glory revealed in the face of Christ. Amen.

HOLY FAMILY OF JESUS, MARY, AND JOSEPH

Today's Focus: Finding True Certainty in Life's Uncertainties

According to the Gospels, the Holy Family lived through times of danger, fear, and uncertainty. But with a strong faithfulness, they endured, did God's will, and continue to be an example for all Christian households.

FIRST READING
Sirach 3:2–6, 12–14

God sets a father in honor over his children;
　a mother's authority he confirms over her sons.
Whoever honors his father atones for sins,
　and preserves himself from them.
When he prays, he is heard;
　he stores up riches who reveres his mother.
Whoever honors his father is gladdened by children,
　and, when he prays, is heard.
Whoever reveres his father will live a long life;
　he who obeys his father brings comfort to his mother.

My son, take care of your father when he is old;
　grieve him not as long as he lives.
Even if his mind fail, be considerate of him;
　revile him not all the days of his life;
kindness to a father will not be forgotten,
　firmly planted against the debt of your sins
　—a house raised in justice to you.

PSALM RESPONSE
Psalm 128:1

Blessed are those who fear the Lord and walk in his ways.

In the shorter form of the reading, the passage in brackets is omitted.

SECOND READING
Colossians 3: 12–21 or 3:12–17

Brothers and sisters: Put on, as God's chosen ones, holy and beloved, heartfelt compassion, kindness, humility, gentleness, and patience, bearing with one another and forgiving one another, if one has a grievance against another; as the Lord has forgiven you, so must you also do. And over all these put on love, that is, the bond of perfection. And let the peace of Christ control your hearts, the peace into which you were also called in one body. And be thankful. Let the word of Christ dwell in you richly, as in all wisdom you teach and admonish one another, singing psalms, hymns, and spiritual songs with gratitude in your hearts to God. And whatever you do, in word or in deed, do everything in the name of the Lord Jesus, giving thanks to God the Father through him.

[Wives, be subordinate to your husbands, as is proper in the Lord. Husbands, love your wives, and avoid any bitterness toward them. Children, obey your parents in everything, for this is pleasing to the Lord. Fathers, do not provoke your children, so they may not become discouraged.]

GOSPEL
Matthew 2:
13–15, 19–23

When the magi had departed, behold, the angel of the Lord appeared to Joseph in a dream and said, "Rise, take the child and his mother, flee to Egypt, and stay there until I tell you. Herod is going to search for the child to destroy him." Joseph rose and took the child and his mother by night and departed for Egypt. He stayed there until the death of Herod, that what the Lord had said through the prophet might be fulfilled,

Out of Egypt I *called my son.*

When Herod had died, behold, the angel of the Lord appeared in a dream to Joseph in Egypt and said, "Rise, take the child and his mother and go to the land of Israel, for those who sought the child's life are dead." He rose, took the child and his mother, and went to the land of Israel. But when he heard that Archelaus was ruling over Judea in place of his father Herod, he was afraid to go back there. And because he had been warned in a dream, he departed for the region of Galilee. He went and dwelt in a town called Nazareth, so that what had been spoken through the prophets might be fulfilled,

He *shall be called a Nazorean.*

❖❖ *Understanding the Word*

The Church celebrates the Holy Family with readings that remind us of our duties to each family member. The book of Sirach, written in Hebrew in the second century BCE and later translated into Greek by the author's grandson, is a compilation of wisdom sayings designed to direct its readers on the right moral path. In today's reading, Sirach outlines the duties that children owe their parents, particularly as the parents age.

The reading from Colossians is part of what scholars call "household codes," which were instructions for orderly and civilized behavior, beginning with the family unit. These "codes" are found throughout Greco-Roman literature. What distinguishes the New Testament household codes is their emphasis on "heartfelt compassion, kindness, humility, gentleness and patience" (Colossians 3:12). The model for behavior is Christ, and so all the members are to conduct themselves accordingly. "Whatever you do, in word or in deed, do everything in the name of the Lord Jesus" (Colossians 3:17).

The Gospel also addresses the appropriate care of the family, but this time rather than a list of duties, the evangelist recounts a harrowing tale of the Holy Family's escape from the murderous clutches of Herod the Great. In a dream, an angel of the Lord directs Joseph to flee to Egypt. Matthew notes that the stay in Egypt actually fulfills a prophecy: "Out of Egypt I called my son." Throughout the Gospel, Matthew is making comparisons between Jesus and Moses. As infants, both must be rescued from murderous tyrants. Matthew even structures the teachings of Jesus into five blocks, as a parallel to the five books of the Torah, traditionally attributed to Moses.

❖ Reflecting on the Word

As on the Fourth Sunday of Advent, here again we have Joseph receiving angelic instruction in a dream: first to flee Bethlehem for Egypt to escape King Herod's murderous plans, and later to return from Egypt once King Herod has died. In addition to paralleling events in the life of Moses, this story confronts us with the precarious and dangerous situation into which Jesus was born. From the moment of Christ's entry into our world, the powers that be seek to take his life. The shadow of the cross falls across the Christmas crib.

The danger in which the child Jesus finds himself drives home for us the way in which God, in the Incarnation, identifies with our human condition. Many families today live in precarious and dangerous situations, whether this as a result of political violence or economic deprivation. Many have to flee their homes, never knowing whether they will be able to return. Some are simply victims of circumstance; others are paying the price of one or more family members standing up for justice. Whatever the reason for their hardship, in Jesus Christ God becomes one with them.

Matthew's story of the trials of the Holy Family reminds us that holiness does not ensure that one's life will never contain uncertainty. Indeed, if we take the Holy Family as our model, then it seems that holiness—whole-hearted dedication to God's will for the world—is likely to make one's life more uncertain, not less. Yet doing the will of God is of such surpassing worth that we should be willing to embrace such uncertainty for its sake.

❖ Consider/Discuss

- How would I treat the homeless and the stranger if I could see the Holy Family in them?
- In what ways is my own life, or the life of my family, uncertain or insecure?

❖ Responding to the Word

Holy God, in Jesus you came to share not only in the love of a human family, but also in the uncertainty and danger of our lives. Help us to see you in all those families who struggle to find safety, and make us will to come to their aid for your sake. Amen.

January 1, 2014

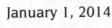

MARY, THE HOLY MOTHER OF GOD

Today's Focus: We Too Must Treasure and
Ponder God's Word

*This celebration affirms the central belief of our faith: that Jesus Christ is fully human
and fully God. As Son of Mary, he took on our full human nature; as Son of God he was
fully divine. Mary is not merely the mother of Jesus, she is the Mother of God.*

**FIRST
READING**
*Numbers 6:
22–27*

The LORD said to Moses: "Speak to Aaron and his sons and tell
them: This is how you shall bless the Israelites. Say to them:
  The LORD bless you and keep you!
  The LORD let his face shine upon you, and be gracious to you!
  The LORD look upon you kindly and give you peace!
So shall they invoke my name upon the Israelites, and I will bless
them."

**PSALM
RESPONSE**
Psalm 67:2a

May God bless us in his mercy.

**SECOND
READING**
Galatians 4:4–7

Brothers and sisters: When the fullness of time had come, God
sent his Son, born of a woman, born under the law, to ransom those
under the law, so that we might receive adoption as sons. As proof
that you are sons, God sent the Spirit of his Son into our hearts,
crying out, "Abba, Father!" So you are no longer a slave but a son,
and if a son then also an heir, through God.

GOSPEL
Luke 2:16–21

The shepherds went in haste to Bethlehem and found Mary and
Joseph, and the infant lying in the manger. When they saw this,
they made known the message that had been told them about
this child. All who heard it were amazed by what had been told
them by the shepherds. And Mary kept all these things, reflecting
on them in her heart. Then the shepherds returned, glorifying and
praising God for all they had heard and seen, just as it had been
told to them. When eight days were completed for his circumcision, he was named Jesus, the name given him by the angel before
he was conceived in the womb.

❖ Understanding the Word

The reading from Numbers is known as the "Priestly Blessing" and recounts the blessing that later Aaronite priests were to say over the people of Israel. Written in poetic form, the blessing outlines God's action toward the people (blessing, making his face shine upon them, lifting up God's countenance) and follows with the results of God's actions (keep you, be gracious, give peace). In response to this blessing, the Israelites were to bear God's name, making them a sign of God's presence, grace, and peace (Numbers 6:27).

In Paul's Letter to the Galatians, the apostle reminds the believers that they are no longer bound by the law of Moses, despite what rival evangelists were claiming. Paul believed that the law of Moses had been given to the Jews as a guide, but with the coming of Christ the law was no longer necessary. God's Son was born of a woman, under the law, so as to release those under the law. As those baptized into Christ, the Galatians are now adopted children of God who have received the Spirit of God, enabling them to call God "Abba."

The Gospel continues the story of the Nativity and seems to focus on the witness of the shepherds. They go to Bethlehem to find verification of the angels' announcement. When they find the Holy Family, they relate what had been told to them about the child, and then they return glorifying and praising God. Sandwiched between this coming and going of the shepherds is Mary's response. She treasured these words and pondered them. When the baby is presented in the temple, Simeon will address Mary directly, "and you yourself a sword will pierce" (Luke 2:35). At the close of Luke's infancy narrative—the finding of Jesus in the temple—once again Mary is said to treasure all these things in her heart (Luke 2:51). Luke presents the role of Mary as both the mother of Jesus and the perfect disciple, one who treasures and ponders God's word.

❖ Reflecting on the Word

Why, one might ask, do we have this feast of Mary on New Year's Day? What does it add to the other Marian feasts such as the Annunciation, the Assumption, Our Lady of Sorrows, the Immaculate Conception, Our Lady of Guadalupe, etc.? Is this an example of what some have called Mariolotry?

What this feast celebrates is the title of Mary as *Theotokos*, Greek for the "God-bearer," which we in the Western tradition typically translate as "Mother of God." This title became very controversial in the fifth century, when the theologian Nestorius and his followers argued that Mary should not be called "Mother of God" but rather "Mother of Jesus," since Mary gave birth to Jesus's humanity, not his divinity, implying that God was above such fundamental human experiences as birth and death. The Council of Chalcedon (451 AD) rejected this line of thinking and affirmed that all that Jesus did and underwent in his human flesh—from his birth to his crucifixion and resurrection—is something that is truly said of God the eternal Son. Because of the Incarnation, we can truly say not only that God was born of Mary, but also that God celebrated at the wedding at Cana of Galilee, wept at the tomb of Lazarus, and suffered and died on the cross.

This feast, like the Immaculate Conception, is as much about Jesus as it is about Mary. In affirming that Mary is "Mother of God," we affirm not only her special role in God's plan of salvation, but also the mystery that lies at the heart of the Christmas season: that in Jesus Christ God truly shares our human condition, that God is with us in the fundamental human experiences of birth and death, joy and sorrow. It is fitting that we celebrate this mystery as we begin a new calendar year.

❖ Consider/Discuss

- Do I have a concept of God that is so lofty that I cannot imagine God knowing "from the inside" what it means to be human?
- How does my concept of God change when I reflect on our belief that every event in Jesus' human life is an event in the life of God?

❖ Responding to the Word

Lord Jesus, in taking on human flesh you have joined yourself in love to all aspects of our human condition except sin. Help us to show that same love to all those whom we will meet in the coming year. Amen.

January 5, 2014

EPIPHANY OF THE LORD

Today's Focus: God's Wisdom Is Present Everywhere

We hear of two kinds of people today: those who are clever or crafty, and those who are truly wise, filled with the wisdom of God. Our goal is to be wise, not merely clever.

FIRST READING
Isaiah 60:1–6

Rise up in splendor, Jerusalem! Your light has come,
    the glory of the Lord shines upon you.
See, darkness covers the earth,
    and thick clouds cover the peoples;
but upon you the Lord shines,
    and over you appears his glory.
Nations shall walk by your light,
    and kings by your shining radiance.
Raise your eyes and look about;
    they all gather and come to you:
your sons come from afar,
    and your daughters in the arms of their nurses.

Then you shall be radiant at what you see,
    your heart shall throb and overflow,
for the riches of the sea shall be emptied out before you,
    the wealth of nations shall be brought to you.
Caravans of camels shall fill you,
    dromedaries from Midian and Ephah;
all from Sheba shall come
    bearing gold and frankincense,
    and proclaiming the praises of the Lord.

PSALM RESPONSE
Psalm 72:11

Lord, every nation on earth will adore you.

SECOND READING
Ephesians 3: 2–3a, 5–6

Brothers and sisters: You have heard of the stewardship of God's grace that was given to me for your benefit, namely, that the mystery was made known to me by revelation. It was not made known to people in other generations as it has now been revealed to his holy apostles and prophets by the Spirit: that the Gentiles are coheirs, members of the same body, and copartners in the promise in Christ Jesus through the gospel.

GOSPEL
Matthew 2:
1–12

When Jesus was born in Bethlehem of Judea, in the days of King Herod, behold, magi from the east arrived in Jerusalem, saying, "Where is the newborn king of the Jews? We saw his star at its rising and have come to do him homage." When King Herod heard this, he was greatly troubled, and all Jerusalem with him. Assembling all the chief priests and the scribes of the people, he inquired of them where the Christ was to be born. They said to him, "In Bethlehem of Judea, for thus it has been written through the prophet:

And you, Bethlehem, land of Judah,
   are by no means least among the rulers of Judah;
since from you shall come a ruler,
   who is to shepherd my people Israel."

Then Herod called the magi secretly and ascertained from them the time of the star's appearance. He sent them to Bethlehem and said, "Go and search diligently for the child. When you have found him, bring me word, that I too may go and do him homage." After their audience with the king they set out. And behold, the star that they had seen at its rising preceded them, until it came and stopped over the place where the child was.

They were overjoyed at seeing the star, and on entering the house they saw the child with Mary his mother. They prostrated themselves and did him homage. Then they opened their treasures and offered him gifts of gold, frankincense, and myrrh. And having been warned in a dream not to return to Herod, they departed for their country by another way.

❖ *Understanding the Word*

As mentioned earlier (see p. 26), the book of Isaiah can be divided into three sections: Chapters 1–39 are the work of Isaiah of Jerusalem, who lived in the eighth century. Chapters 40–55 were composed by "Second" Isaiah, an unnamed prophet writing in the late sixth century. Chapters 56–66 are from another anonymous prophet writing in the name of Isaiah. Today's reading comes from what scholars call "Third" Isaiah and was written when the exiles had returned to Jerusalem. The tenor is one of hope. Deliverance has come. God has renewed the covenant with the Chosen People. God's light will again emanate from Zion and nations will be drawn by this light. A caravan from the East is envisioned bringing gifts of gold and frankincense. The Gospel reading will describe just such a caravan.

The passage from Ephesians picks up this theme of recognition and inclusion depicted in Isaiah. The word that is translated as "Gentiles" in Ephesians is the Greek word *ethne*, which means both "nations" or non-Jews; hence "Gentiles." From an ancient Jewish perspective, one was either a Jew or a member of the *ethne*. Through the preaching of the Gospel, the Gentiles had become fellow heirs and members of the same body, sharing in the promises of the gospel.

In the Gospel reading, more "Gentiles" are encountered. Matthew has magi from the East seek the new king of the Jews. The Greek word *magos* originally referred to a member of the Persian priestly class. It later took on the connotation of those who engage in Eastern philosophy and science—hence magicians and astrologers. Indeed, they report seeing a star rising, which in popular understanding signaled a significant birth. But this star is unusual; it directs the magi to Bethlehem and then stands above the birthplace, which Matthew identifies as a house. The magi pay homage to the infant Jesus, presenting him with gifts befitting his life to come: gold, frankincense, and myrrh. They are warned through a dream not to return to Herod, so they go home by a different route. The magi coming from the East are meant to be understood as Persians, the one empire not conquered by Rome. Thus the magi visiting the infant Jesus foreshadow the inclusion of Gentiles in the later Christian mission.

❖ Reflecting on the Word

The story of the magi and King Herod reminds us of the difference between being "wise" and being "crafty." Though the term "magi" might more literally be translated as "astrologers" (and our word "magician" comes from it), the traditional term "wise men" does capture an aspect of their story. They are wise not simply because they are smart, but because they use their God-given intellectual abilities to seek out God, to read the signs of the times in order to discern what God is doing in the world.

King Herod, in contrast, is not so much wise as he is crafty. Historians agree that Herod was in many ways an effective ruler: rebuilding the Jerusalem temple, maintaining public order, and keeping Roman interference in day-to-day affairs in Palestine to a minimum. They also agree that in large measure his effectiveness as a ruler was a result of his absolute ruthlessness, a merciless resolve that shows itself in today's Gospel. He lies to the magi and plots the murder of a child in what seems to him to be an effective scheme to ensure that he remains in power.

But the wise understand something that the crafty do not. The feast of the Epiphany celebrates the manifestation of God's saving power in the world, not in the form of royal splendor but of a humble child born into lowly circumstances. This is a power that Herod, for all his craftiness, cannot even recognize, but which the magi, showing true wisdom, come to adore.

❖ Consider/Discuss

- What do I associate with the word "wisdom"? How is this different from being merely clever or crafty?
- How does the story of the Epiphany affect the way I see God's saving power manifested in the world today?

❖ Responding to the Word

O God, source of true wisdom, give us discerning minds to see your power at work in the humble, the poor, and the weak. Help us to manifest your love to the world through our words and actions. Amen.

January 12, 2014

BAPTISM OF THE LORD

Today's Focus: "This Is My Son, Whom I Love"

We know that God loves us. In Jesus' baptism we see our own baptismal call to live so that God will also be well pleased with us.

FIRST READING
Isaiah 42:1–4, 6–7

Thus says the LORD:
Here is my servant whom I uphold,
    my chosen one with whom I am pleased,
upon whom I have put my spirit;
    he shall bring forth justice to the nations,
not crying out, not shouting,
    not making his voice heard in the street.
A bruised reed he shall not break,
    and a smoldering wick he shall not quench,
until he establishes justice on the earth;
    the coastlands will wait for his teaching.

I, the LORD, have called you for the victory of justice,
    I have grasped you by the hand;
I formed you, and set you
    as a covenant of the people,
    a light for the nations,
to open the eyes of the blind,
    to bring out prisoners from confinement,
    and from the dungeon, those who live in darkness.

PSALM RESPONSE
Psalm 29:11b

The Lord will bless his people with peace.

SECOND READING
Acts 10:34–38

Peter proceeded to speak to those gathered in the house of Cornelius, saying: "In truth, I see that God shows no partiality. Rather, in every nation whoever fears him and acts uprightly is acceptable to him. You know the word that he sent to the Israelites as he proclaimed peace through Jesus Christ, who is Lord of all, what has happened all over Judea, beginning in Galilee after the baptism that John preached, how God anointed Jesus of Nazareth with the Holy Spirit and power. He went about doing good and healing all those oppressed by the devil, for God was with him."

GOSPEL
Matthew 3:
13–17

Jesus came from Galilee to John at the Jordan to be baptized by him. John tried to prevent him, saying, "I need to be baptized by you, and yet you are coming to me?" Jesus said to him in reply, "Allow it now, for thus it is fitting for us to fulfill all righteousness." Then he allowed him. After Jesus was baptized, he came up from the water and behold, the heavens were opened for him, and he saw the Spirit of God descending like a dove and coming upon him. And a voice came from the heavens, saying, "This is my beloved Son, with whom I am well pleased."

❖ Understanding the Word

Isaiah today introduces the first of four songs that describe the Suffering Servant of the Lord (42:1–9; 49:1–7; 50:4–11; 52:13 — 53:12). Though the actual historical reference may be to an unknown prophet or a collection of individuals, the servant figure symbolizes God's justice and compassion even in the midst of suffering. Christians have long seen the Suffering Servant as a reference to Christ. Indeed, in the baptism accounts, the heavenly voice echoes the words of Isaiah 42:1: "Here is my servant . . . with whom I am pleased," but the servant is now called "beloved Son" in the Gospels.

The reading from Acts picks up in the middle of an important scene. Cornelius, a centurion from Caesarea, experienced a vision and at the urging of an angel sent for Peter (Acts 1:4–8), who also previously had a vision (Acts 10:9–16)—a large sheet containing every kind of animal, reptile, and bird lowered before him. Peter was commanded to slaughter and eat them; what God has made clean cannot be called profane. Inspired by this vision, Peter arrives at the home of this Gentile and begins to proclaim the Good News, beginning with the baptism of Jesus.

The evangelists present Jesus' baptism through slightly different lenses. In Matthew, John the Baptist hesitates, declaring it is he who should be baptized by Jesus, not the other way around. Likely this depicts a question arising in Matthew's community: how could the sinless Jesus need a baptism for the forgiveness of sins? Matthew's Gospel relies heavily on quotes and allusions from the Old Testament, since Matthew intends to demonstrate the continuity between the promises of old and the reality of Christ. To answer John the Baptist's concern, Jesus echoes a theme from the scriptures: "It is fitting for us to fulfill all righteousness." In confirmation, Jesus sees the Spirit of God descending like a dove and coming to rest upon him, and the crowd hears a voice from heaven announcing that this is the beloved Son with whom God is well pleased.

✦ Reflecting on the Word

We end the season of Christmas and begin the period of Ordinary Time, just as we begin the ordinary time of our lives as Christians, with baptism. But Jesus' baptism is also different from our baptism. It does not free him from sin, since he is without sin. Rather, Jesus is baptized by John in order to establish baptism as the way in which we come to share in his holiness.

Jesus's baptism also serves to mark the beginning of his public ministry, and because we share in the ministry of Christ by virtue of our own baptism, it is worth reflecting on the nature of that ministry. The first reading speaks of God's servant as one who will "bring forth justice to the nations," and the second reading describes Jesus as the one through whom God "proclaimed peace." Working for a more just and peaceful world, therefore, is part of what it means to share in the ministry of Jesus.

But the first reading also says that God's servant will not break a bruised reed or quench a smoldering wick, and the second reading tells us that part of Jesus' ministry involved "healing those oppressed by the devil." So to share in the ministry of Jesus involves not only seeking justice and peace, but also doing so in a particular way. Sometimes people's passion for peace and justice leads them to stridency and, as paradoxical as this may seem, to violence. But Jesus embodies a different path, in which even those we perceive as opposing our effort for peace and justice must be seen with compassion, recognizing the weakness of human beings and dealing with them in a way that encourages rather than denounces.

✦ Consider/Discuss

- How in my daily life do I, as a baptized Christian, share in the ministry of Jesus?
- Who are the "bruised reeds" and "smoldering wicks" in my life? In what way am I also a bruised reed?

✦ Responding to the Word

Lord Jesus, beloved Son of God, in whom the Father is well pleased, send to us your Spirit of gentleness and compassion. May we strengthen those who are wavering and be a sign of your peace in the world. Amen.

The liturgical year is punctuated with celebrations of significant moments in the life of Jesus: the annunciation and anticipation of his birth (Advent); his birth, Epiphany, and baptism (Christmas); his journey to the cross (Lent); his passion and death (Triduum); and his resurrection (Easter). Advent leads directly to Christmas as Lent gives way to Holy Week, but between the end of the Christmas season and the beginning of Lent, we enter into Ordinary Time, an English term for the Latin *tempus per annum*, which literally means "time through the year." The weeks of Ordinary Time are interrupted by Lent and then continue after Pentecost Sunday. Though the Baptism of the Lord closes the Christmas season, the following Sunday is numbered as the Second Sunday of Ordinary Time. Special feasts or solemnities that occur during Ordinary Time are known by the feast title and are not numbered (Trinity Sunday, the feast of Christ the King).

Each of the three liturgical years focuses on one of the synoptic Gospels (Matthew, Mark, Luke). Year A follows the Gospel of Matthew, Year B follows the Gospel of Mark (with substantial portions of John), and Year C is Luke. The Gospel of John is also read during some Lenten Sundays and throughout the Easter season.

The selection of a first reading from the Old Testament is chosen to reflect a theme found in the Gospel. In Year A, selections from the prophets (Isaiah, Zephaniah, Hosea, Jeremiah, Zechariah, Ezekiel, Malachi) outnumber readings from wisdom literature (Sirach, Wisdom, Proverbs), the Pentateuch (Leviticus, Deuteronomy, Exodus), and the historical books (First Kings).

The second reading comes from the Letters of St. Paul during Year A. The first four chapters of Paul's First Letter to the Corinthians will be read on the second through eighth Sundays of Ordinary Time. Nearly all of the Letter to the Romans will read between the Ninth and Twenty-fourth Sundays. Excerpts from Philippians and First Thessalonians are read between weeks 25 and 33. The final Sunday of Ordinary Time celebrates the feast of Christ the King. On this Sunday, the second reading is from First Corinthians.

The Gospel selections during Ordinary Time follow the life and teachings of Jesus from his baptism until his arrival in Jerusalem. As noted above, the readings from the Old Testament were chosen because of a similar theme, or in the case of the Gospel of Matthew, because Matthew has cited the Old Testament text in his Gospel. Likely Matthew's community was composed of Jewish Christians who would have been familiar with the Old Testament prophecies and expectations of the coming of the Messiah. Matthew carefully crafts his portrait of Jesus so that he resembles Moses, Israel's greatest prophet and teacher. Matthew's insertion of five teaching blocks into Mark's narrative framework may be an attempt to parallel the teachings of Jesus with the five books of Moses, the Torah.

January 19, 2014

SECOND SUNDAY IN ORDINARY TIME

Today's Focus: Behold the Lamb of God!

With the gentle image of a lamb, John the Baptist introduces Jesus in John's Gospel. We will come to learn that gentle lamb is the sign of God's love, grace, mercy, peace, reconciliation, and eternal life.

FIRST READING
Isaiah 49:3, 5–6

The LORD said to me: You are my servant,
　　Israel, through whom I show my glory.
Now the LORD has spoken
　　who formed me as his servant from the womb,
that Jacob may be brought back to him
　　and Israel gathered to him;
and I am made glorious in the sight of the LORD,
　　and my God is now my strength!
It is too little, the LORD says, for you to be my servant,
　　to raise up the tribes of Jacob,
　　and restore the survivors of Israel;
I will make you a light to the nations,
　　that my salvation may reach to the ends of the earth.

PSALM RESPONSE
Psalm 40:8a, 9a

Here am I, Lord; I come to do your will.

SECOND READING
1 Corinthians 1:1–3

Paul, called to be an apostle of Christ Jesus by the will of God, and Sosthenes our brother, to the church of God that is in Corinth, to you who have been sanctified in Christ Jesus, called to be holy, with all those everywhere who call upon the name of our Lord Jesus Christ, their Lord and ours. Grace to you and peace from God our Father and the Lord Jesus Christ.

GOSPEL
John 1:29–34

John the Baptist saw Jesus coming toward him and said, "Behold, the Lamb of God, who takes away the sin of the world. He is the one of whom I said, 'A man is coming after me who ranks ahead of me because he existed before me.' I did not know him, but the reason why I came baptizing with water was that he might be made known to Israel." John testified further, saying, "I saw the Spirit come down like a dove from heaven and remain upon him. I did not know him, but the one who sent me to baptize with water told me, 'On whomever you see the Spirit come down and remain, he is the one who will baptize with the Holy Spirit.' Now I have seen and testified that he is the Son of God."

❖ Understanding the Word

The reading from the prophet Isaiah is part of the four Suffering Servant Songs attributed to Second Isaiah, an anonymous prophet preaching in the spirit of Isaiah of Jerusalem but nearly two hundred years later. During the time that Second Isaiah was prophesying, the exiles had been liberated by Cyrus the Persian and were hopeful about the future. In this reading, the servant is identified with the ideal personification of an obedient and faithful Israel who will become a light to the nations.

Paul would hope in vain that his Corinthian believers might be a light to the nations. As he begins his letter he identifies the Corinthians as the church of God, the sanctified, and those called to be holy. The exalted introduction is meant to remind the believers of their status as members of the body of Christ, something the various factions have obviously forgotten. The divisions in the Corinthian community arise from their zealous competition over who baptized them (1 Corinthians 1:11–13) and their spiritual gifts (1 Corinthians 12:1–11). They struggle with the appropriate moral behaviors (marry or remain single? eat meat or abstain?) and they defile the Lord's Supper (1 Corinthians 11:18–22). Paul will offer the most effective antidote to schism: "So faith, hope, love remain, these three; but the greatest of these is love" (1 Corinthians 13:13).

In the Gospel reading, the evangelist presents John the Baptist's encounter with Jesus, though the actual baptism isn't narrated. Consistent with the presentation in Matthew, Mark, and Luke, John the Baptist acknowledges Jesus' higher rank (John 1:30). John the Baptist doesn't know Jesus (John 1:31) until a divine sign indicates Jesus' identity. He sees the Spirit come down like a dove and rest upon Jesus, confirming what the Baptist had been told: the one upon whom the Spirit lands will baptize in the Holy Spirit. The Baptist calls Jesus "the Lamb of God, who takes away the sin of the world," an phrase with multiple references. The lamb could refer to the apocalyptic lamb of Revelation 5–7 who will destroy evil. The paschal lamb of Passover (Exodus 12) may be intended. Or the Lamb of God could remind John's readers of the Suffering Servant of Isaiah (53:7, 10) who—like a lamb—is led to slaughter.

❖ Reflecting on the Word

In today's Gospel John identifies Jesus as "the Lamb of God, who takes away the sin of the world." This phrase is familiar to us from the Mass. During the breaking of the bread we pray to Jesus under this title, asking him to grant us mercy and peace. John's words are used to invite us to Communion, where they are combined with a reference to the "Supper of the Lamb" spoken of in the book of Revelation.

These familiar words remind us that the one who takes away our sins is the servant of God who, as the prophet Isaiah says, was led like a lamb to slaughter. This is the servant of whom Isaiah speaks in this Sunday's first reading, the one who will be a light to the nations and a source of salvation for all people. When we implore mercy and peace from Christ the Lamb at the Eucharist, we call to mind both the Suffering Servant of God as well as the victorious Lamb of Revelation. The words that are spoken so often in the liturgy contain the paradoxical mystery at the heart of our faith: saving strength is manifested in the gentle image of a lamb; the heavenly feast is present in a simple sharing of the signs of bread and wine.

As we begin in the following Sundays of Ordinary Time to follow Matthew's story of the life and ministry of Jesus, it is good to bear in mind what John's Gospel tells us: that Jesus is the Lamb, slain and victorious, who bears our sins away. It is through him, as Paul says in the second reading, that we have been sanctified and called to lives of holiness.

❖ Consider/Discuss

- What images does the phrase "Lamb of God" conjure in my mind?
- How should I live my life differently if I believe that Jesus has taken my sins away?

❖ Responding to the Word

Jesus, Lamb of God, bearer of our sins, giver of peace: let us partake of your sacrifice so that we might share in your victory. Amen.

44

January 26, 2014

THIRD SUNDAY IN ORDINARY TIME

Today's Focus: The Reign of God is Present among Us

During the first days of his public ministry, Jesus calls followers to be his disciples. He also begins to show them—and us—what God's reign is about: to teach, to heal, and to proclaim the Good News!

FIRST READING
Isaiah 8:23 — 9:3

First the Lord degraded the land of Zebulun and the land of Naphtali; but in the end he has glorified the seaward road, the land west of the Jordan, the District of the Gentiles.

Anguish has taken wing, dispelled is darkness:
for there is no gloom where but now there was distress.
The people who walked in darkness
have seen a great light;
upon those who dwelt in the land of gloom
a light has shone.
You have brought them abundant joy
and great rejoicing,
as they rejoice before you as at the harvest,
as people make merry when dividing spoils.
For the yoke that burdened them,
the pole on their shoulder,
and the rod of their taskmaster
you have smashed, as on the day of Midian.

PSALM RESPONSE
Psalm 27:1a

The Lord is my light and my salvation.

SECOND READING
1 Corinthians 1:10–13, 17

I urge you, brothers and sisters, in the name of our Lord Jesus Christ, that all of you agree in what you say, and that there be no divisions among you, but that you be united in the same mind and in the same purpose. For it has been reported to me about you, my brothers and sisters, by Chloe's people, that there are rivalries among you. I mean that each of you is saying, "I belong to Paul," or "I belong to Apollos," or "I belong to Cephas," or "I belong to Christ." Is Christ divided? Was Paul crucified for you? Or were you baptized in the name of Paul? For Christ did not send me to baptize but to preach the gospel, and not with the wisdom of human eloquence, so that the cross of Christ might not be emptied of its meaning.

In the shorter form of the reading, the passage in brackets is omitted.

GOSPEL
Matthew
4:12–23 or
4:12–17

When Jesus heard that John had been arrested, he withdrew to Galilee. He left Nazareth and went to live in Capernaum by the sea, in the region of Zebulun and Naphtali, that what had been said through Isaiah the prophet might be fulfilled:
Land of Zebulun and land of Naphtali,
   the way to the sea, beyond the Jordan,
   Galilee of the Gentiles,
the people who sit in darkness have seen a great light,
on those dwelling in a land overshadowed by death
   light has arisen.
From that time on, Jesus began to preach and say, "Repent, for the kingdom of heaven is at hand."

[As he was walking by the Sea of Galilee, he saw two brothers, Simon who is called Peter, and his brother Andrew, casting a net into the sea; they were fishermen. He said to them, "Come after me, and I will make you fishers of men." At once they left their nets and followed him. He walked along from there and saw two other brothers, James, the son of Zebedee, and his brother John. They were in a boat, with their father Zebedee, mending their nets. He called them, and immediately they left their boat and their father and followed him.

He went around all of Galilee, teaching in their synagogues, proclaiming the gospel of the kingdom, and curing every disease and illness among the people.]

❖ Understanding the Word

Isaiah announces the redemption of the land of Zebulun and Naphtali and promises that the yoke that burdened them will be smashed. The two tribal lands of the northern kingdom of Israel had been incorporated into the Assyrian province in the eighth century BCE (before the common era) when the kingdom of Israel joined its neighbor Syria in revolting against its overlord, Assyria. The prophet Isaiah envisions a time when the "people who walked in darkness" will see a great light. The Gospel reading picks up this theme and recognizes that the redemption of Zebulun and Naphtali is realized when Jesus commences his ministry of proclamation in Galilee.

Paul addresses the chief problem among the Corinthian community in today's second reading. They have lost sight of themselves as the body of Christ. They are fighting over the significance of their baptism and forgetting the importance of the gospel. Baptism may be the entry into the mission, but the proclamation of the reign of God is the goal.

Though the synoptic Gospels (Matthew, Mark, and Luke) do not emphasize the point, John the Baptist seems to have been a significant influence in the ministerial life of Jesus. As today's Gospel notes, Jesus departs from his home in Nazareth and begins to preach repentance in Galilee—the region of Zebulun and Naphtali—when he learns that John the Baptist has been arrested. But Jesus doesn't continue to baptize as John did. Jesus' work is proclamation and healing. The preaching has only begun when Jesus calls others to join him. The first four disciples—Peter, Andrew, James, and John—are all fishermen. Jesus invites them to come after him and their response is immediate. They join his preaching and teaching ministry in the region of Galilee, where Jesus proclaims the gospel of the Kingdom of Heaven and cures illnesses and diseases.

❖ Reflecting on the Word

In this Sunday's Gospel, John the Baptist, who was a nearly constant presence throughout the weeks of Advent and Christmas, and even into the beginning of Ordinary Time, now withdraws from the scene and Jesus takes center stage in the unfolding drama, taking up the message that the kingdom of God is at hand. Jesus teaches in synagogues about the Kingdom, and engages in a ministry of healing that demonstrates God's dominion over the forces of death and destruction. Jesus also begins to gather the followers who will become "the Twelve"—an inner circle of disciples who are also a symbolic group representing the restoration of the twelve tribes of Israel. They too are a proclamation of the coming of God's kingdom.

What is striking in Matthew's account is the lack of hesitation with which they respond to Jesus' call to follow him. Peter and Andrew leave their nets "at once;" James and John leave their father Zebedee "immediately." We might be misled by this way of putting things into thinking that the decision to follow Jesus was easy, or maybe even ill-considered. But what Matthew wants to emphasize is the sense of urgency that accompanies Jesus' message. It is a message that demands decision and action.

Of course, we all make decisions and take action in different ways. This might simply be a matter of temperament. Some tend to act quickly and figure things out as they go along; others are a bit more reflective, trying to figure the consequences at the outset. Whatever our natural inclination, however, we need to make sure that we count the costs of being Jesus' disciple, but not let this become an excuse for continually postponing our response to his call.

- What does the phrase "the kingdom of God" mean to me?
- Am I someone who is more inclined to make decisions quickly or slowly? How does this inclination figure into my life as a Christian?

❖ Responding to the Word

Lord Jesus, help us to be ready to answer your call to be your disciples. Let us count the cost of following you, but not delay too long. Amen.

February 2, 2014

PRESENTATION OF THE LORD

Today's Focus: Jesus Christ, Light from light

This feast of light beckons us to see the glory of God's saving power revealed in Jesus. Like Simeon, we have seen salvation in Christ.

FIRST READING
Malachi 3:1–4

Thus says the Lord God:
Lo, I am sending my messenger
    to prepare the way before me;
And suddenly there will come to the temple
    the LORD whom you seek,
And the messenger of the covenant whom you desire.
    Yes, he is coming, says the LORD of hosts.
But who will endure the day of his coming?
    And who can stand when he appears?
For he is like the refiner's fire,
    or like the fuller's lye.
He will sit refining and purifying silver,
    and he will purify the sons of Levi,
Refining them like gold or like silver
    that they may offer due sacrifice to the LORD.
Then the sacrifice of Judah and Jerusalem
    will please the LORD,
    as in the days of old, as in years gone by.

PSALM RESPONSE
Psalm 24:8

Who is this king of glory? It is the Lord!

SECOND READING
Hebrews 2:14–18

Since the children share in blood and flesh, Jesus likewise shared in them, that through death he might destroy the one who has the power of death, that is, the devil, and free those who through fear of death had been subject to slavery all their life. Surely he did not help angels but rather the descendants of Abraham; therefore, he had to become like his brothers and sisters in every way, that he might be a merciful and faithful high priest before God to expiate the sins of the people. Because he himself was tested through what he suffered, he is able to help those who are being tested.

In the shorter form of the reading, the passages in brackets are omitted.
When the days were completed for their purification according to the law of Moses, Mary and Joseph took Jesus up to Jerusalem to present him to the Lord, just as it is written in the law of the Lord,

Every male that opens the womb shall be consecrated to the Lord,

and to offer the sacrifice of

a pair of turtledoves or two young pigeons,

in accordance with the dictate in the law of the Lord.

Now there was a man in Jerusalem whose name was Simeon. This man was righteous and devout, awaiting the consolation of Israel, and the Holy Spirit was upon him. It had been revealed to him by the Holy Spirit that he should not see death before he had seen the Christ of the Lord. He came in the Spirit into the temple; and when the parents brought in the child Jesus to perform the custom of the law in regard to him, he took him into his arms and blessed God, saying:

"Now, Master, you may let your servant go
    in peace, according to your word,
for my eyes have seen your salvation,
    which you prepared in the sight of all the peoples:
a light for revelation to the Gentiles,
    and glory for your people Israel."

[The child's father and mother were amazed at what was said about him; and Simeon blessed them and said to Mary his mother, "Behold, this child is destined for the fall and rise of many in Israel, and to be a sign that will be contradicted—and you yourself a sword will pierce—so that the thoughts of many hearts may be revealed." There was also a prophetess, Anna, the daughter of Phanuel, of the tribe of Asher. She was advanced in years, having lived seven years with her husband after her marriage, and then as a widow until she was eighty-four. She never left the temple, but worshiped night and day with fasting and prayer. And coming forward at that very time, she gave thanks to God and spoke about the child to all who were awaiting the redemption of Jerusalem.

When they had fulfilled all the prescriptions of the law of the Lord, they returned to Galilee, to their own town of Nazareth. The child grew and became strong, filled with wisdom; and the favor of God was upon him.]

❖ Understanding the Word

The reading from the prophet Malachi promises the coming of a messenger who will prepare the way for God. The Lord, the messenger of the covenant, will appear suddenly in the temple. Whether the prophet envisioned two beings—a messenger preparing the way and the Lord, the messenger of the covenant—is uncertain. In the Gospel of Matthew, Jesus quotes this verse from Malachi in reference to John the Baptist (Matthew 11:10), whom he sees as the messenger who has prepared the way. In light of today's Gospel, Malachi's prophecy of the sudden appearance of the Lord in the temple is fulfilled by the presentation of the infant Jesus in the temple.

The reading from Hebrews picks up the temple imagery. Jesus is the high priest who expiates the sins of his people, not because he was divine but because he was human, sharing "in blood and flesh." How to understand Jesus' nature and his saving act became an important theological concern among the early Christians. Jesus was truly human as evidenced by his suffering and death, living in a state lower than the angels. Yet now he is raised above all creation and crowned with glory and honor. The Letter to the Hebrews (most likely a sermon written down later in letter form) attempts to encourage believers who the author fears are in danger of apostasy—renouncing their faith.

According to the laws of Leviticus (12:2–8), a woman who bears a son is considered impure for forty days during which time she cannot touch anything sacred or enter the sanctuary. At the end of the period, a lamb is presented to the temple as a burnt offering and a pigeon or turtledove for a purification offering. If one could not afford a lamb, then two turtledoves could serve as a substitute. The Gospel reading conflates Mary's purification and Jesus' consecration to the Lord as the firstborn son (Exodus 13:2, 12). While fulfilling their religious responsibilities, the family encounters Simeon and Anna, two exemplars of righteousness. Both recognize the extraordinary child. Simeon calls him "a light of revelation to the Gentiles" and Anna speaks about the child to all who are awaiting the redemption of Israel.

❖ Reflecting on the Word

This year, the feast of the Presentation falls on a Sunday, offering the entire Sunday assembly the opportunity to share in the distinctive liturgical features of this day, including the blessing of candles and the procession accompanied by the canticle *Nunc Dimittis* ("Lord, now you let your servant go in peace"), which is also included in the Gospel reading. In some ways, this feast represents the last flicker of the Advent-Christmas season, commemorating the presentation of Jesus in the Jerusalem temple. In Vatican City, the large outdoor manger scene is left in place until this day. It is almost as if the Church just can't give up on celebrating the mystery of God-made-flesh.

The significance of this feast is brought out by the first reading, from Malachi, which speaks of the Lord coming to occupy his temple. Malachi, however, depicts this as an almost terrifying event, in which God's purifying fire will burn away everything that defiles the true worship of God so that a pure offering might be made. Luke's Gospel, in contrast, depicts the Lord coming to his temple in the form of the infant Jesus, seemingly without might or glory. But Simeon, the faithful servant of God who had waited all his life for the Messiah, can recognize in this child the salvation of God, which is a light to the Gentiles and the glory of Israel, the one who makes possible true worship of the Father. Again, we are presented with the mystery of Christmas: the saving power of God made present in the weakness of a child.

Even on this final feast of Christmas, the light of Christ still shines brightly for those who know how to see the glory of God revealed in Jesus. As we immerse ourselves over the next few weeks in Jesus' Sermon on the Mount, it is important to remember that the one who teaches us is Emmanuel, God-with-us.

✤ Consider/Discuss

- Do I live my life, like Simeon, in active anticipation of the revelation of God's glory?
- What hinders me from worshiping God worthily? What worries and anxieties hold me back from giving myself over to God?

✤ Responding to the Word

Lord God, like Simeon we have waited for the revelation of your glory, and we believe that you have given us Jesus as a light to the nations. May our lives reflect his light to all those in darkness. Amen.

February 9, 2014

FIFTH SUNDAY IN ORDINARY TIME

Today's Focus: Adding Flavor, Shedding Light

If you are salt, be salt; if you are light, be light. Jesus calls all disciples to be authentic and true. The images of salt and light lead us to a deeper understanding of discipleship.

FIRST READING
Isaiah 58:7–10

Thus says the LORD:
  Share your bread with the hungry,
    shelter the oppressed and the homeless;
  clothe the naked when you see them,
    and do not turn your back on your own.
  Then your light shall break forth like the dawn,
    and your wound shall quickly be healed;
  your vindication shall go before you,
    and the glory of the LORD shall be your rear guard.
  Then you shall call, and the LORD will answer,
    you shall cry for help, and he will say: Here I am!
  If you remove from your midst
    oppression, false accusation and malicious speech;
  if you bestow your bread on the hungry
    and satisfy the afflicted;
  then light shall rise for you in the darkness,
    and the gloom shall become for you like midday.

PSALM RESPONSE
Psalm 112:4a

The just man is a light in darkness to the upright.

SECOND READING
1 Corinthians 2:1–5

When I came to you, brothers and sisters, proclaiming the mystery of God, I did not come with sublimity of words or of wisdom. For I resolved to know nothing while I was with you except Jesus Christ, and him crucified. I came to you in weakness and fear and much trembling, and my message and my proclamation were not with persuasive words of wisdom, but with a demonstration of Spirit and power, so that your faith might rest not on human wisdom but on the power of God.

GOSPEL
Matthew
5:13–16
Jesus said to his disciples: "You are the salt of the earth. But if salt loses its taste, with what can it be seasoned? It is no longer good for anything but to be thrown out and trampled underfoot. You are the light of the world. A city set on a mountain cannot be hidden. Nor do they light a lamp and then put it under a bushel basket; it is set on a lampstand, where it gives light to all in the house. Just so, your light must shine before others, that they may see your good deeds and glorify your heavenly Father."

❖ Understanding the Word

Not all fasting is for righteousness' sake. A few verses prior to today's first reading, God commands the prophet to announce judgment on those who abuse the laws of God, particularly those who fast improperly (fasting so as to be seen, abusing one's laborers, quarreling and fighting [Isaiah 58:3–4]). The verses of Second Isaiah that are proclaimed today speak of a fast that demonstrates a social ethic. The fast that God chooses is sharing bread with the hungry, offering shelter in one's home for the afflicted and homeless, clothing the naked, and not ignoring one's own family. When such a moral fast is exhibited, then the people of Israel will be vindicated, and God will respond to their cries for help. As a result of this genuine fast, Israel's light will rise in the darkness, its moral life a witness to the nations.

Paul demonstrates the appropriate attitude that Second Isaiah expects of one who stands in right relationship with God. In the reading from First Corinthians, Paul's humility allows God's power to be manifested in his preaching. Unlike most orators in the first century, Paul was not eloquent, unable to demonstrate a "sublimity of words or of wisdom." He came in weakness, fear, and trembling— the appropriate response for one charged with announcing God's good news. The subject of his proclamation was Christ crucified, "a stumbling block to Jews and foolishness to Gentiles" (1 Corinthians 1:23). Paul recognized that the power of his message transcended his own limitations. As the Gospel reading will describe, Paul allowed himself to be as a light shining before others, so that the Corinthians' faith might properly rest on the power of God.

Today's Gospel reading immediately follows the Beatitudes. The first eight address an unidentified "they." But the addressee changes in verse 11. Jesus now speaks to his disciples: "Blessed are you." The metaphors of salt and light in the Gospel reading remind the disciples that they are a visible witness to the gospel that Jesus proclaims. As disciples, they can no more deny their responsibilities than salt can exist without taste. The purpose of salt is to add flavor, the purpose of light is to shine. Jesus reminds the disciples that their purpose is to allow others to see their good deeds and glorify their heavenly Father in response.

Salt is almost certainly the oldest seasoning used by the human race. We have archeological evidence of facilities for the refining of salt as early as 6000 BC. Of course, salt was used for more than seasoning; salting was for many centuries the only way we had to preserve food from decay and corruption. Salt was, in fact, so valuable that a wide variety of cultures have used it for religious purposes. In ancient Egypt, Greece, and Rome salt mixed with water was offered to the gods; in ancient Israel, salt was included in grain offerings and burnt offerings; salt was used to purify and to exorcise; but it also symbolized the table fellowship of a shared meal.

So when Jesus tells his followers that they are the salt of the earth, he is, as is the case with any good metaphor, saying a number of things at the same time. True disciples give our world its flavor; they are the element preserving the world from decay and corruption; they are an offering to God; they are a foretaste of the day when humanity will be gathered around the table in God's kingdom.

But, having told them that they are salt, Jesus also warns them, "If salt loses its taste, with what can it be seasoned? It is no longer good for anything but to be thrown out and trampled underfoot." If the disciples of Jesus lose their power to season and preserve, then they will not serve the purpose for which Jesus has called them. Being a follower of Jesus requires "saltiness," not bland conformity. Disciples should stand out, like a light shining from a hilltop—not to call attention to themselves, but to give glory to God.

❖ Consider/Discuss

- How am I salt? Which of the traditional uses of salt—as a flavoring, a preservative, an offering—best describes how I see my role as a follower of Jesus?
- How do I let my light shine? What are the occasions when I seek to hide it?

❖ Responding to the Word

Lord Jesus, you call us to be salt and light for the world. Let us not lose our flavor; let our light not be hidden, so that we might give glory to your heavenly Father. Amen.

February 16, 2014

SIXTH SUNDAY IN ORDINARY TIME

Today's Focus: Eternal Grace, New Covenant

Jesus is the fulfillment of the scriptures, who challenges us to grow in wisdom and grace.
The love and grace of God are eternal, but now are embodied in Christ in new ways.

FIRST READING
Sirach 15:15–20

Create in

If you choose you can keep the commandments,
    they will save you;
  if you trust in God, you too shall live;
he has set before you fire and water;
    to whichever you choose, stretch forth your hand.
Before man are life and death, good and evil,
    whichever he chooses shall be given him.
Immense is the wisdom of the Lord;
    he is mighty in power, and all-seeing.
The eyes of God are on those who fear him;
    he understands man's every deed.
No one does he command to act unjustly,
    to none does he give license to sin.

PSALM RESPONSE
Psalm 119:1b

Blessed are they who follow the law of the Lord!

SECOND READING
1 Corinthians 2:6–10

Brothers and sisters: We speak a wisdom to those who are mature, not a wisdom of this age, nor of the rulers of this age who are passing away. Rather, we speak God's wisdom, mysterious, hidden, which God predetermined before the ages for our glory, and which none of the rulers of this age knew; for, if they had known it, they would not have crucified the Lord of glory. But as it is written:
What eye has not seen, and ear has not heard,
  and what has not entered the human heart,
  what God has prepared for those who love him,
    this God has revealed to us through the Spirit.

For the Spirit scrutinizes everything, even the depths of God.

GOSPEL
Matthew 5:
17–37 or
5:20–22a,
27–28,
33–34a, 37

Jesus said to his disciples: ["Do not think that I have come to abolish the law or the prophets. I have come not to abolish but to fulfill. Amen, I say to you, until heaven and earth pass away, not the smallest letter or the smallest part of a letter will pass from the law, until all things have taken place. Therefore, whoever breaks one of the least of these commandments and teaches others to do so will be called least in the kingdom of heaven. But whoever obeys and teaches these commandments will be called greatest in the kingdom of heaven.] I tell you, unless your righteousness surpasses that of the scribes and Pharisees, you will not enter the kingdom of heaven.

"You have heard that it was said to your ancestors,
You shall not kill; and whoever kills will be liable to judgment.
But I say to you, whoever is angry with his brother will be liable to judgment; [and whoever says to brother, 'Raqa,' will be answerable to the Sanhedrin; and whoever says, 'You fool,' will be liable to fiery Gehenna. Therefore, if you bring your gift to the altar, and there recall that your brother has anything against you, leave your gift there at the altar, go first and be reconciled with your brother, and then come and offer your gift. Settle with your opponent quickly while on the way to court. Otherwise your opponent will hand you over to the judge, and the judge will hand you over to the guard, and you will be thrown into prison. Amen, I say to you, you will not be released until you have paid the last penny.]

"You have heard that it was said,
You shall not commit adultery.
But I say to you, everyone who looks at a woman with lust has already committed adultery with her in his heart. [If your right eye causes you to sin, tear it out and throw it away. It is better for you to lose one of your members than to have your whole body thrown into Gehenna. And if your right hand causes you to sin, cut it off and throw it away. It is better for you to lose one of your members than to have your whole body go into Gehenna.

"It was also said,
Whoever divorces his wife must give her a bill of divorce.
But I say to you, whoever divorces his wife—unless the marriage is unlawful—causes her to commit adultery, and whoever marries a divorced woman commits adultery.]

"Again you have heard that it was said to your ancestors,
Do not take a false oath,
but make good to the Lord all that you vow.
But I say to you, do not swear at all; [not by heaven, for it is God's throne; nor by the earth, for it is his footstool; nor by Jerusalem, for it is the city of the great King. Do not swear by your head, for you cannot make a single hair white or black.] Let your 'Yes' mean 'Yes,' and your 'No' mean 'No.' Anything more is from the evil one."

The book of Sirach is a collection of moral maxims compiled by a sage in Jerusalem in the early second century BCE. Sirach hoped to demonstrate the superiority of Israel's scripture in a time of growing interest in Greek philosophy. Today's reading reminds us that we have choices, and whatever we decide to do—be it following God's commandments or choosing between life and death—we are given a choice.

By the time Paul is writing, elements of Greek philosophy had pervaded all aspects of the Greco-Roman society in which earliest Christianity took root. Like Sirach before him, Paul attempts to show that true wisdom is not found in the fashions of the day or its rulers. God's wisdom is mysterious and hidden and predetermined before the ages. God's wisdom is revealed to believers through the Spirit.

The Sermon on the Mount from which today's Gospel reading is taken is the first of five teaching blocks found in Matthew's Gospel. The role of the law and the prophets (understood as the "scriptures" in the first century) was particularly important for Matthew's community of Jewish Christians. How were they to interpret the Christ event (passion, death, and resurrection) in light of their own anticipation of the fulfillment of God's promises? Matthew demonstrates that Jesus is the fulfillment of those promises: "I have not come to abolish but to fulfill." Jesus indicates that the law and the prophets become the interpretive lens through which to view one's actions. In today's passage, four examples of behavior are discussed, with each example beginning with a reference to a commandment in the law: "You have heard that it was said to your ancestors . . . " In some cases, Jesus extends the law. The former law that whoever kills is liable for judgment now becomes even stricter: whoever is angry with his or her brother is liable for judgment. In some instances Jesus rejects the standard set by the law. For example, the law forbids taking a false oath. Jesus commands that his disciples are not to take any oaths at all, since an oath is ultimately swearing by God, for all things are of God.

✤ *Reflecting on the Word*

The gospel of Jesus is a gospel of grace. The new law that Jesus gives is not a written code, but is the Holy Spirit who works within us to transform us into God's children, adopted into God's family not because of our own merits but rather out of God's abundant love. This does not mean that the gospel of Jesus places no demands on us. As today's Gospel reading makes clear, if anything the new law of Christ is more stringent in its demands than the law of Moses. It calls not simply for outward conformity, but rather for an inward transformation in which we are conformed to God's Spirit, the Spirit who, as Paul says in the second reading, "scrutinizes everything, even the depths of God."

We all know that it is much easier to go through the motions and grudgingly obey a rule than it is to truly grasp the reason for the rule and let it become part of the fabric of our lives. A child might simply follow a rule to avoid punishment or to obtain a reward, but with maturity and life experience comes an appreciation for the reason behind the rule. The new law requires the hard work of inner transformation, by which we grow into the wisdom and spiritual maturity of which Paul speaks.

The hard work that the new law of Jesus asks of us does not make it any less a gospel of grace, for what Jesus ultimately asks is that we let his Spirit work within us. Our task is to get out of the way and let the Spirit guide us.

✤ Consider/Discuss

- What do I consider the signs of a spiritually mature person?
- Are there rules that I follow without really grasping the reason behind the rule?

✤ Responding to the Word

Holy God, send us the Spirit of wisdom, so that we may grow into a spiritual maturity that will enable us to live the demands of the gospel. Amen.

February 23, 2014

SEVENTH SUNDAY IN ORDINARY TIME

Today's Focus: How Can I Be Perfect?

To be perfect as God is perfect requires us to surpass mere observance of the commandments of the Law. Jesus means what he says: surpass the Law and love your enemies.

FIRST READING
Leviticus 19:1–2, 17–18

The LORD said to Moses, "Speak to the whole Israelite community and tell them: Be holy, for I, the LORD, your God, am holy.

"You shall not bear hatred for your brother or sister in your heart. Though you may have to reprove your fellow citizen, do not incur sin because of him. Take no revenge and cherish no grudge against any of your people. You shall love your neighbor as yourself. I am the LORD."

PSALM RESPONSE
Psalm 103:8a

The Lord is kind and merciful.

SECOND READING
1 Corinthians 3:16–23

Brothers and sisters: Do you not know that you are the temple of God, and that the Spirit of God dwells in you? If anyone destroys God's temple, God will destroy that person; for the temple of God, which you are, is holy.

Let no one deceive himself. If any one among you considers himself wise in this age, let him become a fool, so as to become wise. For the wisdom of this world is foolishness in the eyes of God, for it is written:
God catches the wise in their own ruses,
and again:
The Lord knows the thoughts of the wise,
that they are vain.
So let no one boast about human beings, for everything belongs to you, Paul or Apollos or Cephas, or the world or life or death, or the present or the future: all belong to you, and you to Christ, and Christ to God.

GOSPEL
Matthew 5:38–48

Jesus said to his disciples: "You have heard that it was said,
An eye for an eye and a tooth for a tooth.
But I say to you, offer no resistance to one who is evil. When someone strikes you on your right cheek, turn the other one as well. If anyone wants to go to law with you over your tunic, hand over your cloak as well. Should anyone press you into service for one mile, go for two miles. Give to the one who asks of you, and do not turn your back on one who wants to borrow.

"You have heard that it was said,
You shall love your neighbor and hate your enemy.
But I say to you, love your enemies and pray for those who persecute you, that you may be children of your heavenly Father, for he makes his sun rise on the bad and the good, and causes rain to fall on the just and the unjust. For if you love those who love you, what recompense will you have? Do not the tax collectors do the same? And if you greet your brothers only, what is unusual about that? Do not the pagans do the same? So be perfect, just as your heavenly Father is perfect."

❖ Understanding the Word

The book of Leviticus sets forth the laws concerning the community of Israel and its covenant relationship with God. The primary command is to be holy as God is holy. Such holiness is expressed in love of one's neighbor, which Jesus notes in today's Gospel.

The second reading also speaks of holiness. Paul uses a variety of metaphors to help the Corinthians understand that they are part of a new reality: they belong to Christ and Christ belongs to God. This new relationship has moral expectations. They are to consider themselves God's temple, and as such should remain holy and undefiled, avoiding various immoral behaviors.

Matthew and Luke share a source for today's Gospel, which scholars call "Q," a collection of sayings that Mark did not use, or perhaps did not have available, when he penned his Gospel. In Matthew, we hear a very specific list of behaviors expected of a disciple, behaviors that exceed the Old Testament commandments. They are to offer no resistance when threatened, even to the extent of offering the other cheek when struck. If someone sues over a trivial matter—one's shirt—avoid the conflict and give the coat as well. Roman soldiers traveling through an unfamiliar region could impress a civilian to guide them for one mile. Jesus recognizes this unpopular practice and proposes that the disciple should go an additional mile. Each of these situations builds in difficulty: offer no resistance, turn the other cheek, give up one's covering, provide service to the imperial occupier. The final action is the most shocking: "You have heard that it was said, 'You shall love your neighbor and hate your enemy.' " Jesus doesn't deny that loving one's neighbor is desirable. But he upsets biblical, cultural, and societal expectations. "But I say to you, love your enemies and pray for those who persecute you." His warrant for such extravagant behavior: As children of their heavenly Father, who makes the sun rise on both the good and the bad, they are to strive to be perfect as God is perfect. The Greek word translated as "perfect" is *teleios*, which actually means "having reached an end or achieved completion." By our extravagant behavior that goes beyond the limits of the law, we demonstrate that we are nearing our end, which is union with God.

✤ Reflecting on the Word

The commandment of Jesus with which today's Gospel ends is a bit shocking: "So be perfect, just as your heavenly Father is perfect." Surely Jesus asks too much here. No human being can be perfect in the way that God is perfect. The shock of this commandment is intensified by what has come before it—some of Jesus's most demanding teachings: not retaliating when attacked, giving to those who ask, and loving our enemies. How could any person possibly be perfect in doing these things?

But we have no indication that Jesus does not mean what he says here. Indeed, with regard to loving our enemies Jesus draws a direct parallel between how God acts and how we are to act. Just as God does not discriminate in bestowing the goods of nature between those who love God and those who do not, so too we should not discriminate between friends and enemies when doing good. This may not seem to the world to be an obvious path to happiness and prosperity, but it is undeniably the way of God.

In light of Jesus' command to be perfect as God is perfect, Paul reminds us in the second reading of two things that are important to remember as we seek to follow the teachings of Jesus. First, though these teachings may make us look foolish in the eyes of others, they embody the deep wisdom of God. Second, we are not left without help in striving to live these teachings; we have the Holy Spirit dwelling in us to aid us. We may well fail in living out Jesus' teachings perfectly, but we will surely fail to live them out at all if we decide beforehand that they are impossible.

✤ Consider/Discuss

- What would it mean in practice to love someone whom I considered an enemy? What sort of things might I do?
- How much does the fear of appearing foolish in the eyes of others hold me back from trying to follow the teachings of Jesus?

✤ Responding to the Word

Holy God, you bestow your blessings on all people. Help us to imitate your love: Bless our enemies and those who wish to hurt us; convert their hearts and ours, so that we might live together in peace. Amen.

March 2, 2014

EIGHTH SUNDAY IN ORDINARY TIME

Today's Focus: One Heart, Undivided

God alone can free us from worry about earthly things; what we really need to worry about are the things of heaven. Faith in God frees us from the former so we might seek the latter.

FIRST READING
Isaiah 49:14–15

Zion said, "The LORD has forsaken me;
   my LORD has forgotten me."
Can a mother forget her infant,
   be without tenderness for the child of her womb?
Even should she forget,
   I will never forget you.

PSALM RESPONSE
Psalm 62:6a

Rest in God alone, my soul.

SECOND READING
1 Corinthians 4:1–5

Brothers and sisters: Thus should one regard us: as servants of Christ and stewards of the mysteries of God. Now it is of course required of stewards that they be found trustworthy. It does not concern me in the least that I be judged by you or any human tribunal; I do not even pass judgment on myself; I am not conscious of anything against me, but I do not thereby stand acquitted; the one who judges me is the Lord. Therefore do not make any judgment before the appointed time, until the Lord comes, for he will bring to light what is hidden in darkness and will manifest the motives of our hearts, and then everyone will receive praise from God.

GOSPEL
Matthew 6:24–34

Jesus said to his disciples: "No one can serve two masters. He will either hate one and love the other, or be devoted to one and despise the other. You cannot serve God and mammon. *worth*

"Therefore I tell you, do not worry about your life, what you will eat or drink, or about your body, what you will wear. Is not life more than food and the body more than clothing? Look at the birds in the sky; they do not sow or reap, they gather nothing into barns, yet your heavenly Father feeds them. Are not you more important than they? Can any of you by worrying add a single moment to your life-span? Why are you anxious about clothes? Learn from the way the wild flowers grow. They do not work or spin. But I tell you that not even Solomon in all his splendor was clothed like one of them.

If God so clothes the grass of the field, which grows today and is thrown into the oven tomorrow, will he not much more provide for you, O you of little faith? So do not worry and say, 'What are we to eat?' or 'What are we to drink?'or 'What are we to wear?' All these things the pagans seek. Your heavenly Father knows that you need them all. But seek first the kingdom of God and his righteousness, and all these things will be given you besides. Do not worry about tomorrow; tomorrow will take care of itself. Sufficient for a day is its own evil."

❖ Understanding the Word

The Old Testament frequently recounts the struggles and doubts of Israel. In today's first reading from the book of Isaiah, God, speaking through the prophet, acknowledges the people's fear of being forsaken. "Can a mother forget her infant, be without tenderness for the child of her womb? Even should she forget, I will never forget you." God's providential care endures despite Israel's episodes of unfaithfulness and disobedience.

Paul is often called to defend his ministry as an apostle to the Gentiles, since he had not known the historical Jesus. As he notes in today's reading, he is a trustworthy steward. But the judgment of his trustworthiness is not left up to human courts of law. Rather, when the Lord comes (Jesus' *parousia* or second coming), he will shine a penetrating light that reveals one's true motives.

Today's Gospel is part of a larger section (Matthew 6:19 — 7:11) of instructions to the community, and seems to be loosely related to the Lord's Prayer (Matthew 6:9–13). The passage we hear today shares a theme of anxious concern about one's welfare. In the Lord's Prayer, Jesus taught his disciples to ask for their daily bread, and today's reading is a further explanation of that concept. The astute believer reads scripture aware of two lenses of interpretation. The first recognizes that the narrative comes from the life of Jesus in which Jesus addresses those around him. The second understands that the evangelist is shaping his sources so that they speak to his specific community, which is situated temporally, geographically, and sometimes culturally distant from the actual event. Through these dual lenses, the reader can hear Jesus reminding his disciples that they have chosen to join his charismatic itinerant preaching ministry. Their radical obedience requires that they allow God to provide what they need, and be satisfied with their daily bread. But the reader is also aware that Matthew is addressing the concerns of his somewhat affluent community, which may be overly concerned about the things of this life and miss the point of God's providential care. Likely we are hearing Matthew's editorial voice when Jesus' chides, "O you of little faith," a phrase frequently found in Matthew (8:26, 14:31, 16:8) that challenges the church to deepen its faith.

✤ Reflecting on the Word

Today's Gospel, warning against dividing our hearts between God and worldly goods, begins with the image of God as "master." There is a deep truth contained in this image, for we are called to serve God, carrying out the divine will and seeking the Kingdom. But the image of a master and a servant might also raise the troubling idea that God sees us as no more than lackeys to be exploited. The rest of this section of Jesus' Sermon on the Mount should dispel that notion, for it presents God as the loving provider of all our needs.

The sorts of things Jesus mentions in this passage are fundamental human needs—food, drink, clothing—and he in no way implies that these things are not important for Christians. Rather, what he calls into question is the anxiety and worry that we have about these things, inasmuch as they imply a misunderstanding on our part as to who God is and who we are in relation to God. While God is the master whom we ought to serve, God does not treat us as slaves to be used up and cast aside. Rather, in a surprising reversal of the normal relationship of master and servant, God constantly seeks our good and provides us with what we need to flourish. In the first reading, Isaiah compares God's love to a mother's care for the baby in her arms or the child within her womb, reminding us that God's providential love is even stronger.

Faith in God does not remove practical concerns of food and drink and clothing. But it can remove the worry and anxiety over these things that sometimes dominate our lives and keep us from seeking above all God's kingdom of righteousness.

✤ Consider/Discuss

- What material needs do I worry about the most? What things am I not doing because of these worries?
- How does the image of the mother's love for her child help me to understand God's love better?

✤ Responding to the Word

Generous God, free us from the worry that would hold us back from seeking your kingdom, and give us confidence in your love and care for us. Amen.

The Anglo-Saxon word Lent originally referred to the "spring season" and came to replace the Latin *quadragesima*, meaning "fortieth day," to describe the forty-day fast before Easter. The number forty is used in biblical texts to signal a lengthy period of time. So Moses and the Hebrews wandering in the wilderness for forty years is the biblical way of indicating an extended duration. In the New Testament, Jesus is tempted in the desert (Mark 1:12–13), where he ate nothing for forty days (Luke 4:2) and forty nights (Matthew 4:2).

A forty-day period of Lent appears to have been a widespread practice by the mid-third century, as evidenced in writings of church fathers. The actual duration of the fast varied from locale to locale. St. Gregory, writing in the late sixth century, recognized the rule of abstinence from the flesh of meat and everything that comes from such animals, including milk, cheese, and eggs. This became known as *lacticinia*, which comes from *lac*, the Latin for milk. The practice of giving eggs at Easter originates from the ban on eating eggs.

Both fasting and abstinence are spiritual practices, designed to heighten one's spiritual life and draw a person closer to God. Though most often associated with the avoidance of food, fasting can be the voluntary avoidance of anything we deem good, in order to focus on spiritual matters. Abstinence is the avoidance of particular foods.

Lent begins on Ash Wednesday. On that day, ashes are placed on the forehead to symbolize our recognition of our sinfulness and our willingness to commit to a period of repentance in preparation for Easter. Those have not availed themselves of the sacrament of reconciliation and Eucharist are encouraged to do so during this period. Lent concludes with the commencement of the Triduum on Holy Thursday. Between Ash Wednesday and Holy Thursday, there are actually forty-six days, but Sundays are not included in the count.

The first and second readings during this period reflect the penitential nature of the season, particularly focusing on the origin of sin (First Sunday of Lent), but also offering examples of human faithfulness and endurance (Second Sunday of Lent), God's attentive care (Third Sunday of Lent), and hope (Fourth and Fifth Sundays of Lent). The Gospel lections are selected from both the Gospel of Matthew and the Gospel of John. They include Matthew's account of Jesus' temptation in the wilderness (First Sunday of Lent), the Transfiguration (Second Sunday of Lent), and John's narratives of the Samaritan woman at the well (Third Sunday of Lent), the man born blind (Fourth Sunday of Lent), and the raising of Lazarus (Fifth Sunday of Lent).

March 9, 2014

FIRST SUNDAY OF LENT

Today's Focus: Did the Devil Really Make You Do It?

There is no doubt about it: evil forces are afoot in the world. But too often we use this reality as a reason to shirk our own responsibility for our sins and shortcomings.

FIRST READING
*Genesis 2:7–9;
3:1–7*

The LORD God formed man out of the clay of the ground and blew into his nostrils the breath of life, and so man became a living being.

Then the LORD God planted a garden in Eden, in the east, and placed there the man whom he had formed. Out of the ground the LORD God made various trees grow that were delightful to look at and good for food, with the tree of life in the middle of the garden and the tree of the knowledge of good and evil.

Now the serpent was the most cunning of all the animals that the LORD God had made. The serpent asked the woman, "Did God really tell you not to eat from any of the trees in the garden?" The woman answered the serpent: "We may eat of the fruit of the trees in the garden; it is only about the fruit of the tree in the middle of the garden that God said, 'You shall not eat it or even touch it, lest you die.' " But the serpent said to the woman: "You certainly will not die! No, God knows well that the moment you eat of it your eyes will be opened and you will be like gods who know what is good and what is evil." The woman saw that the tree was good for food, pleasing to the eyes, and desirable for gaining wisdom. So she took some of its fruit and ate it; and she also gave some to her husband, who was with her, and he ate it. Then the eyes of both of them were opened, and they realized that they were naked; so they sewed fig leaves together and made loincloths for themselves.

PSALM RESPONSE
Psalm 51:3a

Be merciful, O Lord, for we have sinned.

In the shorter form of the reading, the passage in brackets is omitted.

SECOND READING
Romans 5:12–19 or 5: 12, 17–19

Brothers and sisters: Through one man sin entered the world, and through sin, death, and thus death came to all men, inasmuch as all sinned—[for up to the time of the law, sin was in the world, though sin is not accounted when there is no law. But death reigned from Adam to Moses, even over those who did not sin after the pattern of the trespass of Adam, who is the type of the one who was to come.

But the gift is not like the transgression. For if by the transgression of the one, the many died, how much more did the grace of God and the gracious gift of the one man Jesus Christ overflow for the many. And the gift is not like the result of the one who sinned. For after one sin there was the judgment that brought condemnation; but the gift, after many transgressions, brought acquittal.] For if, by the transgression of the one, death came to reign through that one, how much more will those who receive the abundance of grace and of the gift of justification come to reign in life through the one Jesus Christ. In conclusion, just as through one transgression condemnation came upon all, so, through one righteous act, acquittal and life came to all. For just as through the disobedience of the one man the many were made sinners, so, through the obedience of the one, the many will be made righteous.

GOSPEL
Matthew 4: 1–11

At that time Jesus was led by the Spirit into the desert to be tempted by the devil. He fasted for forty days and forty nights, and afterwards he was hungry. The tempter approached and said to him, "If you are the Son of God, command that these stones become loaves of bread." He said in reply, "It is written:
> One does not live on bread alone,
>   but on every word that comes forth
>   from the mouth of God."

Then the devil took him to the holy city, and made him stand on the parapet of the temple, and said to him, "If you are the Son of God, throw yourself down. For it is written:
> He will command his angels concerning you
>   and with their hands they will support you,
>   lest you dash your foot against a stone."

Jesus answered him, "Again it is written,
> You shall not put the Lord, your God, to the test."

Then the devil took him up to a very high mountain, and showed him all the kingdoms of the world in their magnificence, and he said to him, "All these I shall give to you, if you will prostrate yourself and worship me." At this, Jesus said to him, "Get away, Satan! It is written:
> The Lord, your God, shall you worship
>   and him alone shall you serve."

Then the devil left him and, behold, angels came and ministered to him.

The reading from Genesis introduces the second of two creation stories found side by side in the Bible. In the first creation story (Genesis 1:1 — 2:3) the making of human beings is God's final act of creation. In today's reading, humanity is the first living being created. The marked difference between these two stories indicates their separate sources: Genesis 1:1 — 2:3 likely coming from the postexilic Priestly editor, and Genesis 2:4–24 emerging from a much earlier narrative tradition known as the Yahwist. In today's reading, before even field or flower, God molds a human being from the clay of the earth. The Hebrew reflects the intimate relationship between the creature and the material of its existence. God forms the *adam* (often translated as "man") from *adamah* (earth). The reading concludes with the cunning serpent encouraging the woman to eat that which God had forbidden. An often-unnoticed part of the story indicates that the man was present during the conversation between the serpent and his wife: "and she also gave some to her husband, who was with her, and he ate it" (3:6). The eating of the forbidden fruit (note: the specific type of fruit is not identified) will haunt the first couple and become the scriptural foundation for the concept of original sin.

In the second reading, St. Paul recognizes the role of Adam in the original trespass. "Through one man sin entered the world, and through sin, death" (Romans 5:12). But the sin of Adam (and Eve) that brought death into the world is reversed by the obedience of Jesus Christ, "so, through the obedience of one, the many were made righteous" (5:19).

In the Gospel, having just been just been baptized, Jesus is led into the desert by the Spirit, where he is tempted by the devil. The serpent of Genesis is known as Satan or the devil in later biblical traditions (Wisdom 2:24; Revelation 12:9), so we are to see a parallel between the serpent's tempting of the first couple and the devil's tempting of Jesus. As Paul noted, Jesus will not succumb to the devil's false promises.

❖ Reflecting on the Word

I remember as a child watching the comedian Flip Wilson on television, whose character Geraldine had as her signature line, "The devil made me do it" —invariably uttered in an attempt at self-exoneration from bad behavior. The first reading might lead us to think that the human race as a whole might attempt such a self-exoneration. After all, if the devil had not tempted Eve and Adam, they would never have disobeyed God and we would not be in the mess that we find ourselves in today.

While not denying the importance of the devil's temptation, however, the Christian tradition has always laid the blame for sin squarely on the shoulders of Adam and Eve themselves, our ancestors in disobedience. While evil forces might provide the occasion for our turning away from God, no demonic power can force us to do anything against our will, no matter how severely they may tempt us. Temptation is something we give in to.

At the same time, sin has made our wills so feeble that we cannot resist temptation without God's grace. As Lent begins, it is important to bear in mind both that our sins are our own responsibility—the devil did not make us do it—and that we need the grace of Christ in order to turn back to God. Lent is an appeal to our freedom, as well as a reminder that we need God's grace in order to use that freedom well.

✤ Consider/Discuss

- Do I ever blame other people or things for my bad actions? Whom or what do I blame?
- What sort of actions can I undertake in order to make Lent a time in which I let God's grace work in my life?

✤ Responding to the Word

Lord Jesus, in the desert you faced the ancient enemy of the human race and showed your power over him. By your grace, help us to face temptation without giving way to it. Amen.

March 16, 2014

SECOND SUNDAY OF LENT

Today's Focus: Lent: A Time to Be Transformed

God comes into our lives in different ways: God's light shining on us, God's word speaking to us. Our job is to allow God into our lives so we will be transformed by grace.

FIRST READING
Genesis 12:1–4a

The LORD said to Abram: "Go forth from the land of your kinsfolk and from your father's house to a land that I will show you.

"I will make of you a great nation,
and I will bless you;
I will make your name great,
so that you will be a blessing.
I will bless those who bless you
and curse those who curse you.
All the communities of the earth
shall find blessing in you."

Abram went as the LORD directed him.

PSALM RESPONSE
Psalm 33:22

Lord, let your mercy be on us, as we place our trust in you.

SECOND READING
2 Timothy 1: 8b–10

Beloved: Bear your share of hardship for the gospel with the strength that comes from God.

He saved us and called us to a holy life, not according to our works but according to his own design and the grace bestowed on us in Christ Jesus before time began, but now made manifest through the appearance of our savior Christ Jesus, who destroyed death and brought life and immortality to light through the gospel.

GOSPEL
Matthew 17: 1–9

Jesus took Peter, James, and John his brother, and led them up a high mountain by themselves. And he was transfigured before them; his face shone like the sun and his clothes became white as light. And behold, Moses and Elijah appeared to them, conversing with him. Then Peter said to Jesus in reply, "Lord, it is good that we are here. If you wish, I will make three tents here, one for you, one for Moses, and one for Elijah." While he was still speaking, behold, a bright cloud cast a shadow over them, then from the cloud came a voice that said, "This is my beloved Son, with whom I am well pleased; listen to him." When the disciples heard this, they fell prostrate and were very much afraid. But Jesus came and touched them, saying, "Rise, and do not be afraid." And when the disciples raised their eyes, they saw no one else but Jesus alone.

As they were coming down from the mountain, Jesus charged them, "Do not tell the vision to anyone until the Son of Man has been raised from the dead."

✤ Understanding the Word

On the promise of God, Abram goes as he is directed, leaving the security of kinfolk and the familiarity of home to travel to an unknown land. Today's first reading introduces the epic journey of one man, who despite the odds, his age, and uncertainty, trusted that God would make him a great nation in which communities of the earth would find blessing. Abram's steadfast commitment is juxtaposed with that of his father, Terah, who had started to venture to Canaan, but instead settled in Haran (Genesis 11:31).

The second reading, purportedly written by Paul to Timothy, continues the theme of call. God's call to a holy life is not based upon personal merit, but is given according to God's own plan. Part of a collection known as the Pastoral Epistles, First and Second Timothy and Titus reflect an early-second-century community that is developing both ecclesial structures and theological understanding.

In the reading from the Gospel, Jesus takes his closest disciples, Peter, James, and John, and leads them up a mountain by themselves. Mountains are significant places in Matthew's Gospel, since the evangelist attempts to present Jesus in Mosaic terms. As Moses received the Law on Mount Sinai, so Jesus has a divine encounter as well. After Moses' experience with the divine, his face would shine so brightly that he had to cover it with a veil (Exodus 34:35). It is not only Jesus' face but his whole being that is transfigured in today's reading. Moses and Elijah, the two great prophets of Israel, representing the Law and the Prophets, appear and begin conversing with Jesus. Peter's response is the impulse to erect tents for each of them. But Jesus is not just one among Israel's great prophets. A bright cloud overshadows them, and a voice is heard, "This is my beloved Son, with whom I am well pleased." Jesus is the beloved Son. At his baptism, Jesus himself had heard the heavenly voice make this announcement. Now his closest disciples are privy. The heavenly voice concludes, "Listen to him." Likely what the disciples are to listen to and heed is Jesus' prediction of his own passion (Matthew 16:21; 17:9–13).

✤ Reflecting on the Word

Lent is a time for transformation; it is a time to let our way of thinking be transfigured. In today's Gospel we not only have the story of the transfiguration of Jesus, but also what we might think of as the "non-transfiguration" of Peter. Peter's response to this event shows in at least two ways that he is still tied to an old way of thinking. First, he thinks that Jesus, Moses, and Elijah are in need of some sort of shelter. Second, he wants to camp out on the mountain of transfiguration rather than make the journey to Jerusalem, where the true glory of Jesus will shine forth on the cross.

What saves him from his un-transfigured way of thinking is the voice of God, speaking from heaven, telling him to listen to Jesus. Most of us do not have the benefit of such an audible voice, but we do have the example of Peter with which scripture presents us. We can learn that what we need to do in order to share in the transfiguration of the world that is glimpsed in Jesus' own transfiguration is to listen to him, the Son in whom God is well pleased.

Lent is traditionally understood as a time of giving things up. Today's Gospel suggests that we need to give up certain old ways of thinking and to listen to Jesus. Our Lenten discipline should not only be one of giving up sweets or smoking or swearing, but one of actively listening to Jesus in prayerful reflection on scripture.

✦ Consider/Discuss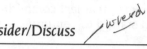

- How do I "imagine" the world being transfigured by the coming of God's kingdom?
- How can I listen more attentively to Jesus? Where do I go to hear his voice?

✦ Responding to the Word

O God, may the light that shines forth from your Son illuminate and transfigure our minds, so that we might come to know you more clearly and share in the glory of your kingdom. Amen.

March 23, 2014

THIRD SUNDAY OF LENT

Today's Focus: Quenching Our Spiritual Thirst

The term "living water" could be thought of as redundant, for we know that without water, there is no life. This essential element recurs throughout scripture to remind us of our need for God's life.

FIRST READING
Exodus 17:3–7

In those days, in their thirst for water, the people grumbled against Moses, saying, "Why did you ever make us leave Egypt? Was it just to have us die here of thirst with our children and our livestock?" So Moses cried out to the LORD, "What shall I do with this people? A little more and they will stone me!" The LORD answered Moses, "Go over there in front of the people, along with some of the elders of Israel, holding in your hand, as you go, the staff with which you struck the river. I will be standing there in front of you on the rock in Horeb. Strike the rock, and the water will flow from it for the people to drink." This Moses did, in the presence of the elders of Israel. The place was called Massah and Meribah, because the Israelites quarreled there and tested the LORD, saying, "Is the LORD in our midst or not?"

PSALM RESPONSE
Psalm 95:8

If today you hear his voice, harden not your hearts.

SECOND READING
Romans 5:1–2, 5–8

Brothers and sisters: Since we have been justified by faith, we have peace with God through our Lord Jesus Christ, through whom we have gained access by faith to this grace in which we stand, and we boast in hope of the glory of God.

And hope does not disappoint, because the love of God has been poured out into our hearts through the Holy Spirit who has been given to us. For Christ, while we were still helpless, died at the appointed time for the ungodly. Indeed, only with difficulty does one die for a just person, though perhaps for a good person one might even find courage to die. But God proves his love for us in that while we were still sinners Christ died for us.

In the shorter form of the reading, the passages in brackets are omitted.

GOSPEL
John 4:5–42 or
4:5–15, 19b–26,
39a, 40–42

Jesus came to a town of Samaria called Sychar, near the plot of land that Jacob had given to his son Joseph. Jacob's well was there. Jesus, tired from his journey, sat down there at the well. It was about noon.

A woman of Samaria came to draw water. Jesus said to her, "Give me a drink." His disciples had gone into the town to buy food. The Samaritan woman said to him, "How can you, a Jew, ask me, a Samaritan woman, for a drink?"—For Jews use nothing in common with Samaritans.—Jesus answered and said to her, "If you knew the gift of God and who is saying to you, 'Give me a drink,' you would have asked him and he would have given you living water." The woman said to him, "Sir, you do not even have a bucket and the cistern is deep; where then can you get this living water? Are you greater than our father Jacob, who gave us this cistern and drank from it himself with his children and his flocks?" Jesus answered and said to her, "Everyone who drinks this water will be thirsty again; but whoever drinks the water I shall give will never thirst; the water I shall give will become in him a spring of water welling up to eternal life." The woman said to him, "Sir, give me this water, so that I may not be thirsty or have to keep coming here to draw water."

[Jesus said to her, "Go call your husband and come back." The woman answered and said to him, "I do not have a husband." Jesus answered her, "You are right in saying, 'I do not have a husband.' For you have had five husbands, and the one you have now is not your husband. What you have said is true." The woman said to him,] "Sir, I can see that you are a prophet. Our ancestors worshiped on this mountain; but you people say that the place to worship is in Jerusalem." Jesus said to her, "Believe me, woman, the hour is coming when you will worship the Father neither on this mountain nor in Jerusalem. You people worship what you do not understand; we worship what we understand, because salvation is from the Jews. But the hour is coming, and is now here, when true worshipers will worship the Father in Spirit and truth; and indeed the Father seeks such people to worship him. God is Spirit, and those who worship him must worship in Spirit and truth." The woman said to him, "I know that the Messiah is coming, the one called the Christ; when he comes, he will tell us everything." Jesus said to her, "I am he, the one speaking with you."

[At that moment his disciples returned, and were amazed that he was talking with a woman, but still no one said, "What are you looking for?" or "Why are you talking with her?" The woman left her water jar and went into the town and said to the people, "Come see a man who told me everything I have done. Could he possibly be the Christ?" They went out of the town and came to him. Meanwhile, the disciples urged him, "Rabbi, eat." But he said to them, "I have food to eat of which you do not know." So the disciples said to one another, "Could someone have brought him something to eat?" Jesus said to them, "My food is to do the will of the one who sent me and to finish his work. Do you not say, 'In four months the harvest will be here'? I tell you, look up and see the fields ripe for the harvest. The reaper is already receiving payment and gathering crops for eternal life, so that the sower and reaper can rejoice together. For here the saying is verified that 'One sows and another reaps.' I sent you to reap what you have not worked for; others have done the work, and you are sharing the fruits of their work."]

Many of the Samaritans of that town began to believe in him because of the word of the woman who testified, "He told me everything I have done." When the Samaritans came to him, they invited him to stay with them; and he stayed there two days. Many more began to believe in him because of his word, and they said to the woman, "We no longer believe because of your word; for we have heard for ourselves, and we know that this is truly the savior of the world."

❖ Understanding the Word

The narrative of the exodus of the Hebrews from Egypt is the foundation story of Israel. But not long after their harrowing escape, the people turn on Moses, their leader. First, they grumble that they have no food (Exodus 16:3), and God provides manna in the morning and quail in the evening. In today's reading, their complaint is thirst. Moses is justified in asking God, "What shall I do with this people?" And as God had provided food, now through the actions of Moses, God provides drink. The place was called Massah (the place of the test) and Meribah (the place of quarreling), and served as a reminder to future Israelites of God's provident care despite the people's grumbling.

The second reading from Paul's Letter to the Romans is another example of God's care, despite humanity's sinful state. Christ's willingness to die for "the ungodly" is beyond imagining. Perhaps a good person may sacrifice his or her life for someone who is just. But for a sinner? Christ's death is evidence of God's love for us; through his death, believers are justified and are at peace with God. As Paul explains, God has poured out the Holy Spirit into the hearts of believers. The presence of the Holy Spirit gives reason to hope that all believers will stand in the glory of God.

The topic of thirst appears again in the Gospel reading. The woman of Samaria meets the man of Galilee at the well of Jacob. The evangelist John may be playing off the motif of meeting one's future spouse at the well. A wife for Isaac is found at the well (Genesis 23:11–14). Jacob met Rachel at a well (Genesis 29:9–12). Moses met Zipporah, the daughter of Jethro, at a well (Exodus 2:16–22). Indeed, Jesus asks the woman about her husbands (she's had five). The evangelist seems to be explaining to his own community how the Samaritans "married" into the Johannine community. But the encounter also serves a larger purpose. The

Samaritan woman is contrasted with Nicodemus in John 3:1–14. Like the Pharisee, she appears at an unusual time. At first she misunderstands Jesus' offer of living water. However, where Nicodemus was stumped by Jesus' teaching, the woman of Samaria engages in a theological conversation with Jesus. Jesus even reveals to her that he is the Messiah. She leaves her water jar behind (perhaps a symbol of having received the "living water"), returns to the town, and invites others to come to Jesus.

✤ Reflecting on the Word

This Sunday's readings all point to Jesus as the one who can quench the deepest thirsts of our souls. The book of Exodus focuses on bodily thirst, with God miraculously providing water for the Israelites in the desert. The Gospel presents Jesus' dialogue with the Samaritan woman at the well, in which he reveals himself as the source of living water. The Letter of Paul to the Romans speaks of the love of God that is poured into our hearts.

Perhaps the metaphor of thirst, even more than the metaphor of hunger, conveys the desperation of the soul's need for God. We might pass a day or two or even more without food and experience only mild discomfort. But cut off from water, we are quickly afflicted with thirst; we experience it as an immediate threat to our life and health. Like the Israelites in the desert, we soon begin to grumble.

The Samaritan woman must already feel the pangs of spiritual thirst. Though initially disconcerted by being addressed by a Jewish man, she engages him in conversation, yearning for the living water that he offers, bringing relief to her life of spiritual longing. Lent is an opportunity to let ourselves feel our spiritual thirst and to welcome the living water that Jesus offers.

✤ Consider/Discuss

- What am I spiritually thirsting for? Acceptance? Wisdom? Forgiveness? Something else?
- Have there been moments when I have felt that the love of God was poured into my heart? Is God's love poured into us even when we don't feel it?

✤ Responding to the Word

Lord Jesus, you offered the Samaritan woman a spring of water welling up to eternal life. Give to us that same living water, so that we might live in God's presence forever. Amen.

March 30, 2014

FOURTH SUNDAY OF LENT

Today's Focus: Seeing Beyond Our Own Blindness

Jesus again takes to task those who criticize the man born blind (or his parents) for sinfulness; also for their inability to see him as something other than blind and begging. What "blinders" do we wear?

FIRST READING
1 Samuel 16: 1b, 6–7, 10–13a

The LORD said to Samuel: "Fill your horn with oil, and be on your way. I am sending you to Jesse of Bethlehem, for I have chosen my king from among his sons."

As Jesse and his sons came to the sacrifice, Samuel looked at Eliab and thought, "Surely the Lord's anointed is here before him." But the LORD said to Samuel: "Do not judge from his appearance or from his lofty stature, because I have rejected him. Not as man sees does God see, because man sees the appearance but the LORD looks into the heart." In the same way Jesse presented seven sons before Samuel, but Samuel said to Jesse, "The LORD has not chosen any one of these." Then Samuel asked Jesse, "Are these all the sons you have?" Jesse replied, "There is still the youngest, who is tending the sheep." Samuel said to Jesse, "Send for him; we will not begin the sacrificial banquet until he arrives here." Jesse sent and had the young man brought to them. He was ruddy, a youth handsome to behold and making a splendid appearance. The LORD said, "There—anoint him, for this is the one!" Then Samuel, with the horn of oil in hand, anointed David in the presence of his brothers; and from that day on, the spirit of the LORD rushed upon David.

PSALM RESPONSE
Psalm 23:1

The Lord is my shepherd; there is nothing I shall want.

SECOND READING
Ephesians 5: 8–14

Brothers and sisters: You were once darkness, but now you are light in the Lord. Live as children of light, for light produces every kind of goodness and righteousness and truth. Try to learn what is pleasing to the Lord. Take no part in the fruitless works of darkness; rather expose them, for it is shameful even to mention the things done by them in secret; but everything exposed by the light becomes visible, for everything that becomes visible is light. Therefore, it says:

"Awake, O sleeper,
and arise from the dead,
and Christ will give you light."

79

In the shorter form of the reading, the passages in brackets are omitted.

GOSPEL
*John 9:1–41 or
9:1, 6–9, 13–17,
34–38*

As Jesus passed by he saw a man blind from birth. [His disciples asked him, "Rabbi, who sinned, this man or his parents, that he was born blind?" Jesus answered, "Neither he nor his parents sinned; it is so that the works of God might be made visible through him. We have to do the works of the one who sent me while it is day. Night is coming when no one can work. While I am in the world, I am the light of the world." When he had said this,] he spat on the ground and made clay with the saliva, and smeared the clay on his eyes, and said to him, "Go wash in the Pool of Siloam"—which means Sent—. So he went and washed, and came back able to see.

His neighbors and those who had seen him earlier as a beggar said, "Isn't this the one who used to sit and beg?" Some said, "It is," but others said, "No, he just looks like him." He said, "I am." [So they said to him, "How were your eyes opened?" He replied, "The man called Jesus made clay and anointed my eyes and told me, 'Go to Siloam and wash.' So I went there and washed and was able to see." And they said to him, "Where is he?" He said, "I don't know."]

They brought the one who was once blind to the Pharisees. Now Jesus had made clay and opened his eyes on a sabbath. So then the Pharisees also asked him how he was able to see. He said to them, "He put clay on my eyes, and I washed, and now I can see." So some of the Pharisees said, "This man is not from God, because he does not keep the sabbath." But others said, "How can a sinful man do such signs?" And there was a division among them. So they said to the blind man again, "What do you have to say about him, since he opened your eyes?" He said, "He is a prophet."

[Now the Jews did not believe that he had been blind and gained his sight until they summoned the parents of the one who had gained his sight. They asked them, "Is this your son, who you say was born blind? How does he now see?" His parents answered and said, "We know that this is our son and that he was born blind. We do not know how he sees now, nor do we know who opened his eyes. Ask him, he is of age; he can speak for himself." His parents said this because they were afraid of the Jews, for the Jews had already agreed that if anyone acknowledged him as the Christ, he would be expelled from the synagogue. For this reason his parents said, "He is of age; question him."

So a second time they called the man who had been blind and said to him, "Give God the praise! We know that this man is a sinner." He replied, "If he is a sinner, I do not know. One thing I do know is that I was blind and now I see." So they said to him, "What did he do to you? How did he open your eyes?" He answered them, "I told you already and you did not listen. Why do you want to hear it again? Do you want to become his disciples, too?" They ridiculed him and said, "You are that man's disciple; we are disciples of Moses! We know that God spoke to Moses, but we do not know where this one is from." The man answered and said to them, "This is what is so amazing, that you do not know where he is from, yet he opened my eyes. We know that God does not listen to sinners, but if one is devout and does his will, he listens to him. It is unheard of that anyone ever opened the eyes of a person born blind. If this man were not from God, he would not be able to do anything."] They answered and said to him, "You were born totally in sin, and are you trying to teach us?" Then they threw him out.

When Jesus heard that they had thrown him out, he found him and said, "Do you believe in the Son of Man?" He answered and said, "Who is he, sir, that I may believe in him?" Jesus said to him, "You have seen him, the one speaking with you is he." He said, "I do believe, Lord," and he worshiped him. [Then Jesus said, "I came into this world for judgment, so that those who do not see might see, and those who do see might become blind."

Some of the Pharisees who were with him heard this and said to him, "Surely we are not also blind, are we?" Jesus said to them, "If you were blind, you would have no sin; but now you are saying, 'We see,' so your sin remains."]

❖ Understanding the Word

The reading from the first book of Samuel introduces David, the youngest son of Jesse of Bethlehem. At the request of the people, God had allowed the prophet Samuel to anoint Saul as ruler over the people (1 Samuel 10:1), but Saul proved unworthy. Samuel is sent to Bethlehem to anoint a new king from among the sons of Jesse. Judging by appearance, Samuel mistakes the oldest as the Lord's chosen. But God corrects him, "Not as man sees does God see." It is the youngest son, David, whom God has chosen. As Samuel anoints him, the Spirit of the Lord rushes upon him. David will prove a worthy ruler, but he must first deal with Saul's jealousy, for as the Spirit descended upon David, so it withdrew from Saul. After Saul's death, David will be made king of Judah (2 Samuel 2:4).

The Letter to the Ephesians purported to be have been written by Paul actually comes from the second generation of Pauline Christians. Writing in the voice of the Apostle, the author reminds the community to live according to the light, which produces goodness, justice, and truth—virtues that even pagans admire.

The Gospel reading from John introduces the narrative of the man born blind. This is the sixth sign or miracle that Jesus has performed (water into wine in Cana, 2:1–11; royal official's son restored to life, 4:46–54; healing of the crippled man at Bethesda, 5:1–9; feeding the multitude, 6:1–15; walking on the water, 6:16–21). Each sign serves to reveal Jesus' identity and confirm his disciples' belief in him. But with each sign, those who do not believe strengthen their animosity toward him. After the seventh and final sign, the raising of Lazarus (11:1–14), the chief priests and Pharisees gather the Great Council and decide to have Jesus put to death (11:53). The man healed in today's Gospel is twice brought before the Pharisees to explain who restored his vision. With his new sight, he recognizes his healer as a prophet and a man from God. And now it is the Pharisees, unable to recognize Jesus as the Son of Man, who are truly blind.

It is striking that in the story of the man born blind the man's neighbors enter into a debate—once he is healed—as to whether it is in fact the same man. It is as if they have difficulty recognizing him once the blindness that was for them his defining feature is gone. It is also noteworthy that they refer to him as "the one who used to sit and beg." For them, he was not a person with a name and a story, but simply a part of the landscape, wholly defined by his blindness and his begging. Furthermore, despite the fact that they know nothing about him, and seem to want to know nothing about him, they presume that his blindness must be the result of sin—either his sin or that of his parents.

Part of the irony of the story is that it is the man's neighbors who are really the blind ones. It is they who cannot see beyond their presumptions and prejudices and truly perceive the blind man. Moreover, they cannot truly see Jesus, saying that they know that he is a sinner. As Jesus heals the man's physical blindness, he is also trying to heal the blindness of the bystanders by giving them the eyes of faith, so they can see what the blind man now sees: that if Jesus were not from God he would not be able to do anything.

Though we might think of healing physical blindness as a great miracle, the Gospel of John seems to be saying that it is spiritual blindness that truly needs to be overcome, and it is the healing of spiritual blindness that is the greatest miracle.

✤ Consider/Discuss

- Do I tend to reduce people to single characteristics, whether these are physical features or single events in their lives, as if these defined them?
- What would it mean to see others through eyes that had been healed of all spiritual blindness?

✤ Responding to the Word

Lord Jesus, Light of the world, you who have come to heal our blindness: give us eyes to see others truly, so that we may know them even as you know them. Amen.

April 6, 2014

FIFTH SUNDAY OF LENT

Today's Focus: Awake! Arise!

We use the term "rising" for getting out of bed in the morning, and for what we believe will happen to us on the last day. The Resurrection calls us to other "awakenings" in daily living as well.

FIRST READING
Ezekiel 37: 12–14

Thus says the LORD GOD: O my people, I will open your graves and have you rise from them, and bring you back to the land of Israel. Then you shall know that I am the LORD, when I open your graves and have you rise from them, O my people! I will put my spirit in you that you may live, and I will settle you upon your land; thus you shall know that I am the LORD. I have promised, and I will do it, says the LORD.

PSALM RESPONSE
Psalm 130:7

With the Lord there is mercy and fullness of redemption.

SECOND READING
Romans 8:8–11

Brothers and sisters: Those who are in the flesh cannot please God. But you are not in the flesh; on the contrary, you are in the spirit, if only the Spirit of God dwells in you. Whoever does not have the Spirit of Christ does not belong to him. But if Christ is in you, although the body is dead because of sin, the spirit is alive because of righteousness. If the Spirit of the one who raised Jesus from the dead dwells in you, the one who raised Christ from the dead will give life to your mortal bodies also, through his Spirit dwelling in you.

GOSPEL
*John 11:1–45
or 11: 3–7, 17,
20–27, 33b–45*

[Now a man was ill, Lazarus from Bethany, the village of Mary and her sister Martha. Mary was the one who had anointed the Lord with perfumed oil and dried his feet with her hair; it was her brother Lazarus who was ill.] So the sisters sent word to Jesus saying, "Master, the one you love is ill." When Jesus heard this he said, "This illness is not to end in death, but is for the glory of God, that the Son of God may be glorified through it." Now Jesus loved Martha and her sister and Lazarus. So when he heard that he was ill, he remained for two days in the place where he was. Then after this he said to his disciples, "Let us go back to Judea." [The disciples said to him, "Rabbi, the Jews were just trying to stone you, and you want to go back there?" Jesus answered, "Are there not twelve hours in a day? If one walks during the day, he does not stumble, because he sees the light of this world. But if one walks at night, he stumbles, because the light is not in him." He said this, and then told them, "Our friend Lazarus is asleep, but I am going to awaken him." So the disciples said to him, "Master, if he is asleep, he will be saved." But Jesus was talking about his death, while they thought that he meant ordinary sleep. So then Jesus said to them clearly, "Lazarus has died. And I am glad for you that I was not there, that you may believe. Let us go to him." So Thomas, called Didymus, said to his fellow disciples, "Let us also go to die with him."]

When Jesus arrived, he found that Lazarus had already been in the tomb for four days. [Now Bethany was near Jerusalem, only about two miles away. And many of the Jews had come to Martha and Mary to comfort them about their brother.] When Martha heard that Jesus was coming, she went to meet him; but Mary sat at home. Martha said to Jesus, "Lord, if you had been here, my brother would not have died. But even now I know that whatever you ask of God, God will give you." Jesus said to her, "Your brother will rise." Martha said to him, "I know he will rise, in the resurrection on the last day." Jesus told her, "I am the resurrection and the life; whoever believes in me, even if he dies, will live, and everyone who lives and believes in me will never die. Do you believe this?" She said to him, "Yes, Lord. I have come to believe that you are the Christ, the Son of God, the one who is coming into the world."

[When she had said this, she went and called her sister Mary secretly, saying, "The teacher is here and is asking for you." As soon as she heard this, she rose quickly and went to him. For Jesus had not yet come into the village, but was still where Martha had met him. So when the Jews who were with her in the house comforting her saw Mary get up quickly and go out, they followed her, presuming that she was going to the tomb to weep there. When Mary came to where Jesus was and saw him, she fell at his feet and said to him, "Lord, if you had been here, my brother would not have died." When Jesus saw her weeping and the Jews who had come with her weeping,] he became perturbed and deeply troubled, and said, "Where have you laid him?" They said to him, "Sir, come and see." And Jesus wept. So the Jews said, "See how he loved him." But some of them said, "Could not the one who opened the eyes of the blind man have done something so that this man would not have died?"

So Jesus, perturbed again, came to the tomb. It was a cave, and a stone lay across it. Jesus said, "Take away the stone." Martha, the dead man's sister, said to him, "Lord, by now there will be a stench; he has been dead for four days." Jesus said to her, "Did I not tell you that if you believe you will see the glory of God?" So they took away the stone. And Jesus raised his eyes and said, "Father, I thank you for hearing me. I know that you always hear me; but because of the crowd here I have said this, that they may believe that you sent me." And when he had said this, he cried out in a loud voice, "Lazarus, come out!" The dead man came out, tied hand and foot with burial bands, and his face was wrapped in a cloth. So Jesus said to them, "Untie him and let him go."

Now many of the Jews who had come to Mary and seen what he had done began to believe in him.

❖ Understanding the Word

Speaking to the exiles in Babylon, the prophet Ezekiel proclaims a vision of hope. Dry bones wholly without life are knit together again. Graves are opened and the dead are not only raised but brought back to the land of Israel. God's spirit will be placed in this new people and they will come to life. This figurative description of the exiles' return to the land is viewed by some as the foundation of Jewish and Christian understanding of resurrection from the dead.

Paul's Letter to the Romans continues the theme of a new creation. But it is not new sinews on dry bones or bodies emerging from graves. Rather, Paul understands that baptism into Christ makes the believer one with Christ. Earlier in the letter, he had written, "We were indeed buried with him through baptism into death, so that, just as Christ was raised from the dead by the glory of the Father, we too might live in newness of life" (Romans 6:4). The Spirit of God dwells within the believer, so that the "fleshly" things of the world are no longer of import. If God's spirit could raise Jesus from the dead, that same spirit will raise the body of believers. Though Paul's writing sounds dualistic, he means to distinguish between the things of God (the spiritual) and the things of this world (the fleshly).

The Gospel presents a poignant picture of Jesus, who, despite his love for Lazarus, delays his return until Lazarus has died in order that his disciples might come to greater belief. Sandwiched between Lazarus' death and Jesus' raising of him is Jesus' encounter with Martha, Lazarus' sister. In conversation between Jesus and the Samaritan woman, Jesus had identified himself as the Messiah. Here in another theological discussion with Martha he declares: "I am the resurrection and the life." Martha responds affirmatively, "I have come to believe that you are the Christ, the Son of God." And yet this Messiah is not beyond human emotion. Jesus begins to weep at the tomb of Lazarus, causing the onlookers to remark, "See how he loved him." The final sign in John's Gospel reveals Jesus as a human Messiah, and points to his own death and resurrection.

In today's Gospel, Jesus says, "Our friend Lazarus is asleep, but I am going to awaken him," imagery that echoes the Letter to the Ephesians (5:14): "Awake, O sleeper, and arise from the dead, and Christ will give you light." Physical death is portrayed as a kind of sleep from which Christ has the power to awaken us. But in the context of Lent this imagery also implies that the life of sin from which Christ comes to raise us is a kind of dream, an illusion. It is the illusion that we are the source and meaning of our own existence; it is the dream—or nightmare—that we can exist without God.

If we read the story of Lazarus not simply as a story about Jesus's victory over bodily death, but also his victory over sin, then we can see ourselves like Lazarus, lying in the tomb of our own evil actions, bound by them the way that Lazarus is bound by his burial cloths. We also see Jesus weeping, grieving by the tomb in which the deadly power of sin has enclosed us. And we hear his cry, "Come out!" as an invitation to us to rise from our sins and turn back to God.

The seasons of Lent and Easter display for us the drama of death and resurrection. But it is a drama in which we participate, as we pass over from a life of sin into the new life that Jesus offers to us, a life that we begin to live now. The promise God makes through the prophet Ezekiel, "I will open your graves and have you rise from them," is a promise that has already been kept in our salvation from sin.

❖ *Consider/Discuss*

- In what ways is sin like death? In what ways is it like sleeping?
- What are the signs that we are awakening from sin?

❖ *Responding to the Word*

Lord Jesus, you wept at the tomb of your friend Lazarus and called him forth to life. Call us too from the death of sin to live the risen life you offer. Amen.

It's Time to Order
Living the Word 2015: Year B

By now you have discovered what a prayerful and valuable scriptural resource *Living the Word* provides for you each Sunday of the year.

Don't miss a single week! Subscribe to *Living the Word 2015* today for yourself, your staff, parishioners, family, and friends, and share the gift of God's Word.

Order now to receive the same low price as 2014:

100 or more copies .... $6.95 each
25–99 copies .... $8.95 each
10–24 copies .... $9.95 each
2–9 copies .... $10.95 each
Single copies... $14.95

MAKE A COPY OF THIS ORDER FORM AND FAX IT TODAY TO
888-957-3291 OR SCAN AND SEND TO WLPCS@JSPALUCH.COM.
(This will keep your current book intact!)

OR, CALL WLP CUSTOMER CARE AT
800-566-6150 TO PLACE YOUR ORDER.

[ ] Yes, I'd like to order *Living the Word 2015: Year B*. Please send me _____ copies at _____ each, plus shipping, handling and any applicable sales tax.

NAME _____ POSITION _____

PARISH/INSTITUTION_____

ADDRESS _____

CITY _____ STATE _____ ZIP _____

PHONE _____ FAX_____ E-MAIL_____

Please keep a copy of your order for reference.

Living the Word 2015 will be shipped and billed after October 1, 2014.

Add $7.95 for orders up to $20.00. Add 15% of total for orders over $20.00. Payment in U.S. currency only. No cash or stamps, please. Make checks payable to World Library Publications. Prices subject to change without notice. **Applicable sales tax will be added to orders based on individual state tax requirements.**

World Library Publications
the music and liturgy division of J.S.Paluch Company, Inc.
3708 River Road, Suite 400 • Franklin Park, IL 60131-2158
800-566-6150 • wlpcs@jspaluch.com • wlpmusic.com

LTWB15

April 13, 2014

PALM SUNDAY OF THE PASSION OF THE LORD

Today's Focus: The Know-How We Need for Christian Living

As we enter Holy Week, we begin to encounter many examples in the scriptures that reveal to us Jesus' way to die to ourselves, so we might have life everlasting.

FIRST READING
Isaiah 50:4–7

The Lord GOD has given me
 a well-trained tongue,
that I might know how to speak to the weary
 a word that will rouse them.
Morning after morning
 he opens my ear that I may hear;
and I have not rebelled,
 have not turned back.
I gave my back to those who beat me,
 my cheeks to those who plucked my beard;
my face I did not shield
 from buffets and spitting.

The Lord GOD is my help,
 therefore I am not disgraced;
I have set my face like flint,
 knowing that I shall not be put to shame.

PSALM RESPONSE
Psalm 22:2a

My God, my God, why have you abandoned me?

SECOND READING
Philippians 2: 6–11

Christ Jesus, though he was in the form of God,
 did not regard equality with God
 something to be grasped.
Rather, he emptied himself,
 taking the form of a slave,
 coming in human likeness;
 and found human in appearance,
 he humbled himself,
 becoming obedient to the point of death,
 even death on a cross.
Because of this, God greatly exalted him
 and bestowed on him the name
 which is above every name,
 that at the name of Jesus
 every knee should bend,
 of those in heaven and on earth and under the earth,
 and every tongue confess that
 Jesus Christ is Lord,
 to the glory of God the Father.

GOSPEL
Matthew
26:14 — 27:66
or 27:11–54

[One of the Twelve, who was called Judas Iscariot, went to the chief priests and said, "What are you willing to give me if I hand him over to you?" They paid him thirty pieces of silver, and from that time on he looked for an opportunity to hand him over.

On the first day of the Feast of Unleavened Bread, the disciples approached Jesus and said, "Where do you want us to prepare for you to eat the Passover?" He said, "Go into the city to a certain man and tell him, 'The teacher says, "My appointed time draws near; in your house I shall celebrate the Passover with my disciples." ' " The disciples then did as Jesus had ordered, and prepared the Passover.

When it was evening, he reclined at table with the Twelve. And while they were eating, he said, "Amen, I say to you, one of you will betray me." Deeply distressed at this, they began to say to him one after another, "Surely it is not I, Lord?" He said in reply, "He who has dipped his hand into the dish with me is the one who will betray me. The Son of Man indeed goes, as it is written of him, but woe to that man by whom the Son of Man is betrayed. It would be better for that man if he had never been born." Then Judas, his betrayer, said in reply, "Surely it is not I, Rabbi?" He answered, "You have said so."

While they were eating, Jesus took bread, said the blessing, broke it, and giving it to his disciples said, "Take and eat; this is my body." Then he took a cup, gave thanks, and gave it to them, saying, "Drink from it, all of you, for this is my blood of the covenant, which will be shed on behalf of many for the forgiveness of sins. I tell you, from now on I shall not drink this fruit of the vine until the day when I drink it with you new in the kingdom of my Father." Then, after singing a hymn, they went out to the Mount of Olives.

Then Jesus said to them, "This night all of you will have your faith in me shaken, for it is written:
    I *will strike the shepherd,*
        and the sheep of the flock will be dispersed;
but after I have been raised up, I shall go before you to Galilee." Peter said to him in reply, "Though all may have their faith in you shaken, mine will never be." Jesus said to him, "Amen, I say to you, this very night before the cock crows, you will deny me three times." Peter said to him, "Even though I should have to die with you, I will not deny you." And all the disciples spoke likewise.

Then Jesus came with them to a place called Gethsemane, and he said to his disciples, "Sit here while I go over there and pray." He took along Peter and the two sons of Zebedee, and began to feel sorrow and distress. Then he said to them, "My soul is sorrowful even to death. Remain here and keep watch with me." He advanced a little and fell prostrate in prayer, saying, "My Father, if it is possible, let this cup pass from me; yet, not as I will, but as you will." When he returned to his disciples he found them asleep. He said to Peter, "So you could not keep watch with me for one hour?

Watch and pray that you may not undergo the test. The spirit is willing, but the flesh is weak." Withdrawing a second time, he prayed again, "My Father, if it is not possible that this cup pass without my drinking it, your will be done!" Then he returned once more and found them asleep, for they could not keep their eyes open. He left them and withdrew again and prayed a third time, saying the same thing again. Then he returned to his disciples and said to them, "Are you still sleeping and taking your rest? Behold, the hour is at hand when the Son of Man is to be handed over to sinners. Get up, let us go. Look, my betrayer is at hand."

While he was still speaking, Judas, one of the Twelve, arrived, accompanied by a large crowd, with swords and clubs, who had come from the chief priests and the elders of the people. His betrayer had arranged a sign with them, saying, "The man I shall kiss is the one; arrest him." Immediately he went over to Jesus and said, "Hail, Rabbi!" and he kissed him. Jesus answered him, "Friend, do what you have come for." Then stepping forward they laid hands on Jesus and arrested him. And behold, one of those who accompanied Jesus put his hand to his sword, drew it, and struck the high priest's servant, cutting off his ear. Then Jesus said to him, "Put your sword back into its sheath, for all who take the sword will perish by the sword. Do you think that I cannot call upon my Father and he will not provide me at this moment with more than twelve legions of angels? But then how would the Scriptures be fulfilled which say that it must come to pass in this way?" At that hour Jesus said to the crowds, "Have you come out as against a robber, with swords and clubs to seize me? Day after day I sat teaching in the temple area, yet you did not arrest me. But all this has come to pass that the writings of the prophets may be fulfilled." Then all the disciples left him and fled.

Those who had arrested Jesus led him away to Caiaphas the high priest, where the scribes and the elders were assembled. Peter was following him at a distance as far as the high priest's courtyard, and going inside he sat down with the servants to see the outcome. The chief priests and the entire Sanhedrin kept trying to obtain false testimony against Jesus in order to put him to death, but they found none, though many false witnesses came forward. Finally two came forward who stated, "This man said, 'I can destroy the temple of God and within three days rebuild it.' " The high priest rose and addressed him, "Have you no answer? What are these men testifying against you?" But Jesus was silent. Then the high priest said to him, "I order you to tell us under oath before the living God whether you are the Christ, the Son of God." Jesus said to him in reply, "You have said so. But I tell you:

From now on you will see 'the Son of Man
    seated at the right hand of the Power'
    and 'coming on the clouds of heaven.' "

Then the high priest tore his robes and said, "He has blasphemed! What further need have we of witnesses? You have now heard the blasphemy; what is your opinion?" They said in reply, "He deserves to die!" Then they spat in his face and struck him, while some slapped him, saying, "Prophesy for us, Christ: who is it that struck you?"

Now Peter was sitting outside in the courtyard. One of the maids came over to him and said, "You too were with Jesus the Galilean." But he denied it in front of everyone, saying, "I do not know what you are talking about!" As he went out to the gate, another girl saw him and said to those who were there, "This man was with Jesus the Nazarene." Again he denied it with an oath, "I do not know the man!" A little later the bystanders came over and said to Peter, "Surely you too are one of them; even your speech gives you away." At that he began to curse and to swear, "I do not know the man." And immediately a cock crowed. Then Peter remembered the word that Jesus had spoken: "Before the cock crows you will deny me three times." He went out and began to weep bitterly.

When it was morning, all the chief priests and the elders of the people took counsel against Jesus to put him to death. They bound him, led him away, and handed him over to Pilate, the governor.

Then Judas, his betrayer, seeing that Jesus had been condemned, deeply regretted what he had done. He returned the thirty pieces of silver to the chief priests and elders, saying, "I have sinned in betraying innocent blood." They said, "What is that to us? Look to it yourself." Flinging the money into the temple, he departed and went off and hanged himself. The chief priests gathered up the money, but said, "It is not lawful to deposit this in the temple treasury, for it is the price of blood." After consultation, they used it to buy the potter's field as a burial place for foreigners. That is why that field even today is called the Field of Blood. Then was fulfilled what had been said through Jeremiah the prophet,

And they took the thirty pieces of silver,
the value of a man with a price on his head,
a price set by some of the Israelites,
and they paid it out for the potter's field
just as the Lord had commanded me.

Now] Jesus stood before the governor, who questioned him, "Are you the king of the Jews?" Jesus said, "You say so." And when he was accused by the chief priests and elders, he made no answer. Then Pilate said to him, "Do you not hear how many things they are testifying against you?" But he did not answer him one word, so that the governor was greatly amazed.

Now on the occasion of the feast the governor was accustomed to release to the crowd one prisoner whom they wished. And at that time they had a notorious prisoner called Barabbas. So when they had assembled, Pilate said to them, "Which one do you want me to release to you, Barabbas, or Jesus called Christ?" For he knew that it was out of envy that they had handed him over. While he was still seated on the bench, his wife sent him a message, "Have nothing to do with that righteous man. I suffered much in a dream today because of him." The chief priests and the elders persuaded the crowds to ask for Barabbas but to destroy Jesus. The governor said to them in reply, "Which of the two do you want me to release to you?" They answered, "Barabbas!" Pilate said to them, "Then what shall I do with Jesus called Christ?" They all said, "Let him be crucified!" But he said, "Why? What evil has he done?" They only shouted the louder, "Let him be crucified!" When Pilate saw that he was not succeeding at all, but that a riot was breaking out instead, he took water and washed his hands in the sight of the crowd, saying, "I am innocent of this man's blood. Look to it yourselves." And the whole people said in reply, "His blood be upon us and upon our children." Then he released Barabbas to them, but after he had Jesus scourged, he handed him over to be crucified.

Then the soldiers of the governor took Jesus inside the praetorium and gathered the whole cohort around him. They stripped off his clothes and threw a scarlet military cloak about him. Weaving a crown out of thorns, they placed it on his head, and a reed in his right hand. And kneeling before him, they mocked him, saying, "Hail, King of the Jews!" They spat upon him and took the reed and kept striking him on the head. And when they had mocked him, they stripped him of the cloak, dressed him in his own clothes, and led him off to crucify him.

As they were going out, they met a Cyrenian named Simon; this man they pressed into service to carry his cross.

And when they came to a place called Golgotha—which means Place of the Skull—, they gave Jesus wine to drink mixed with gall. But when he had tasted it, he refused to drink. After they had crucified him, they divided his garments by casting lots; then they sat down and kept watch over him there. And they placed over his head the written charge against him: This is Jesus, the King of the Jews. Two revolutionaries were crucified with him, one on his right and the other on his left. Those passing by reviled him, shaking their heads and saying, "You who would destroy the temple and rebuild it in three days, save yourself, if you are the Son of God, and come down from the cross!" Likewise the chief priests with the scribes and elders mocked him and said, "He saved others; he cannot save himself. So he is the king of Israel! Let him come down from the cross now, and we will believe in him. He trusted in God; let him deliver him now if he wants him. For he said, 'I am the Son of God.' " The revolutionaries who were crucified with him also kept abusing him in the same way.

From noon onward, darkness came over the whole land until three in the afternoon. And about three o'clock Jesus cried out in a loud voice, "Eli, Eli, *lema sabachthani?*" which means, "My God, my God, why have you forsaken me?" Some of the bystanders who heard it said, "This one is calling for Elijah." Immediately one of them ran to get a sponge; he soaked it in wine, and putting it on a reed, gave it to him to drink. But the rest said, "Wait, let us see if Elijah comes to save him." But Jesus cried out again in a loud voice, and gave up his spirit.

And behold, the veil of the sanctuary was torn in two from top to bottom. The earth quaked, rocks were split, tombs were opened, and the bodies of many saints who had fallen asleep were raised. And coming forth from their tombs after his resurrection, they entered the holy city and appeared to many. The centurion and the men with him who were keeping watch over Jesus feared greatly when they saw the earthquake and all that was happening, and they said, "Truly, this was the Son of God!" [There were many women there, looking on from a distance, who had followed Jesus from Galilee, ministering to him. Among them were Mary Magdalene and Mary the mother of James and Joseph, and the mother of the sons of Zebedee.

When it was evening, there came a rich man from Arimathea named Joseph, who was himself a disciple of Jesus. He went to Pilate and asked for the body of Jesus; then Pilate ordered it to be handed over. Taking the body, Joseph wrapped it in clean linen and laid it in his new tomb that he had hewn in the rock. Then he rolled a huge stone across the entrance to the tomb and departed. But Mary Magdalene and the other Mary remained sitting there, facing the tomb. The next day, the one following the day of preparation, the chief priests and the Pharisees gathered before Pilate and said, "Sir, we remember that this impostor while still alive said, 'After three days I will be raised up.' Give orders, then, that the grave be secured until the third day, lest his disciples come and steal him and say to the people, 'He has been raised from the dead.' This last imposture would be worse than the first." Pilate said to them, "The guard is yours; go, secure it as best you can." So they went and secured the tomb by fixing a seal to the stone and setting the guard.]

The role of the prophet is to speak for God, despite the costs. Isaiah 50 is one of four songs that describe the Suffering Servant of the Lord (42:1–9; 49:1–7; 50:4–11; 52:13 — 53:12), and is attributed to Second Isaiah, an anonymous prophet preaching in the spirit of Isaiah of Jerusalem but two centuries later. Christians see the Suffering Servant as foreshadowing the passion of Christ.

The theme of humility and obedience is echoed in Paul's Letter to the Philippians. Incorporating an older hymn, Paul reminds the Philippian faithful that they are to have the same attitude as Christ, whose obedience to God led to his exaltation. Paul's correspondence with the Philippians evidences a fondness for the community, his first converts on European soil. As such, this reading is meant to encourage them to continue their "partnership for the Gospel" (Philippians 1:5).

Palm Sunday begins with the reading of the jubilant march into Jerusalem with palms held high and hosannas ringing out (Matthew 21:1–11). But very quickly, the Gospel reminds us that this is more properly called Passion Sunday and begins Holy Week. The long form of the Gospel includes several scenes: Judas' deal to hand Jesus over, the Passover supper, the prayer at Gethsemane, the arrest in the garden, the Jewish trial and Peter's denial, Judas' death, the trial before Pilate, the Crucifixion, the burial, and the guarding of the tomb. Matthew's Passion has several unique aspects, not found in the other two Synoptic Gospels or John. Only Matthew suggests that greed was Judas' motive for betraying Jesus. Judas' payment of thirty pieces of silver is the same amount as the cost of a slave (Exodus 21:32). In Zechariah 11:12, it is the wage of the shepherd who gives the money back to the treasury. Judas too will fling the money into the temple when he regrets his act of betrayal. The chief priests and elders will use it to buy a cemetery for foreigners. Matthew writes that this was to fulfill the prophecy of Jeremiah, though it more accurately reflects Zechariah 11:13—"Then the LORD said to me, Throw it in the treasury—the handsome price at which they valued me. So I took the thirty pieces of silver and threw them into the treasury in the house of the LORD." Only Matthew recounts that the chief priests and Pharisees requested of Pilate that Jesus' tomb be guarded. The empty tomb will be even more miraculous given the presence of guards and the sealed tomb.

❖ Reflecting on the Word

In today's second reading Paul recounts for the Philippians the pattern of humility and exaltation that can be discerned in the life, death, and resurrection of Jesus. Unfortunately, the Church's Lectionary omits the verse with which Paul begins his account, in which he tells his readers, "Have among yourselves the same attitude that is also yours in Christ Jesus" (Philippians 2:5). The word that gets translated here as possessing an "attitude" is the Greek *phroneite*, which refers to the kind of thinking we do that allows us to know how to act in the world. It is not the kind of abstract "knowing that" that we use with regard to facts, but the concrete "knowing how" involved in living our lives well.

What Paul seems to be saying is that we should seek to possess the kind of "know how" that Jesus displayed in choosing a life of humility over a life of self-glorification. The radical humility that Jesus shows in his taking the form of a slave, in his willingness to follow the divine will even to the cross, is one that we are called to imitate in our own lives. It is by our imitation of the pattern of living that Jesus has set that we acquire the "know how" to face even life's daily challenges.

When we hear Matthew's account of the passion of Jesus, we are called not just to admiration of the love Jesus shows, but imitation of it. We may or may not be called to make the kind of supreme sacrifice that Jesus made, but we are all called to make our own Jesus' prayer to his Father, "not as I will, but as you will" (Matthew 26:39). In this way, we learn what it means to live as adopted sons and daughters of God.

❖ Consider/Discuss

- How in my daily life might I have the same attitude that Jesus showed in his suffering and death?
- When have I been able to pray, "not as I will, but as you will"?

❖ Responding to the Word

Lord Jesus, help us to reject what you rejected in embracing your cross: attachment to riches, honor, and glory. Help us even more to love what you loved: patience, humility, and obedience. We ask this in your name. Amen.

Notes

After the forty days of Lent and Holy Week, Easter is a joyous celebration of resurrection and light. The Gospels uses *pascha*, the Aramaic form for the Hebrew word for Passover, *pesach*, to refer to the passion and death of Jesus. By the fifth century, the term was used to include the celebration of the Resurrection. Christ is the new *pascha*, the new Passover. Like the term Lent, the word Easter has pagan roots, and may have originally referred to a Teutonic goddess of the rising light of day. According to St. Bede, by the eighth century the church used the word "Easter" to signify Christ, our light rising from the grave.

The fifty-day season of Easter begins with the Vigil and concludes with Pentecost. The first eight days after Easter constitute the Octave of Easter and are celebrated as Solemnities of the Lord. (Solemnities are the highest-ranking feast days in the liturgical calendar and celebrate an event in the life of Jesus.)

The readings of the Easter season reflect the theme of resurrection. For most of the year the first reading is taken from the Old Testament, but during the Easter season the Acts of the Apostles is read. This is a second New Testament volume, written by the same author who penned the Gospel of Luke. It follows the spread of the gospel from Jerusalem to Rome through the inspired preaching of the apostles, naming Peter and Paul. Acts begins with the resurrected Jesus meeting the apostles on the Mount of Olives and commissioning them to preach to all the nations. The coming of the Spirit in Chapter 2 empowers and directs the apostles, so that they are able to proclaim in various languages, boldly and without fear. This coming of the Spirit is celebrated at Pentecost, which will close the Easter season.

The second reading is almost exclusively from First Peter, a letter attributed to the apostle Peter but written long after his death. First Peter addresses a Gentile community that is experiencing suffering. Scholars propose that the root of the community's suffering may be sporadic persecutions under the Emperor Domitian. However, the letter itself indicates that the believers are experiencing difficulties with their Gentile neighbors. The suffering may result from social exclusion (1 Peter 4:3–4). The author borrows images and metaphors from the Old Testament to instill in the believers a new sense of identity. "You are 'a chosen race, a royal priesthood, a holy nation, a people of his own, so that you may announce the praises' of him who called you out of darkness into his wonderful light" (1 Peter 2:9).

April 20, 2014

EASTER SUNDAY OF THE RESURRECTION OF THE LORD

Today's Focus: God's Love Is More Powerful Than Our Sin

If we take the time to look, we can see signs of God's life and love all around. The life of Jesus Christ was filled with these signs; the supreme one is his resurrection.

FIRST READING
Acts 10:34a, 37–43

Peter proceeded to speak and said: "You know what has happened all over Judea, beginning in Galilee after the baptism that John preached, how God anointed Jesus of Nazareth with the Holy Spirit and power. He went about doing good and healing all those oppressed by the devil, for God was with him. We are witnesses of all that he did both in the country of the Jews and in Jerusalem. They put him to death by hanging him on a tree. This man God raised on the third day and granted that he be visible, not to all the people, but to us, the witnesses chosen by God in advance, who ate and drank with him after he rose from the dead. He commissioned us to preach to the people and testify that he is the one appointed by God as judge of the living and the dead. To him all the prophets bear witness, that everyone who believes in him will receive forgiveness of sins through his name.

PSALM RESPONSE
Psalm 118:24

This is the day the Lord has made; let us rejoice and be glad.

SECOND READING
Colossians 3: 1–4

Brothers and sisters: If then you were raised with Christ, seek what is above, where Christ is seated at the right hand of God. Think of what is above, not of what is on earth. For you have died, and your life is hidden with Christ in God. When Christ your life appears, then you too will appear with him in glory.

– or –

1 Corinthians 5: 6b–8

Brothers and sisters: Do you not know that a little yeast leavens all the dough? Clear out the old yeast, so that you may become a fresh batch of dough, inasmuch as you are unleavened. For our paschal lamb, Christ, has been sacrificed. Therefore, let us celebrate the feast, not with the old yeast, the yeast of malice and wickedness, but with the unleavened bread of sincerity and truth.

GOSPEL
John 20:1–9

On the first day of the week, Mary of Magdala came to the tomb early in the morning, while it was still dark, and saw the stone removed from the tomb. So she ran and went to Simon Peter and to the other disciple whom Jesus loved, and told them, "They have taken the Lord from the tomb, and we don't know where they put him." So Peter and the other disciple went out and came to the tomb. They both ran, but the other disciple ran faster than Peter and arrived at the tomb first; he bent down and saw the burial cloths there, but did not go in. When Simon Peter arrived after him, he went into the tomb and saw the burial cloths there, and the cloth that had covered his head, not with the burial cloths but rolled up in a separate place. Then the other disciple also went in, the one who had arrived at the tomb first, and he saw and believed. For they did not yet understand the Scripture that he had to rise from the dead.

✤ Understanding the Word

In the first reading, Peter is in Caesarea Maritima, a Greco-Roman city on the coast of Israel. He had been summoned to the house of the Gentile centurion Cornelius, whom we are told was a God-fearer, one who worshiped with the Jews but was not Jewish. Peter begins his speech by recounting the story of Jesus' public life and assures Cornelius' household that Peter and the apostles are witnesses of all that Jesus said and did, and that they have been commissioned by Jesus to preach to the people. Peter's speech serves to validate the ministerial work of the apostles, confirming that they have received "power when the holy Spirit [came] upon them" (Acts 1:8). The proclamation of the gospel to a Gentile and his family in this Greco-Roman city fulfills the prophecy of Simeon that Jesus would be "a light for revelation to the Gentiles" (Luke 2:32), and opens the way of the gospel for all Gentiles.

Though there are two choices for second readings, both Colossians 3:1–4 and 1 Corinthians 5:6–8 speak of the same theme: the newness that comes with being part of the body of Christ. In Colossians, we are reminded that our focus should be on the things of heaven, since our life is now in Christ and Christ is seated at God's right hand. In First Corinthians, we are to be fresh dough without old yeast. Christ is the Passover who was sacrificed and we are to respond with the bread of sincerity and truth.

The Gospel of John recounts the discovery of the empty tomb by Mary Magdalene. All four of our Gospels attributed this discovery to Mary, but Paul will announce that Cephas or Peter was the first one to whom Jesus appeared (1 Corinthians 15:5). Later texts by Gnostic writers (a heresy that only a few with secret knowledge would be saved) pit Peter against Mary Madalene, as they vied with each other for Jesus' affection and authority in the post-Resurrection community. Today's Gospel highlights the important roles of both parties. Mary visits the tomb of Jesus, but we are not told why. In the synoptic Gospels, Mary and the other women come to anoint Jesus, but in John's Gospel, Jesus is anointed before his burial (John 19:40). Likely, Mary comes to mourn (John 20:11). When she discovers the empty tomb, she runs to Simon Peter and the beloved disciple. The men hasten to the tomb and verify what Mary has told them. In the Greco-Roman context, the testimony of a woman did not hold up in court. Rather, two male witnesses were needed to corroborate a fact. In our Gospel, the community—represented by Mary and Simon and the beloved disciple—is brought together in their grief and confusion. Very shortly, this same community will come to "understand the Scripture that [Jesus] had to rise from the dead" (John 20:9).

❖ Reflecting on the Word

Recent scholarship concerning the origins of Christianity indicates that from the earliest days of the Christian community its members were making bold claims concerning the identity of Jesus, claiming for him a role in salvation that could only be true of God. An earlier generation of scholars had tended to think that the identification of Jesus with God was something that developed only gradually within Christianity, but this seems not to be the case. From the outset, Christians apparently sought to affirm the divine status of Jesus.

This raises the question of what possibly could have led the first generation of Christians, almost all of whom were Jewish, to identify Jesus of Nazareth with the God who made a covenant with Abraham and his descendants, who freed the Israelites from captivity in Egypt, and who promised through the prophets to bless all the families of nations. The answer in the New Testament is unambiguous. It was the resurrection of Jesus from the dead. This was the sign that Jesus had done what only God could do—break the power of sin and death. It is from this event that all of our beliefs about Jesus flow: that he is "God from God, light from light . . . begotten not made, consubstantial with the Father." All of these phrases are different ways of affirming that the Resurrection has revealed Jesus as the Lord of life and death.

The Resurrection tells us something about Jesus, but it also tells us something about the God whom we encounter in the person of Jesus. The God we know in Jesus Christ is a God who is love, a love that is more powerful than our sin, a love that can triumph over death, a love that seeks to share itself with us so that we too can triumph over sin and death. This is the message of Easter that we are called to share.

❖ Consider/Discuss

- What signs do I see in the world and in my life that Jesus has triumphed over death?
- In what ways could I serve as a sign to others that God is love?

❖ Responding to the Word

Lord God, in raising Jesus from the dead you have revealed the triumphant presence of your love in the midst of hatred and death. Give us the grace to share the good news of Easter with all those we meet. We ask this through Christ our Lord. Amen.

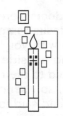

April 27, 2014

SECOND SUNDAY OF EASTER (OR SUNDAY OF DIVINE MERCY)

Today's Focus: Seeing Is Not Always Believing

In today's world, we look for evidence that things are true. When it comes to the Resurrection, the only evidence that others have of its truth is the witness of those who follow the Risen Lord.

FIRST READING
Acts 2:42–47

They devoted themselves to the teaching of the apostles and to the communal life, to the breaking of bread and to the prayers. Awe came upon everyone, and many wonders and signs were done through the apostles. All who believed were together and had all things in common; they would sell their property and possessions and divide them among all according to each one's need. Every day they devoted themselves to meeting together in the temple area and to breaking bread in their homes. They ate their meals with exultation and sincerity of heart, praising God and enjoying favor with all the people. And every day the Lord added to their number those who were being saved.

PSALM RESPONSE
Psalm 118:1

Give thanks to the Lord for he is good, his love is everlasting.

SECOND READING
1 Peter 1:3–9

Blessed be the God and Father of our Lord Jesus Christ, who in his great mercy gave us a new birth to a living hope through the resurrection of Jesus Christ from the dead, to an inheritance that is imperishable, undefiled, and unfading, kept in heaven for you who by the power of God are safeguarded through faith, to a salvation that is ready to be revealed in the final time. In this you rejoice, although now for a little while you may have to suffer through various trials, so that the genuineness of your faith, more precious than gold that is perishable even though tested by fire, may prove to be for praise, glory, and honor at the revelation of Jesus Christ. Although you have not seen him you love him; even though you do not see him now yet believe in him, you rejoice with an indescribable and glorious joy, as you attain the goal of your faith, the salvation of your souls.

GOSPEL
John 20:19–31

On the evening of that first day of the week, when the doors were locked, where the disciples were, for fear of the Jews, Jesus came and stood in their midst and said to them, "Peace be with you." When he had said this, he showed them his hands and his side. The disciples rejoiced when they saw the Lord. Jesus said to them again, "Peace be with you. As the Father has sent me, so I send you." And when he had said this, he breathed on them and said to them, "Receive the Holy Spirit. Whose sins you forgive are forgiven them, and whose sins you retain are retained."

Thomas, called Didymus, one of the Twelve, was not with them when Jesus came. So the other disciples said to him, "We have seen the Lord." But he said to them, "Unless I see the mark of the nails in his hands and put my finger into the nailmarks and put my hand into his side, I will not believe."

Now a week later his disciples were again inside and Thomas was with them. Jesus came, although the doors were locked, and stood in their midst and said, "Peace be with you." Then he said to Thomas, "Put your finger here and see my hands, and bring your hand and put it into my side, and do not be unbelieving, but believe." Thomas answered and said to him, "My Lord and my God!" Jesus said to him, "Have you come to believe because you have seen me? Blessed are those who have not seen and have believed."

Now, Jesus did many other signs in the presence of his disciples that are not written in this book. But these are written that you may come to believe that Jesus is the Christ, the Son of God, and that through this belief you may have life in his name.

❖ Understanding the Word

The first reading from the Acts of the Apostles describes an almost utopian community. The author of Acts, whom we call Luke, portrays the disciples and apostles as living a communal life, attending to the needs of each member and worshiping in their homes and in the temple. The witness of these believers draws others to join them. The presence of the Holy Spirit makes this idyllic experience possible.

This portrait of an inspired community is further developed in the second reading from First Peter. By means of the resurrection of Jesus Christ, believers are given a new birth to an imperishable inheritance. But this birth is only partially experienced, since the birth to salvation is only complete in the last days. First Peter presents itself as a letter from the apostle Peter, written from Rome (Babylon in 5:13 is symbol for Rome) to Christians in Asia Minor at a time of persecution. Likely it was written in the name of Peter but perhaps as late as 90–95 CE (Common Era). The letter may actually have been a baptismal sermon set in the format of a letter. The Gospel reading presents the evangelist John's narration of the coming of the Spirit. Jesus is present and offers his spirit, unlike Luke's Pentecost account in Chapter 2 of Acts of the Apostles, when Jesus is absent. The disciples are together behind locked doors when Jesus appears before them.

He offers a typical Jewish greeting: *Shalom*—Peace be with you. After showing them his wounds, he repeats the greeting. Jesus then commissions the disciples. As the Father has sent him, so he now empowers and sends the disciples. The resurrected Jesus breathes the Holy Spirit upon them, and with that they share in his power. The story doesn't then depict the great works enacted by this now inspired group of disciples, as will be narrated in Acts. Instead, we hear of one disciple, Thomas, who missed the encounter. His doubt is only erased when Jesus returns a week later. Instead of simply showing his wounds as Jesus did the first time, he now invites Thomas to touch them. Thomas responds with an exclamation of belief: "My Lord and my God." In this passage, the evangelist John doesn't place the emphasis on the giving of the Spirit or Thomas' disbelief. Rather, the important moment comes when Jesus offers a blessing on all those who have not seen and yet believe. The blessing is for us.

✤ *Reflecting on the Word*

Both the second reading and the Gospel give us an opportunity to reflect on "seeing" and "believing." In the Gospel, Thomas says that he will not believe unless he sees the risen Jesus himself. Jesus obliges him by appearing to him, but also says, "Blessed are those who have not seen and have believed." In the second reading, the author makes much the same point: "Even though you do not see him now yet believe in him, you rejoice with an indescribable and glorious joy." In both of these readings, it is a willingness to believe what goes beyond the evidence of our eyes that is praised.

But it remains part of human nature to desire a sign, some evidence prompting us to an act of faith. In the first reading, from the Acts of the Apostles, it seems that people come to faith in the risen Jesus because of the kind of life that they see his followers living. They see people dedicated to living a life together, who willingly share their goods, and who break bread with each other "with exultation and sincerity of heart." Because of the witness of the Christian community in Jerusalem, "the Lord added to their number those who were being saved." They were the sign that Jesus was truly risen.

Even today it remains the role of the Church to be a sign of the resurrection of Jesus, which can prompt those who witness our love and joy to believe in the risen life of the one whom they cannot see. The Church is not simply a place where we go to be spiritually nourished; it is a reality in which we all have the role of serving as a sign of the reality of Easter.

- How might followers of Jesus respond to those who say that they will not believe in God without possessing concrete evidence? What evidence might we point to for the reality of God?
- In what ways does the depiction of the church in Acts still serve as a model for what the Church should be?

❖ Responding to the Word

God of love, may your Holy Spirit inspire us to live lives of generosity that grow from the joy of the Resurrection. We ask this is Jesus' name. Amen.

May 4, 2014

THIRD SUNDAY OF EASTER

Today's Focus: Speak to Us, Feed Us

At every Sunday Mass, we re-enact today's Gospel, as we come together to walk with Christ, to hear him speak, and to recognize him in the bread broken and the cup poured out.

FIRST READING
Acts 2:14, 22–23

Then Peter stood up with the Eleven, raised his voice, and proclaimed: "You who are Jews, indeed all of you staying in Jerusalem. Let this be known to you, and listen to my words. You who are Israelites, hear these words. Jesus the Nazarene was a man commended to you by God with mighty deeds, wonders, and signs, which God worked through him in your midst, as you yourselves know. This man, delivered up by the set plan and foreknowledge of God, you killed, using lawless men to crucify him. But God raised him up, releasing him from the throes of death, because it was impossible for him to be held by it. For David says of him:

I saw the Lord ever before me,
 with him at my right hand I shall not be disturbed.
Therefore my heart has been glad and my tongue has exulted;
 my flesh, too, will dwell in hope,
because you will not abandon my soul to the netherworld,
 nor will you suffer your holy one to see corruption.
You have made known to me the paths of life;
 you will fill me with joy in your presence.

"My brothers, one can confidently say to you about the patriarch David that he died and was buried, and his tomb is in our midst to this day. But since he was a prophet and knew that God had sworn an oath to him that he would set one of his descendants upon his throne, he foresaw and spoke of the resurrection of the Christ, that neither was he abandoned to the netherworld nor did his flesh see corruption. God raised this Jesus; of this we are all witnesses. Exalted at the right hand of God, he received the promise of the Holy Spirit from the Father and poured him forth, as you see and hear."

PSALM RESPONSE
Psalm 16:11a

Lord, you will show us the path of life.

SECOND READING
1 Peter 1:17–21

Beloved: If you invoke as Father him who judges impartially according to each one's works, conduct yourselves with reverence during the time of your sojourning, realizing that you were ransomed from your futile conduct, handed on by your ancestors, not with perishable things like silver or gold but with the precious blood of Christ as of a spotless unblemished lamb.

He was known before the foundation of the world but revealed in the final time for you, who through him believe in God who raised him from the dead and gave him glory, so that your faith and hope are in God.

GOSPEL
Luke 24:13–35

That very day, the first day of the week, two of Jesus' disciples were going to a village seven miles from Jerusalem called Emmaus, and they were conversing about all the things that had occurred. And it happened that while they were conversing and debating, Jesus himself drew near and walked with them, but their eyes were prevented from recognizing him. He asked them, "What are you discussing as you walk along?" They stopped, looking downcast. One of them, named Cleopas, said to him in reply, "Are you the only visitor to Jerusalem who does not know of the things that have taken place there in these days?" And he replied to them, "What sort of things?" They said to him, "The things that happened to Jesus the Nazarene, who was a prophet mighty in deed and word before God and all the people, how our chief priests and rulers both handed him over to a sentence of death and crucified him. But we were hoping that he would be the one to redeem Israel; and besides all this, it is now the third day since this took place. Some women from our group, however, have astounded us: they were at the tomb early in the morning and did not find his body; they came back and reported that they had indeed seen a vision of angels who announced that he was alive. Then some of those with us went to the tomb and found things just as the women had described, but him they did not see." And he said to them, "Oh, how foolish you are! How slow of heart to believe all that the prophets spoke! Was it not necessary that the Christ should suffer these things and enter into his glory?" Then beginning with Moses and all the prophets, he interpreted to them what referred to him in all the Scriptures. As they approached the village to which they were going, he gave the impression that he was going on farther. But they urged him, "Stay with us, for it is nearly evening and the day is almost over." So he went in to stay with them. And it happened that, while he was with them at table, he took bread, said the blessing, broke it, and gave it to them. With that their eyes were opened and they recognized him, but he vanished from their sight. Then they said to each other, "Were not our hearts burning within us while he spoke to us on the way and opened the Scriptures to us?" So they set out at once and returned to Jerusalem where they found gathered together the eleven and those with them who were saying, "The Lord has truly been raised and has appeared to Simon!" Then the two recounted what had taken place on the way and how he was made known to them in the breaking of bread.

Peter is the chief spokesperson for the newly reconstituted Twelve (Acts 1:15–26). After the coming of the Spirit, he addresses those Jews who have gathered in Jerusalem for the feast of Pentecost. He provides a summary of Jesus' life, death, and resurrection, but the focus remains on God's action. It is God who sent Jesus. God worked through him to effect miracles, wonders, and signs. The purpose and plan of God led to Jesus' being delivered to pagans and crucified. But God freed him from that death and raised him to new life. As his scriptural support, Peter refers to David, who acknowledged that God is "ever before me."

The reading from First Peter shares with Acts the focus on God's actions. As a father, God will judge justly. This same God delivered believers from their former ways, not by paying in silver or gold, but by offering Christ's blood as the Passover lamb. First Peter is a circulating letter, meant to be read among various communities (1 Peter 1:1). These believers are sojourners in a strange land (1 Peter 1:17) because their faith now sets them apart from the pagan society of which they were once members.

The Gospel reading describes the profound disappointment of the two disciples on the road to Emmaus. They are approached by another traveler whom the reader knows to be Jesus, but the two despondent travelers do not. When Jesus asks what they are discussing, Cleopas retells the story of Jesus' passion, ending with the most amazing news: the tomb in which the body was placed was found empty! The stranger now chastises them for not believing what the prophets had announced. He then begins to recount the passages of the Old Testament that referred to Jesus. Throughout the narrative, the reader is surprised that Cleopas and his partner (some scholars suggest it is his wife) don't recognize Jesus. But Luke is stressing that without recourse to scripture, no one could have anticipated the Resurrection. In fact, in order to understand Jesus' true identity and his Messiahship, one must begin with scripture. It is in the course of breaking and blessing the bread that the two disciples recognize Jesus. "Were not our hearts burning within us while he spoke to us on the way and opened the Scriptures to us?"

✣ Reflecting on the Word

While we believe that Jesus instituted the Eucharist at the Last Supper, all of the meals that the Gospels recount—from his dining with sinners to his feeding of the multitudes—can enrich our understanding of the Eucharist. The meal that the risen Jesus eats with his disciples at Emmaus is a particularly rich source for reflection. Here we see the risen Jesus walking unrecognized with his followers, trying to explain to them the baffling events in which they find themselves, and seeming to meet with little success. It is only when they invite him to stay and break bread with them that they recognize him. When he takes, blesses, and gives the bread their eyes are suddenly opened to know him and the burning truth that he had imparted to them on the road, and then he vanishes.

The experience of the disciples journeying to Emmaus is our experience, too. As the First Eucharistic Prayer for Various Needs puts it: "as once for the disciples, so now for us, [Jesus] opens the Scriptures and breaks the bread." The pattern of the Emmaus experience is reflected in the structure of the eucharistic celebration: we recount the words of scripture and seek to understand how they cast light on what is happening in our lives; but it is only in the breaking of the bread that our eyes are truly opened to the meaning of God's revelation and the meaning of our lives. The Liturgy of the Word and the Liturgy of the Table form a unity; the scriptural word of God prepares our hearts to receive Christ, the living Word, sacramentally, and our reception of the living Word opens our eyes to the meaning of the scriptural word and to its implications for us.

Just as for the disciples at Emmaus, word and sacrament together empower us to proclaim the good news of the risen Jesus, to tell of how we met him on the way, and of how he was made known to us in the breaking of bread.

✤ Consider/Discuss

- Have I ever felt my heart "burning within me" and only later realized that God has been present?
- How do I see the unity and relationship of the Liturgy of the Word and the Liturgy of the Eucharist?

✤ Responding to the Word

Lord Jesus, be present among us as you were present to your disciples at Emmaus, so that you might open our minds to understand the scriptures and empower us to bear witness to your resurrection. Amen.

May 11, 2014

FOURTH SUNDAY OF EASTER

Today's Focus: The Shepherd's Voice

While the comparison of us to a flock of sheep isn't necessarily the most flattering, it does grant us one remarkable characteristic: the ability to hear and heed the voice of our Shepherd.

FIRST READING
Acts 2:14a, 36–41

Then Peter stood up with the Eleven, raised his voice, and proclaimed: "Let the whole house of Israel know for certain that God has made both Lord and Christ, this Jesus whom you crucified."

Now when they heard this, they were cut to the heart, and they asked Peter and the other apostles, "What are we to do, my brothers?" Peter said to them, "Repent and be baptized, every one of you, in the name of Jesus Christ for the forgiveness of your sins; and you will receive the gift of the Holy Spirit. For the promise is made to you and to your children and to all those far off, whomever the Lord our God will call." He testified with many other arguments, and was exhorting them, "Save yourselves from this corrupt generation." Those who accepted his message were baptized, and about three thousand persons were added that day.

PSALM RESPONSE
Psalm 23:1

The Lord is my shepherd; there is nothing I shall want.

SECOND READING
1 Peter 2:20b–25

Beloved: If you are patient when you suffer for doing what is good, this is a grace before God. For to this you have been called, because Christ also suffered for you, leaving you an example that you should follow in his footsteps.
He committed no sin, and no deceit was found in his mouth.

When he was insulted, he returned no insult; when he suffered, he did not threaten; instead, he handed himself over to the one who judges justly. He himself bore our sins in his body upon the cross, so that, free from sin, we might live for righteousness. By his wounds you have been healed. For you had gone astray like sheep, but you have now returned to the shepherd and guardian of your souls.

GOSPEL
John 10:1–10

Jesus said: "Amen, amen, I say to you, whoever does not enter a sheepfold through the gate but climbs over elsewhere is a thief and a robber. But whoever enters through the gate is the shepherd of the sheep. The gatekeeper opens it for him, and the sheep hear his voice, as the shepherd calls his own sheep by name and leads them out. When he has driven out all his own, he walks ahead of them, and the sheep follow him, because they recognize his voice. But they will not follow a stranger; they will run away from him, because they do not recognize the voice of strangers." Although Jesus used this figure of speech, the Pharisees did not realize what he was trying to tell them.

So Jesus said again, "Amen, amen, I say to you, I am the gate for the sheep. All who came before me are thieves and robbers, but the sheep did not listen to them. I am the gate. Whoever enters through me will be saved, and will come in and go out and find pasture. A thief comes only to steal and slaughter and destroy; I came so that they might have life and have it more abundantly."

❖ *Understanding the Word*

At the conclusion of his speech to the Jews who had gathered on Pentecost, Peter announces that God has made Jesus both Lord and Messiah. Their response is heartfelt. "What are we to do, my brothers?" (Acts 2:37). Peter responds that one must reform, be baptized in the name of Jesus Christ for the forgiveness of sins, and receive the Holy Spirit. As the narrative of Acts continues, baptism isn't always accompanied by the gift of the Spirit. The Ethiopian eunuch will ask for baptism but not receive the Spirit (Acts 8:36–39). Cornelius and his household will receive the Spirit and then be baptized (Acts 10:45–47).

In the second reading, the author uses images from scripture, particularly the Servant Song from Isaiah, to remind his readers that suffering for what is right is acceptable to God. They should be encouraged, having been given Christ's suffering as an example for their own. The readers of First Peter may have suffered from the sporadic persecutions under the Emperor Domitian. Or their sufferings may have stemmed from being ostracized by the mainstream Gentile society (1 Peter 4:3–4). Despite their current situation, the author reminds his readers that by Christ's wounds they have been healed.

Like the first reading, the Gospel talks about entrance into the community of believers, here described as the sheepfold. In John's Gospel, Jesus uses a series of "I am" statements to explain his identity. These "I am" statements are meant to mirror the self-naming of God to Moses. When Moses asked for God's name, God replied, "I am who I am" (Exodus 3:14). In today's reading, Jesus announces, "I am the gate for the sheep . . . I am the gate. Whoever enters through me will be safe." In John 6:35, Jesus is the bread of life. In John 8:12, he is the light of the world. He is the good shepherd in John 10:11, and the resurrection and the life in John 11:25. In John 14:6, Jesus is the way, the truth, and the life. Finally, in John 15:1, Jesus is the true vine. Jesus follows each "I am" with the benefit for believers. In today's reading, Jesus is the gate that guards against thieves who come to steal and slaughter. As the gate for this new community, Jesus assures believers that they have life and have it to the full.

110

❖ Reflecting on the Word

On the whole, no one likes being described as "sheep-like." It conveys not only intellectual dullness, but also a tendency to follow the herd and an inability to think or care for oneself. Rightly or wrongly, we think of sheep as needing far more care and protection than, for example, cattle, as well as a tendency to wander. As the second reading says, "you had gone astray like sheep."

This might or might not be a fair assessment of actual sheep, but it is not the aspect of sheep that today's Gospel reading focuses on. While the vulnerability of sheep to theft and harm is mentioned, it is their ability to distinguish the shepherd's voice from the voice of strangers that Jesus emphasizes. Rather than dull creatures who will follow whoever happens to come along, sheep are presented as discerning listeners, attuned to the voice of their master, able to tell the true shepherd from the thief who "comes only to steal and slaughter and destroy."

When Christians are called on to look to Jesus as their shepherd, and thus to think of themselves as sheep, they are not being asked to succumb to an unthinking herd mentality, but to listen discerningly to the call of Christ. God wants us to come to know the voice of Jesus, so that we will not mistake it for other voices.

❖ Consider/Discuss

- How can I tell the voice of Jesus from other voices that might call to me?
- What are some of the perils of falling into the "herd instinct"?

❖ Responding to the Word

O God, you sent Jesus to us to guard your flock from those who would steal or slaughter or destroy. Help us always to seek his protection and listen for his voice. Amen.

May 18, 2014

FIFTH SUNDAY OF EASTER

Today's Focus: Jesus Christ—Architect

The scriptures today are filled with architecture/house/building-related images. Like the structures we use or inhabit regularly, we sometimes take for granted the beauty or usefulness of spiritual structures.

FIRST READING
Acts 6:1–7

As the number of disciples continued to grow, the Hellenists complained against the Hebrews because their widows were being neglected in the daily distribution. So the Twelve called together the community of the disciples and said, "It is not right for us to neglect the word of God to serve at table. Brothers, select from among you seven reputable men, filled with the Spirit and wisdom, whom we shall appoint to this task, whereas we shall devote ourselves to prayer and to the ministry of the word." The proposal was acceptable to the whole community, so they chose Stephen, a man filled with faith and the Holy Spirit, also Philip, Prochorus, Nicanor, Timon, Parmenas, and Nicholas of Antioch, a convert to Judaism. They presented these men to the apostles who prayed and laid hands on them. The word of God continued to spread, and the number of the disciples in Jerusalem increased greatly; even a large group of priests were becoming obedient to the faith.

PSALM RESPONSE
Psalm 33:22

Lord, let your mercy be on us, as we place our trust in you.

SECOND READING
1 Peter 2:4–9

Beloved: Come to him, a living stone, rejected by human beings but chosen and precious in the sight of God, and, like living stones, let yourselves be built into a spiritual house to be a holy priesthood to offer spiritual sacrifices acceptable to God through Jesus Christ. For it says in Scripture:
> Behold, I am laying a stone in Zion,
> a cornerstone, chosen and precious,
> and whoever believes in it shall not be put to shame.

Therefore, its value is for you who have faith, but for those without faith:
> The stone that the builders rejected
> has become the cornerstone,

and
> A stone that will make people stumble,
> and a rock that will make them fall.

They stumble by disobeying the word, as is their destiny.

You are "a chosen race, a royal priesthood, a holy nation, a people of his own, so that you may announce the praises" of him who called you out of darkness into his wonderful light.

GOSPEL
John 14:1–12

Jesus said to his disciples: "Do not let your hearts be troubled. You have faith in God; have faith also in me. In my Father's house there are many dwelling places. If there were not, would I have told you that I am going to prepare a place for you? And if I go and prepare a place for you, I will come back again and take you to myself, so that where I am you also may be. Where I am going you know the way." Thomas said to him, "Master, we do not know where you are going; how can we know the way?" Jesus said to him, "I am the way and the truth and the life. No one comes to the Father except through me. If you know me, then you will also know my Father. From now on you do know him and have seen him." Philip said to him, "Master, show us the Father, and that will be enough for us." Jesus said to him, "Have I been with you for so long a time and you still do not know me, Philip? Whoever has seen me has seen the Father. How can you say, 'Show us the Father'? Do you not believe that I am in the Father and the Father is in me? The words that I speak to you I do not speak on my own. The Father who dwells in me is doing his works. Believe me that I am in the Father and the Father is in me, or else, believe because of the works themselves. Amen, amen, I say to you, whoever believes in me will do the works that I do, and will do greater ones than these, because I am going to the Father."

❖ Understanding the Word

The idyllic community that Acts portrays very quickly encounters a problem. In today's reading, the Hellenist Jewish Christians complain that their widows are not being cared for as well as the Jewish Christian widows. Underlying the problem is the issue of culture and identity. The Jewish Christians were those who first followed Jesus. As Jews living in the Holy Land, they tended to practice Jewish rituals and traditions more strictly. Jews who lived outside of Israel in the so-called "Diaspora" (from the Greek for "scattering" or "dispersion") spoke Greek and tended to be more sympathetic to the Greco-Roman culture. To respond to the growing needs and cultural diversity among the members, the Twelve proposed that seven men be selected to serve as deacons (from the Greek word for "service"). The deacons are to "wait on tables," meeting the physical needs of the community, while the Twelve engage in the ministry of the word. However, the deacons Stephen and Philip distinguish themselves for their preaching. Stephen will become the first martyr (Acts 7:54–60), and Philip will proclaim Christ to the Samaritans (8:4–8).

The First Letter of Peter also reflects a community coming to understand its new identity. The author repeatedly uses images and metaphors from scripture in order to strengthen the community's understanding of itself as the new Israel. In today's reading, the believers are living stones, forming a building for the spirit, and making them into a holy priesthood. They are a chosen race (Isaiah 43:20–21), a royal priesthood and consecrated nation (Exodus 19:6), a people claimed by God (Malachi 3:17). The titles once given to Israel are now claimed for Christians, whom God has called from darkness into the marvelous light of the Resurrection.

The Gospel reading comes from the portion of John's Gospel known as the Book of Glory (John 13 — 20:31), wherein Jesus directs his attention to his coming glorification (passion). In John 14 — 16, he speaks intimately to his disciples in the form of a farewell address that includes several themes. First, Jesus announces the imminence of his departure (John 13:33; 14:2–3; 16:16). Second, the announcement is met with distress by his disciples (John 14:1, 27; 16:6–7, 22). Jesus then recalls what he has said earlier (John 13:33, 14:10; 15:3, 20) and promises that the Paraclete will interpret for them what he has said and done (John 14:26; 16:14–15). Finally, there is a directive to keep God's commandments (John 14:15, 21, 23; 15:10).

❖ Reflecting on the Word

Architecture is perhaps unique among art forms in the fact that it is art that we inhabit. Over time, we can let slip from our minds the beauty of spaces that we occupy on a regular basis, but their beauty and artistry still affect us on a subconscious level, shaping our way of being and feeling. Perhaps this is why buildings are such important metaphors in scripture. Like a great work of architecture, the Christian faith is something that we are called not simply to admire from the outside, but to occupy, to inhabit, and to let shape us on levels both conscious and unconscious.

We see one such metaphor in First Peter, where the Christian community is compared to a building—a "spiritual house"—of which Christ forms the cornerstone, upon which the whole edifice rests. We are called to make the life and worship of the Church our home, the structure that shapes us spiritually.

We see the same image of a house in the Gospel reading. Among some more literally-minded Christians the reference of Jesus to the "many dwelling places" in his Father's "house" has prompted speculation as to the nature of structures in which the redeemed will dwell for eternity. This is perhaps encouraged by the well-known King James translation of "dwelling places" as "mansions," which conjures images of luxurious rewards being prepared for the followers of Jesus, as well as speculation as to the dimensions and construction materials. St. Thomas Aquinas cut through such idle speculation by pointing out that when Jesus refers to his Father's house, it is really a metaphor for God; it is into this house that we will all be gathered (see *Commentary on John* 14.1). Our destiny is not to live in any created dwelling place, but to share in the life of the eternal God. It is by dwelling in the "spiritual house" of the Christian community on earth—through worship and mutual love—that we come to dwell with God in eternity.

❖ Consider/Discuss

- What sort of places do I find "sacred"? How does architecture, whether sacred or secular, speak to me of God?
- How do I imagine eternal life?

❖ Responding to the Word

Lord Jesus, great cornerstone of God's people, help us to dwell in your love and to be shaped by our worship of you. Amen.

114

May 25, 2014

SIXTH SUNDAY OF EASTER

Today's Focus: Come, Holy Spirit!

The Easter season heads toward—in a way, has its destiny in—the celebration of Pentecost, the descent of the Holy Spirit. As St. Paul tells us, the Risen Christ is "alive in the Spirit."

FIRST READING
Acts 8:5–8, 14–17

Philip went down to the city of Samaria and proclaimed the Christ to them. With one accord, the crowds paid attention to what was said by Philip when they heard it and saw the signs he was doing. For unclean spirits, crying out in a loud voice, came out of many possessed people, and many paralyzed or crippled people were cured. There was great joy in that city.

Now when the apostles in Jerusalem heard that Samaria had accepted the word of God, they sent them Peter and John, who went down and prayed for them, that they might receive the Holy Spirit, for it had not yet fallen upon any of them; they had only been baptized in the name of the Lord Jesus. Then they laid hands on them and they received the Holy Spirit.

PSALM RESPONSE
Psalm 66:1

Let all the earth cry out to God with joy.

SECOND READING
1 Peter 3:15–18

Beloved: Sanctify Christ as Lord in your hearts. Always be ready to give an explanation to anyone who asks you for a reason for your hope, but do it with gentleness and reverence, keeping your conscience clear, so that, when you are maligned, those who defame your good conduct in Christ may themselves be put to shame. For it is better to suffer for doing good, if that be the will of God, than for doing evil. For Christ also suffered for sins once, the righteous for the sake of the unrighteous, that he might lead you to God. Put to death in the flesh, he was brought to life in the Spirit.

*Realize Philip - good Jew-
Realization △*

*Once you see God -
Looking at JC -
What did they see*

*Not in Glory-
but king in JC*

What do we see

115

GOSPEL
John 14:15–21

Jesus said to his disciples: "If you love me, you will keep my commandments. And I will ask the Father, and he will give you another Advocate to be with you always, the Spirit of truth, whom the world cannot accept, because it neither sees nor knows him. But you know him, because he remains with you, and will be in you. I will not leave you orphans; I will come to you. In a little while the world will no longer see me, but you will see me, because I live and you will live. On that day you will realize that I am in my Father and you are in me and I in you. Whoever has my commandments and observes them is the one who loves me. And whoever loves me will be loved by my Father, and I will love him and reveal myself to him."

❖ Understanding the Word

After the martyrdom of Stephen, a persecution arose so that many believers had to leave Jerusalem. The persecution had an unintended effect. With the scattering of the disciples, the word was proclaimed even further. Philip, a Greek-speaking Jewish Christian who had been chosen to be a deacon, traveled to Samaria, where he proclaimed Jesus as the Messiah. The miracles and healings he performed brought the Samaritans to faith. The apostles who remained in Jerusalem sent Peter and John to investigate. Since the Samaritans had only been baptized, the two apostles imposed hands on them and the Samaritans received the Holy Spirit. This brief narrative indicates that as the gospel spread, the church developed structures to support the mission. Evangelists proclaimed the message and apostles verified the success and authenticity of the new believers.

In the second reading, First Peter presents the community with advice on how to live as Christians in a hostile world. They are to venerate the Lord in their hearts, while the Gentiles venerated the emperor publicly. Our English translation doesn't pick up the legal tone of the following verse. The Greek more properly reads: If someone asks you to give an account (*logos*) for your hope, be ready to offer a defense (*apologia*). But it is a defense marked by gentleness and respect. Christians should have a clear conscience, so that those who libel their way of life will be disappointed. Better to suffer for good deeds rather than evil ones.

The Gospel reading reminds us that Jesus has not left us bereft of his presence. He will ask his Father to send another Advocate, the transliteration of the actual Greek word that means helper or intercessor. This Advocate is also described as the Spirit of truth who will remain with believers though the world will not recognize it. Jesus promised he would not leave the community orphaned, but would return. The Synoptics interpret Jesus' return through the lens of eschatology (the anticipation of the end–times and the final judgment). But the Johannine community recognized that the Spirit was the presence of the resurrected Christ in their midst. Some scholars interpret this as "realized eschatology"—Jesus Christ, who will come in glory at the end of time, is present and experienced now.

116

The feast of Pentecost is two weeks away, so in today's readings we are already preparing for the coming of the Holy Spirit. Indeed, Pentecost is where Easter has been heading all along. As today's second reading says this, "put to death in the flesh," Jesus was "brought to life in the Spirit." This means that the Holy Spirit is already active in the resurrection of Jesus, and continues to be active in the lives of those who share in that resurrection through faith.

The ongoing activity of the Holy Spirit in our lives is the fulfillment of Jesus' promise to his disciples in today's Gospel reading that he will not leave them orphans. Due to various social safety nets, orphans in the developed world today do not face the kind of immediate threat that they would have in Jesus' world. In places like sub-Saharan Africa, however, where an estimated twelve percent of all children are orphans, largely due to the AIDS epidemic, the dire situation of parentless children is very evident as they are left to face a dangerous world alone, without the guidance and protection of their parents.

When Jesus says that he will not leave the disciples orphans, he is recognizing their need for guidance and their defenselessness with regard to the dangers they will face from a world hostile to the gospel. He speaks of the Spirit as "another Advocate" who will remain with them and stand by them always. It is this Spirit on whom we must lean as we seek to find our way in the world.

❖ Consider/Discuss

- An old spiritual sings, "Sometimes I feel like a motherless child." Have I ever felt "orphaned"?
- How would I live my life differently if I were fully confident that I had the Spirit of God beside me as my Advocate?

❖ *Responding to the Word*

Holy Spirit, stand by us when we feel alone and defenseless. Give us confidence in God's love. We ask this in Jesus' name. Amen.

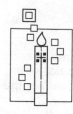

May 29 or June 1, 2014

THE ASCENSION OF THE LORD

Many dioceses in the United States celebrate the Ascension on June 1, replacing the Seventh Sunday of Easter.

Today's Focus: Why Are You Standing There Looking Up?

The urgency of the mission given to the early church is shown by the angels' questioning of the disciples. Rather than beginning this mission with Jesus far away, they will come to know him near in a new way.

FIRST READING
Acts 1:1–11

In the first book, Theophilus, I dealt with all that Jesus did and taught until the day he was taken up, after giving instructions through the Holy Spirit to the apostles whom he had chosen. He presented himself alive to them by many proofs after he had suffered, appearing to them during forty days and speaking about the kingdom of God. While meeting with them, he enjoined them not to depart from Jerusalem, but to wait for "the promise of the Father about which you have heard me speak; for John baptized with water, but in a few days you will be baptized with the Holy Spirit."

When they had gathered together they asked him, "Lord, are you at this time going to restore the kingdom to Israel?" He answered them, "It is not for you to know the times or seasons that the Father has established by his own authority. But you will receive power when the Holy Spirit comes upon you, and you will be my witnesses in Jerusalem, throughout Judea and Samaria, and to the ends of the earth." When he had said this, as they were looking on, he was lifted up, and a cloud took him from their sight. While they were looking intently at the sky as he was going, suddenly two men dressed in white garments stood beside them. They said, "Men of Galilee, why are you standing there looking at the sky? This Jesus who has been taken up from you into heaven will return in the same way as you have seen him going into heaven."

PSALM RESPONSE
Psalm 47:6

God mounts his throne to shouts of joy: a blare of trumpets for the Lord.

SECOND READING
Ephesians 1:17–23

Brothers and sisters: May the God of our Lord Jesus Christ, the Father of glory, give you a Spirit of wisdom and revelation resulting in knowledge of him. May the eyes of your hearts be enlightened, that you may know what is the hope that belongs to his call, what are the riches of glory in his inheritance among the holy ones, and what is the surpassing greatness of his power for us who believe, in accord with the exercise of his great might, which he worked in Christ, raising him from the dead and seating him at his right hand in the heavens, far above every principality, authority, power, and dominion, and every name that is named not only in this age but also in the one to come. And he put all things beneath his feet and gave him as head over all things to the church, which is his body, the fullness of the one who fills all things in every way.

GOSPEL
Matthew 28:16–20

The eleven disciples went to Galilee, to the mountain to which Jesus had ordered them. When they saw him, they worshiped, but they doubted. Then Jesus approached and said to them, "All power in heaven and on earth has been given to me. Go, therefore, and make disciples of all nations, baptizing them in the name of the Father, and of the Son, and of the Holy Spirit, teaching them to observe all that I have commanded you. And behold, I am with you always, until the end of the age."

❖ Understanding the Word

Both the Gospel of Luke and the Acts of the Apostles were penned by the same person, whom tradition calls Luke. Each volume begins with a prologue addressed to the writer's patron, Theophilus. Today's first reading reminds Theophilus of the content of the Gospel, and then echoes its conclusion: remain in Jerusalem and await the Holy Spirit. After the prologue, the narrative begins. The disciples ask Jesus if he is now going to restore the rule of Israel, something that was expected of the Messiah. But Jesus defers that decision to the Father. Rather, the disciples are to await the Holy Spirit and then become witnesses to the ends of the earth. Shortly after Jesus' commission, he is lifted up into a cloud and taken from their sight. The resurrected Jesus will make no more appearances in the Acts of the Apostles.

The reading from the Letter to the Ephesians provides a theological interpretation for the Ascension. Christ has been seated at the right hand of God in heaven, above every principality, power, virtue, domination, and every name. Christ's ascension is the completion of his exaltation. God has placed all things under Christ's feet and exalted him as head of the church.

Whereas Luke placed Jesus' ascension on a mount outside Jerusalem, Matthew situates the narrative on a mountain in Galilee. The difference reflects the evangelists' theologies, rather than their sources. For Luke, Jerusalem represents the center of Israel's history and religious traditions. It is impossible for a prophet to die outside of Jerusalem (Luke 13:33). For Matthew, placing Jesus in Galilee fulfills scripture (Matthew 4:15–16), and it is in Galilee that Jesus begins to preach (Matthew 4:17). In Matthew 26:32, Jesus tells his disciples that after he is raised, they are to return to Galilee. When Mary Magdalene and the other Mary discover the empty tomb, the angel of the Lord directs them to tell the disciples that Jesus is risen from the dead and is going before them to Galilee, where they will see him (Matthew 28:7). In today's reading, the eleven disciples have traveled to Galilee, to a mountain to which Jesus had directed them. Like the mountain of Sinai on which Moses received the Ten Commandments, this mountain of Galilee becomes a place of revelation. Jesus appears and announces that all authority in heaven and on earth has been given to him. The disciples are therefore to go and make disciples of all nations. They are to baptize in the name of the Father, Son, and Holy Spirit, and to teach the new believers to observe all that Jesus had commanded. The Gospel of Matthew concludes with a promise from Jesus, "I am with you always, until the end of the age."

❖ *Reflecting on the Word*

"Why are you standing there looking at the sky?" The question of the angels seems a bit unfair. After all, the disciples have just seen Jesus ascend into heaven. We can hardly blame them if they stood there craning their necks and wondering if what they had just seen was real. Still, the angels chide them because, as our Gospel reading indicates, they have work to do: "Go, therefore, and make disciples of all nations." This is a big job; there is no time to waste.

Yet if we look carefully at the first reading, we see that the chief thing that the apostles need to do is to hurry up and wait—wait for "the promise of the Father," the Holy Spirit who will empower them to be Jesus' witnesses. This is an important point, because the Ascension does not mean that Jesus has left and now it is up to us to do his work. Unless we, like the apostles, wait for the Spirit, we can do nothing. But if we are filled with the Spirit, then even the daunting task of making disciples of all nations is possible.

Pope Benedict XVI noted that the Ascension is not so much the departure of Jesus as it is "the beginning of a new nearness." In the Ascension, Jesus becomes "the one who fills all things in every way," and it is through the Ascension that his promise to be with his disciples always, until the end of the age, can be fulfilled. Rather than an occasion to mourn the departure of Jesus, the feast of the Ascension is a day to rejoice in how close to us he has drawn.

- How do I try to fulfill Jesus's command to make disciples of all nations? What could I do that I am not doing now?
- Do I experience Jesus as someone who lived long ago or lives now in a distant heaven, or do I experience the "new nearness" that the Ascension makes possible?

✜ Responding to the Word

Almighty God, you have drawn our humanity into your eternity in raising Jesus to eternal glory. Help us to live joyfully in your glory, and by our joy become signs of your love to the world. Amen.

June 1, 2014

SEVENTH SUNDAY OF EASTER

Today's Focus: Gathered in an Upper Room

The followers of Jesus gathered in that upper room did not—as we do today—have the capacity to record and communicate to the outside world what they were experiencing. But they waited in patience—together.

FIRST READING
Acts 1:12–14

After Jesus had been taken up to heaven the apostles returned to Jerusalem from the mount called Olivet, which is near Jerusalem, a sabbath day's journey away.

When they entered the city they went to the upper room where they were staying, Peter and John and James and Andrew, Philip and Thomas, Bartholomew and Matthew, James son of Alphaeus, Simon the Zealot, and Judas son of James. All these devoted themselves with one accord to prayer, together with some women, and Mary the mother of Jesus, and his brothers.

PSALM RESPONSE
Psalm 27:13

I believe I shall see the good things of the Lord in the land of the living.

SECOND READING
1 Peter 4:13–16

Beloved: Rejoice to the extent that you share in the sufferings of Christ, so that when his glory is revealed you may also rejoice exultantly. If you are insulted for the name of Christ, blessed are you, for the Spirit of glory and of God rests upon you. But let no one among you be made to suffer as a murderer, a thief, an evildoer, or as an intriguer. But whoever is made to suffer as a Christian should not be ashamed but glorify God because of the name.

GOSPEL
John 17:1–11a

Jesus raised his eyes to heaven and said, "Father, the hour has come. Give glory to your son, so that your son may glorify you, just as you gave him authority over all people, so that your son may give eternal life to all you gave him. Now this is eternal life, that they should know you, the only true God, and the one whom you sent, Jesus Christ. I glorified you on earth by accomplishing the work that you gave me to do. Now glorify me, Father, with you, with the glory that I had with you before the world began.

"I revealed your name to those whom you gave me out of the world. They belonged to you, and you gave them to me, and they have kept your word. Now they know that everything you gave me is from you, because the words you gave to me I have given to them, and they accepted them and truly understood that I came from you, and they have believed that you sent me. I pray for them. I do not pray for the world but for the ones you have given me, because they are yours, and everything of mine is yours and everything of yours is mine, and I have been glorified in them. And now I will no longer be in the world, but they are in the world, while I am coming to you."

✦ Understanding the Word

The Acts of the Apostles presents an idyllic portrait of the community of believers after the resurrection of Jesus and before the coming of the Spirit. The eleven apostles, some women (likely those who had traveled with Jesus in Galilee [Luke 8:1–3]), Mary the mother of Jesus, and his brothers (Acts 1:14) have devoted themselves to common prayer. In the Gospel, Jesus sought moments for prayer to gain strength and guidance (Luke 5:15f; 6:12; 22:39–46). Like their founder, the early community follows suit. In prayer, they will select a successor to Judas Iscariot (Acts 1:24) and in prayer they will organize their communal life (Acts 2:42).

The second reading comes from First Peter, a text attributed to the Apostle Peter but written long after his death. The community addressed is suffering persecution simply because they bear the name "Christian." Since they did not worship the Roman gods, Christians were considered atheists by the Roman authorities. The author encourages these believers that suffering is a blessing and a sign of God's favor, for "the Spirit of glory and of God rests upon you" (v. 14).

The reading from the Gospel of John is known as the prayer of Jesus. After completing a long discourse to his disciples in Chapters 13–16, Jesus now turns to his Father. He acknowledges that his hour has come; it is the time of his glorification. But the focus of the prayer is not solely on Jesus' relationship with God. Rather, Jesus prays for his disciples. He has revealed God's name to them (v. 6) and Jesus asks that God protect them in God's name (v. 12). Knowing the name of God is a particular sign of God's favor. The prophet Isaiah had proclaimed, "Therefore my people shall know my name on that day, that it is I who speak" (52:6). Scholars see in this prayer the signs of a covenant. Jesus, God's envoy, has accomplished the task for which the Father sent him. He has passed on to the disciples everything that God had made known to him. The disciples are now in a covenant relationship with the Father, who will allow them to continue the work of Jesus in making God known to the world (vv. 21–26).

The reading from Acts captures the moment, after the ascension of Jesus and prior to the descent of the Spirit, when the apostles and Mary gather in the upper room, praying fervently, yet probably not yet clear on what the coming of the promised Spirit will mean for them. Having come to believe in the risen Jesus, they still await the power of the Spirit from on high.

Perhaps gathered in that room they were recalling the words of Jesus recounted in our Gospel reading—words in which Jesus spoke of how he was already leaving this world and returning to the Father, and of how his disciples belong to God the Father. These strange but comforting words seemed to suspend them in a moment of uncertainty. Would belonging to the Father mean that they would meet a painful death like Jesus' death, or would it mean being glorified as Jesus was glorified? Or would it perhaps, somehow, mean both?

At times we are all like the apostles and Mary in today's first reading, caught in a moment of suspense. Though we have been given the fullness of the Spirit, we still await the world transformed, of which the risen Jesus is the first fruits. And we know that in this time of waiting, we may face suffering. Indeed, our second reading seems to say that it is in the degree to which we suffer with Christ that we will share in his glory. Meanwhile, we wait for the Spirit.

❖ *Consider/Discuss*

- What does it mean to belong to God?
- What are the different ways in which one might suffer with Christ?

❖ *Responding to the Word*

Holy Spirit, we await your coming with eager anticipation, knowing that you will lead us into all truth, so that we may truly belong to God our Father, through Christ our Lord. Amen.

June 8, 2014

PENTECOST

Today's Focus: Caesar's Final and the Church's First Breath

Today Jesus breathes the Holy Spirit on his followers, following his resurrection. That Holy Spirit, the Church's very breath, is still breathed on us and into us today.

FIRST READING
Acts 2:1–11

When the time for Pentecost was fulfilled, they were all in one place together. And suddenly there came from the sky a noise like a strong driving wind, and it filled the entire house in which they were. Then there appeared to them tongues as of fire, which parted and came to rest on each one of them. And they were all filled with the Holy Spirit and began to speak in different tongues, as the Spirit enabled them to proclaim.

Now there were devout Jews from every nation under heaven staying in Jerusalem. At this sound, they gathered in a large crowd, but they were confused because each one heard them speaking in his own language. They were astounded, and in amazement they asked, "Are not all these people who are speaking Galileans? Then how does each of us hear them in his native language? We are Parthians, Medes, and Elamites, inhabitants of Mesopotamia, Judea and Cappadocia, Pontus and Asia, Phrygia and Pamphylia, Egypt and the districts of Libya near Cyrene, as well as travelers from Rome, both Jews and converts to Judaism, Cretans and Arabs, yet we hear them speaking in our own tongues of the mighty acts of God."

PSALM RESPONSE
Psalm 104:30

Lord, send out your Spirit, and renew the face of the earth.

SECOND READING
1 Corinthians 12:3b–7, 12–13

Brothers and sisters: No one can say, "Jesus is Lord," except by the Holy Spirit. There are different kinds of spiritual gifts but the same Spirit; there are different forms of service but the same Lord; there are different workings but the same God who produces all of them in everyone. To each individual the manifestation of the Spirit is given for some benefit.

As a body is one though it has many parts, and all the parts of the body, though many, are one body, so also Christ. For in one Spirit we were all baptized into one body, whether Jews or Greeks, slaves or free persons, and we were all given to drink of one Spirit.

125

GOSPEL
John 20:19–23
On the evening of that first day of the week, when the doors were locked, where the disciples were, for fear of the Jews, Jesus came and stood in their midst and said to them, "Peace be with you." When he had said this, he showed them his hands and his side. The disciples rejoiced when they saw the Lord. Jesus said to them again, "Peace be with you. As the Father has sent me, so I send you." And when he had said this, he breathed on them and said to them, "Receive the Holy Spirit. Whose sins you forgive are forgiven them, and whose sins you retain are retained."

❖ *Understanding the Word*

In the first reading, the disciples have gathered in one place. Passover is long gone and Pentecost is "being fulfilled." This Jewish pilgrim feast, also called the Festival of Weeks, celebrated the first fruits of the field and was later associated with the giving of the Law. Here in Acts, the giving of the Law on Mount Sinai—the moment at which the wandering former slaves became a people covenanted to God—is transformed into the giving of the Spirit—the moment at which we become a people who are to witness to the ends of the earth that Jesus is Lord and Christ. The experience is described as a sound—a strong, driving wind—and as a visual representation—tongues of fire, which separate and rest on all in the room. All are filled with Holy Spirit and immediately speak in foreign tongues. The commission Jesus had given—to proclaim him to the ends of the earth (Acts 1:8)—can now be realized, for the disciples have the gifts of the Holy Spirit to empower them.

The Apostle Paul recognized the important role of the Spirit in the proclamation of the gospel and the building up of the church. In the second reading, Paul explains that though there are different gifts of the Spirit, each gift is given for the good of the whole. This same Spirit is found in all the baptized, regardless of their ethnicity (Jew or Greek) or their status (slave or free). The Corinthian community seemed to have fought over which gifts of the Spirit were superior, leading Paul to remind them to keep love as their goal (1 Corinthians 14:1).

Before his death, Jesus had told his disciples that an Advocate would come and help them interpret and live his commands after his death (John 14:16). In today's Gospel, the promised Advocate comes as the Holy Spirit. Throughout the Gospel, Jesus has explained his unique relationship with the Father, and invited the disciples into that relationship. As the Father had loved Jesus, so Jesus loved his disciples (John 15:9). What Jesus has heard from the Father, he made known to the disciples (John 15:15). Now as the Father had sent Jesus, so Jesus sends the disciples. He breathes on them and says, "Receive the Holy Spirit." The disciples are now united with the Father, as Jesus had prayed: "And I have given them the glory you gave me, so that they may be one, as we are one, I in them and you in me, that they may be brought to perfection as one" (John 17:22–23).

"Caesar's last breath" is an example commonly used in chemistry classrooms to explain molecular diffusion. The average human breath, including the last breath exhaled by the dying Julius Caesar, contains 1,022 molecules of air and the world as a whole contains 1,044 molecules of air. Presuming a number of things, such as a relatively even diffusion of air molecules over time, we find that there is a 98.2 percent chance that at least one of the molecules of air in your lungs came from Caesar's last breath. Presumably, therefore, there is also a 98.2 percent chance that at least one of the molecules of air in your lungs came from that breath that Christ breathed out upon the disciples in the upper room when he said, "Receive the Holy Spirit."

Those odds are very good—but that is not the basis for our belief that we have received Christ's Spirit. God doesn't really leave such things to chance; the Spirit's work, mysterious as it is, is not really like the random diffusion of molecules. We don't have to wonder if we have a molecule of Christ's breath in our bodies, because the Spirit of Christ has drawn us into his mystical body. As Paul reminds us in our second reading, "in one Spirit we were all baptized into one body." All the baptized have been drawn into the body of Christ, and now live in that place where the Holy Spirit dwells, the Spirit that fills and gives life to Christ's body.

And this body of Christ into which we have been drawn exhales us out into the world, to live as Christ's followers and so to be his witnesses.

✦ Consider/Discuss

- How do I let God breathe me into the body of Christ?
- How do I let God breathe me out into the world?

✦ Responding to the Word

God our Father, send us your Spirit so that we might truly be living members of the body of Christ, your Son. Amen.

Notes

128

After the Easter season, which concludes with the celebration of Pentecost, three Sundays commemorate the solemnities of the Most Holy Trinity, the Most Holy Body and Blood of Christ, and Saints Peter and Paul. The Gospel readings for these celebrations reflect the theme of the Sunday. On Trinity Sunday, we are reminded that "God so loved the world that he sent his only Son" (John 3:16–18). The following Sunday highlights the Eucharist. In the Gospel reading from John 6:51–58, Jesus announces that he is the living bread come down from heaven. The Gospel reading for the celebrations of Saints Peter and Paul recounts Peter's designation as the Rock upon which the church will be built. After these solemnities, the liturgical calendar returns to Ordinary Time.

The first readings for the Sundays of Ordinary Time (14–22) are most often taken from the prophetic books (Zechariah, Isaiah, Jeremiah). On the Sixteenth Sunday, we read from the book of Wisdom (12:13, 16–19). The following Sunday we hear of Solomon's request for wisdom (1 Kings 3:5, 7–12). The story of Elijah's finding God in the whisper (1 Kings 19:9a, 11–13a) is read on the Nineteenth Sunday.

Chapters 8 and 9 and much of Chapters 11 and 12 of Paul's Letter to the Romans comprise the second readings for these Sundays in Ordinary Time. In these chapters, Paul encourages the community of Rome to trust the presence of the Holy Spirit to aid them in their struggles in the current age. Like many early Christians, Paul believed in an apocalyptic eschatology (a calamitous view of the end-times), which held that the present age—filled with sin and suffering—would be replaced by the age to come. This new age would be initiated by the Messiah and completed when the Son of Man returned to judge the living and the dead.

The Gospel passages are taken from Matthew, chapters 11–16. In the narrative of this Gospel, Jesus concludes his ministry in Galilee and begins his journey to Jerusalem. Along the way, Jesus teaches his disciples in parables. Several of these parables are unique to Matthew, and may reflect some of the struggles being experienced by members of the Matthean community (Matthew 13:24–52). Chapter 13 is the third of five discourses (4:23 — 7:29; 10:1 — 11:1; 18:1 – 35; 24:1 — 25:46), which Matthew places in his Gospel to replicate the five books of Moses. In Chapter 16, the tone of the journey to Jerusalem takes a somber turn. When Jesus makes the first of three Passion predictions, Peter is scandalized. "No such things shall ever happen to you," he avows (Matthew 16:22). Jesus quickly rebukes Peter, and follows with an explanation of the conditions of true discipleship—"Whoever wishes to come after me must deny himself, take up his cross, and follow me" (Matthew 16:24).

June 15, 2014

THE MOST HOLY TRINITY

Today's Focus: More Than Mere Math

One God in three persons, or three persons who are one God? More important than how the numbers add up is the mystery of the Triune God of love.

FIRST READING
Exodus 34:4b–6, 8–9

Early in the morning Moses went up Mount Sinai as the LORD had commanded him, taking along the two stone tablets.

Having come down in a cloud, the LORD stood with Moses there and proclaimed his name, "LORD." Thus the LORD passed before him and cried out, "The LORD, the LORD, a merciful and gracious God, slow to anger and rich in kindness and fidelity." Moses at once bowed down to the ground in worship. Then he said, "If I find favor with you, O LORD, do come along in our company. This is indeed a stiff-necked people; yet pardon our wickedness and sins, and receive us as your own."

PSALM RESPONSE
Dn 3:52b

Glory and praise for ever!

SECOND READING
2 Corinthians 13:11–13

Brothers and sisters, rejoice. Mend your ways, encourage one another, agree with one another, live in peace, and the God of love and peace will be with you. Greet one another with a holy kiss. All the holy ones greet you.

The grace of the Lord Jesus Christ and the love of God and the fellowship of the Holy Spirit be with all of you.

GOSPEL
John 3:16–18

God so loved the world that he gave his only Son, so that everyone who believes in him might not perish but might have eternal life. For God did not send his Son into the world to condemn the world, but that the world might be saved through him. Whoever believes in him will not be condemned, but whoever does not believe has already been condemned, because he has not believed in the name of the only Son of God.

The first reading picks up the story of the giving of the Law after the debacle of the golden calf (Exodus 32). In Moses' lengthy absence as he communed with God on Mount Sinai, the people began to doubt his return. In their fear and anxiety, they convinced Aaron to build and worship a golden calf, an image of the pagan gods. Moses broke the original commandments upon his discovery of this travesty. But despite their sin, Moses again ascends Sinai in today's reading. For a second time he petitions God on their behalf, "yet pardon our wickedness and sins, and receive us as your own."

The Second Letter to the Corinthians is a composite of at least five letter fragments written by the Apostle Paul and his apostolic teams. Today's reading is the conclusion of the so-called "Letter of Tears," in which Paul strongly reprimands the Corinthians and charges them to mend their ways and live in peace. The Corinthians have questioned Paul's legitimacy as an apostle, since he does not preach with the same eloquence as the "super-apostles" (2 Corinthians 11:5). These outsider preachers have upset the community, causing them to question what they first learned from Paul.

In the first reading, Moses intercedes for the people's sin. In the second, Paul chastises the people for their behavior. In the Gospel, the evangelist states clearly that God's love has not abated, despite human mistakes. "For God so loved the world . . . " The passage is part of a conversation between Jesus and a would-be disciple, Nicodemus, who comes to Jesus at night. Johannine imagery of light and dark gives the reader clues as to how to interpret the encounter. Nicodemus doesn't understand Jesus' invitation to be born again. So Jesus explains more fully: "For God did not send his Son into the world to condemn the world, but that the world might be saved through him." After Jesus' death, Nicodemus will appear again. This time, he stands in the light. Through the cross, he has come to insight, and he brings the spices to help in Jesus' burial (John 19:39).

❖ *Reflecting on the Word*

The doctrine of the Trinity strikes many, both Christians and non-Christians, as one of the more exotic and esoteric of Christian doctrines. Somehow, three divine persons add up to one God. But today's scriptures cut to the heart of the matter. The doctrine of the Trinity is our way of understanding the truth that we live every day as Christians: that God the Father has saved us through his Son Jesus Christ and made us into one people, united in the Holy Spirit. It is the experience of this salvation that is at the root of our knowledge of God as Trinity.

Of course, the Trinity is not simply a scheme that we come up with as a way of talking about our experience of salvation. It is also, we believe, how God really is. God is, from all eternity, a communion of love shared among Father, Son, and Spirit. It is because God includes us in this eternal love through becoming one of us in Jesus that we have eternal life. Our salvation is nothing less than our inclusion in the love that is the Holy Trinity. This is one reason why Paul exhorts the Corinthians to "encourage one another, agree with one another, and live in peace." It is through actions such as these that our lives mirror the communion of love that is the Trinity.

So the Trinity is what must be true of God if our experience of salvation is true: through the grace of Jesus Christ we become partakers of the love of God in the communion that the Holy Spirit establishes among us and between us and God. The doctrine of the Trinity might be thought of as the affirmation that who God shows himself to be in the story of salvation is who God truly is in eternity.

✢ Consider/Discuss

- How do I relate to the image of God as Father? What role does this image play in my prayer life?
- How do the life and example of Jesus direct and shape my understanding of God and my life as a Christian?
- Where do I see the Holy Spirit at work in the world around me?

✢ Responding to the Word

God of love, help me to seek your presence day by day, so I may come to live in you, and one day live with you for eternity. Amen.

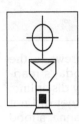

June 22, 2014

THE MOST HOLY
BODY AND BLOOD OF CHRIST

Today's Focus: Echoes of the Resurrection

The feast of Easter has concluded, but we hear and experience its vibrant presence in the mystery of the Risen Christ present as our Eucharistic feast.

FIRST READING
Deuteronomy 8:2–3, 14b–16a

Moses said to the people: "Remember how for forty years now the LORD, your God, has directed all your journeying in the desert, so as to test you by affliction and find out whether or not it was your intention to keep his commandments. He therefore let you be afflicted with hunger, and then fed you with manna, a food unknown to you and your fathers, in order to show you that not by bread alone does one live, but by every word that comes forth from the mouth of the LORD.

"Do not forget the LORD, your God, who brought you out of the land of Egypt, that place of slavery; who guided you through the vast and terrible desert with its saraph serpents and scorpions, its parched and waterless ground; who brought forth water for you from the flinty rock and fed you in the desert with manna, a food unknown to your fathers."

PSALM RESPONSE
Psalm 147:12

Praise the Lord, Jerusalem.

SECOND READING
1 Corinthians 10:16–17

Brothers and sisters: The cup of blessing that we bless, is it not a participation in the blood of Christ? The bread that we break, is it not a participation in the body of Christ? Because the loaf of bread is one, we, though many, are one body, for we all partake of the one loaf.

GOSPEL
John 6:51–58

Jesus said to the Jewish crowds: "I am the living bread that came down from heaven; whoever eats this bread will live forever; and the bread that I will give is my flesh for the life of the world."

The Jews quarreled among themselves, saying, "How can this man give us his flesh to eat?" Jesus said to them, "Amen, amen, I say to you, unless you eat the flesh of the Son of Man and drink his blood, you do not have life within you. Whoever eats my flesh and drinks my blood has eternal life, and I will raise him on the last day. For my flesh is true food, and my blood is true drink. Whoever eats my flesh and drinks my blood remains in me and I in him. Just as the living Father sent me and I have life because of the Father, so also the one who feeds on me will have life because of me. This is the bread that came down from heaven. Unlike your ancestors who ate and still died, whoever eats this bread will live forever."

133

The book of Deuteronomy recounts the wanderings of the Hebrews in the desert and the subsequent giving of the Law of the Covenant. In today's reading, Moses reminds the sometimes grumbling Hebrews that God may discipline, but God always protects. Their clothes may be in tatters, but their feet did not swell during their arduous journey. In their hunger, God provided manna, a food unknown to them. Moses acknowledges that "not by bread alone does one live, but by every word that comes forth from the mouth of the LORD" (Deuteronomy 8:3). Their trials tested them. Would the Israelites keep the commandments and recognize God's word as the true source of life?

In Paul's First Letter to the Corinthians, he encourages unity in mind and heart. Some members have fought over the superiority of their spiritual gifts (1 Corinthians 12:4–6). Others are ignoring the needs of the lesser members (1 Corinthians 11:18–22). Paul recognizes that it is the body and blood of Jesus that is the unifying force for the community. He concludes, "Because the loaf of bread is one, we, though many, are one body, for we all partake of the one loaf" (1 Corinthians 10:17).

But the unifying force of the Eucharist is not recognized by all. In the Gospel of John, Jesus makes an astounding series of statements. He is the living water (John 4:10). He is the way, the truth and the life (John 14:6). He is the true vine (John 15:1). In today's reading, Jesus is the living bread. Earlier in the chapter, Jesus had fed the multitude. Now in the synagogue in Capernaum, those who had been fed ask him for yet another sign. They cite Moses' giving their ancestors manna in the desert. Jesus corrects their misunderstanding: "Amen, amen, I say to you, it was not Moses who gave the bread from heaven; my Father gives you the true bread from heaven" (John 6:32). When Jesus identifies himself as this true bread and his blood as true drink, which must be consumed, many of his disciples are scandalized. "This saying is hard; who can accept it?" they ask (John 6:60), and they return to their former ways of life.

❖   *Reflecting on the Word*

The season of Easter ends with Pentecost Sunday. But the solemnities celebrated on the following two Sundays, the feast of the Most Holy Trinity and (in the United States) the feast of the Most Holy Body and Blood of Christ, might be though of as "echoes" that resound from our Easter celebration. The mystery of the Trinity is revealed in the events of Easter, in which we are brought by the Spirit through the cross and resurrection of Jesus into the Father's love. In Eucharist the risen Christ remains with us in the gift of his Body and Blood.

The feast of Corpus Christi, as this day is commonly known, might be thought of as forming a kind of bookend with Holy Thursday. On Holy Thursday we focus on the institution of the Eucharist in the context of Jesus' impending sacrificial death. On Corpus Christi our attention is drawn to the abiding Eucharistic presence of Christ among us, the life-giving flesh and blood through which Christ remains in us and we in him. Many of the traditions associated with this day, including Eucharistic adoration and processions with the Blessed Sacrament, provide an opportunity to reflect on the Eucharist as the "bread that came down from heaven," the fulfillment in Christ of the gift of manna on which the Israelites fed during their forty years of wandering in the wilderness.

Ultimately, the presence of Christ in the Eucharist is a mystery. But it is not simply the mystery of how Jesus can be with us under the appearances of bread and wine. This mystery is part of the greater mystery: the mystery of God's love for us, God's desire to be with us every day in the most intimate way possible. When we say "Amen" to the minister of Communion's proclamation "The Body of Christ," we are saying yes to this saving mystery.

❖ Consider/Discuss

- What is the significance of Jesus choosing to remain with us in the form of food and drink?
- How do I show my appreciation for the gift of the Eucharist? Do I spend any time in reflection before Mass? Am I attentive during Mass? Am I careful to receive the Eucharist as the great gift and mystery it is?

❖ Responding to the Word

Lord Jesus Christ, help me to say yes to you present in the sacrament of the Eucharist, so I may also say yes to your presence with me day by day. Amen.

June 29, 2014

SAINTS PETER AND PAUL, APOSTLES

Today's Focus: Two Christians, Every Christian

Each of us has a bit of Peter and a bit of Paul in us as we live out our discipleship; together they established a strong Christian presence in the world—a work we are called on to continue today.

FIRST READING
Acts 12:1–11

In those days, King Herod laid hands upon some members of the church to harm them. He had James, the brother of John, killed by the sword, and when he saw that this was pleasing to the Jews he proceeded to arrest Peter also. —It was the feast of Unleavened Bread.— He had him taken into custody and put in prison under the guard of four squads of four soldiers each. He intended to bring him before the people after Passover. Peter thus was being kept in prison, but prayer by the church was fervently being made to God on his behalf.

On the very night before Herod was to bring him to trial, Peter, secured by double chains, was sleeping between two soldiers, while outside the door guards kept watch on the prison. Suddenly the angel of the Lord stood by him and a light shone in the cell. He tapped Peter on the side and awakened him, saying, "Get up quickly." The chains fell from his wrists. The angel said to him, "Put on your belt and your sandals." He did so. Then he said to him, "Put on your cloak and follow me." So he followed him out, not realizing that what was happening through the angel was real; he thought he was seeing a vision. They passed the first guard, then the second, and came to the iron gate leading out to the city, which opened for them by itself. They emerged and made their way down an alley, and suddenly the angel left him.

PSALM RESPONSE
Psalm 34:5b

The angel of the Lord will rescue those who fear him.

SECOND READING
2 Timothy 4:6–8 17–18

I, Paul, am already being poured out like a libation, and the time of my departure is at hand. I have competed well; I have finished the race; I have kept the faith. From now on the crown of righteousness awaits me, which the Lord, the just judge, will award to me on that day, and not only to me, but to all who have longed for his appearance.

The Lord stood by me and gave me strength, so that through me the proclamation might be completed and all the Gentiles might hear it. And I was rescued from the lion's mouth. The Lord will rescue me from every evil threat and will bring me safe to his heavenly Kingdom. To him be glory forever and ever. Amen.

GOSPEL
Matthew
16:13–19

When Jesus went into the region of Caesarea Philippi he asked his disciples, "Who do people say that the Son of Man is?" They replied, "Some say John the Baptist, others Elijah, still others Jeremiah or one of the prophets." He said to them, "But who do you say that I am?" Simon Peter said in reply, "You are the Christ, the Son of the living God." Jesus said to him in reply, "Blessed are you, Simon son of Jonah. For flesh and blood has not revealed this to you, but my heavenly Father. And so I say to you, you are Peter, and upon this rock I will build my church, and the gates of the netherworld shall not prevail against it. I will give you the keys to the kingdom of heaven. Whatever you bind on earth shall be bound in heaven; and whatever you loose on earth shall be loosed in heaven."

❖ Understanding the Word

The first persecution of the early Christians occurred under Herod Agrippa, who martyred James, the brother of John, and imprisoned Peter. Today's first reading recounts the miraculous rescue of Peter from prison. The author of the Acts of the Apostles, whom we call Luke, goes into great detail to emphasize the extraordinary event. Peter is doubly chained between two soldiers and guarded by four squads of four soldiers. Suddenly an angel appears, awakens Peter, and tells him to dress. The chains fall from his wrists, and he follows the angel's directions. Not until Peter is safely outside the prison does he fully realize that he has encountered an angel who has rescued him. Later in Acts, Paul will also experience a miraculous prison break, except that he does not leave, but rather converts his jailer (Acts 16:23–34).

The Second Letter to Timothy is a doubly pseudonymous work. It purports to be written by the Apostle Paul to his younger co-worker, Timothy, when in fact the letter was likely written some fifty years after Paul's death. The reading from Second Timothy describes an elderly Paul in prison, who looks back on his life and acknowledges that he has fought well, won the race, and kept the faith. By his words, he hopes to encourage Timothy to remain steadfast in his own pursuit of faith.

All three of the Synoptic Gospels (Matthew, Mark, and Luke) include the story of Jesus' question to his disciples: Who do you say that I am? However, only Matthew includes the special commission to Peter. Unlike the other two evangelists, Matthew is likely writing for a Jewish Christian community that was struggling with bridging its Jewish past with its Christian future. James of Jerusalem and those who advocated that Gentile Christians be circumcised stood opposite Paul, who admitted Gentile Christians without circumcision. Peter represented the middle ground, and so Matthew encourages his community to see in Peter the proper foundation for their church.

137

Saints Peter and Paul make an interesting pair. Peter: the impetuous one who acts first and reflects later, caught up as he is in his love for Jesus. Paul: the cerebral one who asks us to think through the implications of the love we have experienced in Christ. They represent not simply two different types of Christians, but two aspects of every Christian's life.

The story of Peter at Caesarea Philippi shows him confessing faith in Jesus as Messiah, even though he does not yet fully grasp all that this means. He simply knows that, in his first-century Jewish context, this was the most exalted title he can give to Jesus. He does not yet grasp that this will mean that Jesus must suffer and die and be raised again, but time and trials will teach Peter the full meaning of the faith that he has so boldly confessed, the faith upon which the Church will be built.

While the Gospel reading presents Peter at the beginning of his life as a follower of Jesus, our second reading present Paul near the end of his life. He reflects on how his life has been poured out for the sake of the gospel, and how God has stood by him and given him strength. Unlike Peter's impetuous profession of faith, Paul's is one that arises from considered reflection on the path on which God has led him throughout his life. But the faith he expresses is the same as that of Peter: Jesus is the fulfillment of human longing, the anointed one who will lead us into God's kingdom.

❖ Consider/Discuss

- Do I incline more toward the impetuous faith of Peter or the reflective faith of Paul? How might I incorporate both aspects into my faith life?

- What does Paul mean when he says that his life is "poured out like a libation"? What would that mean in my life?

❖ Responding to the Word

In the waters of Baptism, Holy Spirit, I was sealed with your fire and love to spread the Good News of salvation in Christ. Strengthen me, as you strengthened Saints Peter and Paul, for this grace-filled mission. Amen.

July 6, 2014

FOURTEENTH SUNDAY IN ORDINARY TIME

Today's Focus: Headlines Then, Headlines Now

We hear today that not much has changed in the world: war and violence and life's burdens are present everywhere, but it is through making the presence of our loving God known that peace can come to reign.

FIRST READING
Zechariah 9:9–10

Thus says the LORD:
    Rejoice heartily, O daughter Zion,
        shout for joy, O daughter Jerusalem!
See, your king shall come to you;
    a just savior is he,
    meek, and riding on an ass,
        on a colt, the foal of an ass.
He shall banish the chariot from Ephraim,
    and the horse from Jerusalem;
the warrior's bow shall be banished,
    and he shall proclaim peace to the nations.
His dominion shall be from sea to sea,
    and from the River to the ends of the earth.

PSALM RESPONSE
Psalm 145:1

I will praise your name for ever, my king and my God.

SECOND READING
Romans 8:9, 11–13

Brothers and sisters: You are not in the flesh; on the contrary, you are in the spirit, if only the Spirit of God dwells in you. Whoever does not have the Spirit of Christ does not belong to him. If the Spirit of the one who raised Jesus from the dead dwells in you, the one who raised Christ from the dead will give life to your mortal bodies also, through his Spirit that dwells in you. Consequently, brothers and sisters, we are not debtors to the flesh, to live according to the flesh. For if you live according to the flesh, you will die, but if by the Spirit you put to death the deeds of the body, you will live.

GOSPEL
Matthew
11:25–30

At that time Jesus exclaimed: "I give praise to you, Father, Lord of heaven and earth, for although you have hidden these things from the wise and the learned you have revealed them to little ones. Yes, Father, such has been your gracious will. All things have been handed over to me by my Father. No one knows the Son except the Father, and no one knows the Father except the Son and anyone to whom the Son wishes to reveal him.

"Come to me, all you who labor and are burdened, and I will give you rest. Take my yoke upon you and learn from me, for I am meek and humble of heart; and you will find rest for yourselves. For my yoke is easy, and my burden light."

❖ Understanding the Word

The reading from the prophet Zechariah promises the coming of the Messiah. But this not the Messiah whom many have envisioned. He is not the conquering hero. Rather, he promises peace and demonstrates meekness. The warrior messiah would enter the city riding a horse and chariot, the vehicle of war. But Zechariah promises a messiah riding on a young donkey. His poetic description of "an ass, on a colt, the foal of an ass" is misinterpreted by Matthew, who picks up the imagery for Jesus' triumphal entry into Jerusalem. Matthew has Jesus awkwardly riding two animals: "they brought the ass and the colt and laid their cloaks over them, and [Jesus] mounted" (Matthew 21:7).

A few verses before today's reading from the Letter to the Romans, Paul had written, "There is no condemnation for those who are in Christ Jesus. For the law of the spirit of life in Christ Jesus has freed you from the law of sin and death" (Romans 8:1–2). The concerns of the flesh are no longer those of the Christian who now shares in Christ's spirit. The same spirit of God that raised Jesus dwells in the believers, so they can rightly trust that the same spirit will bring them to new life as well. But Paul places this statement within a conditional clause: "if the spirit . . . dwells in you." It is left up to the individual believer to affirm the Spirit's presence, and so shun living according to the flesh.

In the verses preceding today's Gospel passage, Jesus has cursed the obstinate residents of Chorazin, Bethsaida, and Capernaum who did not repent despite his many deeds of power (Matthew 11:21–24). But his harsh words do not close the door completely. He suddenly turns to his Father in prayer, thanking God for hiding things from the wise but revealing them to children. Then Jesus invites those who are heavily burdened to come to him, promising an easy yoke. Jesus demonstrates that he is gentle and humble of heart, for a path to redemption is still open to the people of Israel, but only if they choose to set aside their "wisdom" and become like children.

In his *Confessions*, St. Augustine describes the extreme grief he felt as a young man over the death of a friend. He states that his grief became a "hard riddle," one that caused him to fret, sigh, weep, and torment himself, allowing him neither rest nor counsel, for he was dragging around a "torn and bloody soul." His soul was impatient at being dragged around, yet he could find no place to lay his burden down (Book 4). Augustine gives us one version of what it means to be one of those "who labor and are burdened"—one of those to whom Jesus promises rest. This is a form of burden that many of us can identify with rather readily. We can be burdened by ourselves, wondering if life is worth the grief that lacerates our souls, the anxiety that nips at our heels, the impatience that clouds our minds. Jesus invites all who bear such burdens to come to him to be refreshed.

The first reading focuses on a different sort of burden: the violence and conflict that have plagued the human race throughout its history. The king whose coming is prophesied will banish the war chariot and the bow and proclaim peace. For those of us who live in situations of relative security, it might be more difficult to identify with this sort of burden. But for many people in the world, who live in places torn by war and other forms of strife, the situation described by the prophet Zechariah is all too familiar. Jesus comes to lift this burden as well, for he is the peace-bringing king of whom Zechariah speaks.

Whether we think of the psychological forces that burden our souls or the forces of violence and conflict that afflict so many people in the world, we should look to Jesus as the one who can teach us the way to true peace. He invites us to learn from him and to take his yoke upon us, so that we might join in his mission of lifting the burdens of others.

❖   Consider/Discuss

- What internal burdens do I carry around with me? What external burdens weigh me down?
- What can I learn from Jesus that will lift my burdens and help me to lift the burdens of others?

❖   Responding to the Word

Lord Jesus Christ, grant me the faith and humility to come to you with my own burdens and the burdens of the world around me. With your strength and love, ease my own load so I can work to better the world around me. Amen.

July 13, 2014

FIFTEENTH SUNDAY IN ORDINARY TIME

Today's Focus: Patience Today, Joy Tomorrow

Perhaps one of the most difficult character traits to live out when times are tough is that of patience. Patience, however, helps us endure—indeed, helps us suffer—our trials as we await the joy that comes after.

FIRST READING
Isaiah 55:10–11

Thus says the Lord:
Just as from the heavens
    the rain and snow come down
and do not return there
    till they have watered the earth,
    making it fertile and fruitful,
giving seed to the one who sows
    and bread to the one who eats,
so shall my word be
    that goes forth from my mouth;
my word shall not return to me void,
    but shall do my will,
    achieving the end for which I sent it.

PSALM RESPONSE
Luke 8:8

The seed that falls on good ground will yield a fruitful harvest.

SECOND READING
Romans 8:18–23

Brothers and sisters: I consider that the sufferings of this present time are as nothing compared with the glory to be revealed for us. For creation awaits with eager expectation the revelation of the children of God; for creation was made subject to futility, not of its own accord but because of the one who subjected it, in hope that creation itself would be set free from slavery to corruption and share in the glorious freedom of the children of God. We know that all creation is groaning in labor pains even until now; and not only that, but we ourselves, who have the firstfruits of the Spirit, we also groan within ourselves as we wait for adoption, the redemption of our bodies.

In the shorter form of the reading, the passages in brackets are omitted.

GOSPEL
Matthew
13:1–23
or 13:1–9

On that day, Jesus went out of the house and sat down by the sea. Such large crowds gathered around him that he got into a boat and sat down, and the whole crowd stood along the shore. And he spoke to them at length in parables, saying: "A sower went out to sow. And as he sowed, some seed fell on the path, and birds came and ate it up. Some fell on rocky ground, where it had little soil. It sprang up at once because the soil was not deep, and when the sun rose it was scorched, and it withered for lack of roots. Some seed fell among thorns, and the thorns grew up and choked it. But some seed fell on rich soil, and produced fruit, a hundred or sixty or thirtyfold. Whoever has ears ought to hear."

[The disciples approached him and said, "Why do you speak to them in parables?" He said to them in reply, "Because knowledge of the mysteries of the kingdom of heaven has been granted to you, but to them it has not been granted. To anyone who has, more will be given and he will grow rich; from anyone who has not, even what he has will be taken away. This is why I speak to them in parables, because

they look but do not see and hear but do not listen or understand.
Isaiah's prophecy is fulfilled in them, which says:
You shall indeed hear but not understand,
you shall indeed look but never see.
Gross is the heart of this people,
they will hardly hear with their ears,
they have closed their eyes,
lest they see with their eyes
and hear with their ears
and understand with their hearts and be converted,
and I heal them.

"But blessed are your eyes, because they see, and your ears, because they hear. Amen, I say to you, many prophets and right-eous people longed to see what you see but did not see it, and to hear what you hear but did not hear it.

"Hear then the parable of the sower. The seed sown on the path is the one who hears the word of the kingdom without understand-ing it, and the evil one comes and steals away what was sown in his heart. The seed sown on rocky ground is the one who hears the word and receives it at once with joy. But he has no root and lasts only for a time. When some tribulation or persecution comes because of the word, he immediately falls away. The seed sown among thorns is the one who hears the word, but then worldly anxiety and the lure of riches choke the word and it bears no fruit. But the seed sown on rich soil is the one who hears the word and understands it, who indeed bears fruit and yields a hundred or sixty or thirtyfold."]

As the reading from Isaiah demonstrates, the word of God is spoken only to accomplish the end for which it is sent. Earlier in Chapter 55, God had invited the thirsty and poor to seek the Lord and call upon him (Isaiah 55:1–2, 6). They are to turn to God, who is generous and forgiving (Isaiah 55:7). Today's reading serves as confirmation of what God has promised. The images of rain and snow and fertile earth remind the exiles to whom Second Isaiah wrote that they could trust the slow but sure work of God, for God's word is never without effect.

In Romans 8, Paul explains the power of the Spirit. Those led by the Spirit of God are children of God, who received not a spirit of slavery but one of adoption (Romans 8:14–15). The Spirit itself testifies that the believers are heirs of God and joint heirs with Christ through suffering with him (Romans 8:16). And as we see in today's reading, Creation also awaits the full revelation of God (Romans 8:19–22). Though believers possess the Spirit as firstfruits, we are still awaiting the full redemption of our bodies. No power on earth or in heaven will be able to separate the faithful from the love of God in Christ Jesus (Romans 8:39).

Matthew Chapter 13 begins a new discourse section in the Gospel, placed within a narrative setting. Previously, Jesus had encountered opposition from various sources (questions from John the Baptist, 11:2–3; unrepentant towns, 11:20–24; critical Pharisees, 12:2; 24; demanding scribes who join the Pharisees in their challenge of Jesus, 12:38; and perhaps even his own family, 12:46). In this new chapter, Jesus uses parables to address the gathered crowd. The parables serve to sift the true disciples from those who seek but cannot truly recognize Jesus. "Knowledge of the mysteries of the kingdom of heaven has been granted to you, but to them it has not been granted."

❖ Reflecting on the Word

The nineteenth-century poet Gerard Manley Hopkins began a poem with the words, "Patience, hard thing!" And indeed it is. Our English word "patience" is derived from the Latin word *passio*, meaning "suffering." The hardest thing about patience is that it requires that we loosen our grip on our situation and let what will come arrive in its own time. Patience means surrendering all attempts to force a solution; it means letting time take over so situations may run their course. In our second reading, St. Paul speaks of the contrast between our present suffering and our future redemption, deriving solace and hope from that future while recognizing that ours is a time of patience, a time of suffering. We, along with all creation, groan in our waiting.

The familiar parable of the sower in today's Gospel reading is usually seen, not incorrectly, as being about the different ways in which people respond to Jesus' proclamation of God's word. But it also is a story about patience, because the seed that is sown, if it falls on good soil, takes time to come to fruition; and that time is a time in which the sprouting seeds suffer tribulation, persecution, anxiety, and worldly cares that threaten to destroy them. In the time of waiting we must cultivate patience, that hard thing. But we can be confident that our patience, as difficult as it may be, is not in vain. We have faith that we will some day "share in the glorious freedom of the children of God," because we trust that God's word, which has been scattered abroad, will achieve the end for which God has sent it.

✤ Consider/Discuss

- What people and situations try my patience most?
- What difficulties have I seen resolved by patient waiting? What difficulties have required direct action on my part in order to resolve them?

✤ Responding to the Word

Grant me patience, O Lord, the fruit of your Holy Spirit's presence in my life. Walk with me daily, so I come to understand the joy of doing your will. Amen.

July 20, 2014

SIXTEENTH SUNDAY IN ORDINARY TIME

Today's Focus: Tending the Field, Awaiting the Harvest

Last week's gift of patience comes in handy today, as we learn that it isn't during grow-ing time, but at harvest time, that weeds are best sorted out. All of us are a mixture of holiness and sinfulness, needing to tend what helps us to grow.

FIRST READING
Wisdom 12:13, 16–19

There is no god besides you who have the care of all,
    that you need show you have not unjustly condemned.
For your might is the source of justice;
    your mastery over all things makes you lenient to all.
For you show your might when the perfection
      of your power is disbelieved;
    and in those who know you, you rebuke temerity.
But though you are master of might,
      you judge with clemency,
    and with much lenience you govern us;
for power, whenever you will, attends you.
And you taught your people, by these deeds,
    that those who are just must be kind;
and you gave your children good ground for hope
    that you would permit repentance for their sins.

PSALM RESPONSE
Psalm 86:5a

Lord, you are good and forgiving.

SECOND READING
Romans 8:26–27

Brothers and sisters: The Spirit comes to the aid of our weak-ness; for we do not know how to pray as we ought, but the Spirit himself intercedes with inexpressible groanings. And the one who searches hearts knows what is the intention of the Spirit, because he intercedes for the holy ones according to God's will.

GOSPEL
Matthew
13:24–43
or 13:24–30

Jesus proposed another parable to the crowds, saying: "The kingdom of heaven may be likened to a man who sowed good seed in his field. While everyone was asleep his enemy came and sowed weeds all through the wheat, and then went off. When the crop grew and bore fruit, the weeds appeared as well. The slaves of the householder came to him and said, 'Master, did you not sow good seed in your field? Where have the weeds come from?' He answered, 'An enemy has done this.' His slaves said to him, 'Do you want us to go and pull them up?' He replied, 'No, if you pull up the weeds you might uproot the wheat along with them. Let them grow together until harvest; then at harvest time I will say to the harvesters, "First collect the weeds and tie them in bundles for burning; but gather the wheat into my barn." ' "

[He proposed another parable to them. "The kingdom of heaven is like a mustard seed that a person took and sowed in a field. It is the smallest of all the seeds, yet when full-grown it is the largest of plants. It becomes a large bush, and the 'birds of the sky come and dwell in its branches.' "

He spoke to them another parable. "The kingdom of heaven is like yeast that a woman took and mixed with three measures of wheat flour until the whole batch was leavened."

All these things Jesus spoke to the crowds in parables. He spoke to them only in parables, to fulfill what had been said through the prophet:
  I *will open my mouth in parables,*
  I *will announce what has lain hidden from the foundation of the world.*

Then, dismissing the crowds, he went into the house. His disciples approached him and said, "Explain to us the parable of the weeds in the field." He said in reply, "He who sows good seed is the Son of Man, the field is the world, the good seed the children of the kingdom. The weeds are the children of the evil one, and the enemy who sows them is the devil. The harvest is the end of the age, and the harvesters are angels. Just as weeds are collected and burned up with fire, so will it be at the end of the age. The Son of Man will send his angels, and they will collect out of his kingdom all who cause others to sin and all evildoers. They will throw them into the fiery furnace, where there will be wailing and grinding of teeth. Then the righteous will shine like the sun in the kingdom of their Father. Whoever has ears ought to hear."]

The book of Wisdom is traditionally attributed to King Solomon, and much of ancient Near Eastern wisdom teachings concern the proper role of the king. In today's reading, God is the exemplar that a good ruler is to follow. God's might is the source of justice, but a justice that allows for clemency. God's people have been taught that justice is preceded by kindness. Thus sinners have hope that God will accept true repentance.

In the second reading, Paul writes of the Spirit's aid in "our weakness." In Romans 8:18, Paul explained, "the sufferings of this present time are as nothing compared with the glory to be revealed for us." Paul and other early Christians believed in apocalyptic eschatology, which held that the present age—filled with sin and suffering—would be replaced by the age to come. This new age would be initiated by the Messiah and completed when the Son of Man returned to judge the living and the dead. "Our weakness" is the difficulty of being in the flesh but of the Spirit. In other words, though believers are initiated into Christ and will share in the glories to come, until that time they cannot escape the trials and tribulations of this age. But the believers, caught between these two ages, are aided by the Spirit who intercedes on their behalf.

The Gospel presents three parables of Jesus: the story of the wheat and weeds, and two briefer parables about the Kingdom of God. The latter two are found in Mark and Luke. The first one, however, is unique to Matthew. After good seed is sown in a field, an enemy secretly plants weeds. Both weeds and wheat grow together and are separated at the harvest. At the disciples' urging, Jesus explains the eschatological (end-times) meaning of the parable. The weeds are evildoers and those who have turned their back on the faith (apostasy). These will be cast into the fire, while the saints will enter the Kingdom. Matthew's community seems to have had an internal struggle among its membership. Rather than ripping out the weeds, the parable reminds Matthew's community that it is not they, but the Son of Man, who distinguishes the good from the bad.

✥ Reflecting on the Word

Last week's Gospel reading presented us with a parable about sowing. This week we have a parable that speaks of tending the growing plants as we await the harvest. We are not to pull up the weeds lest we pull up the crop as well; we are, rather, to await the time of harvest, at which time the weeds will be separated out. As Jesus interprets this parable for his disciples, it tells us why, for the time being, God allows evil to co-exist alongside the good in the world.

St. Augustine applied this parable to the church. Like the world in general, the church is a mixed bag of good and evil. Why does God allow this? Doesn't God want us to make the church an enclave of purity in a sinful world, eliminating the wrong-headed and half-hearted? Our parable suggests that even, maybe especially, within the church, saints and sinners cannot always be easily distinguished from one another. Appearances can be deceiving, and someone who appears saintly can in fact be the worst of sinners and someone who seems to be a sinner could be destined by God to become a great saint. Perhaps what we at first see to be a weed might turn out to be a valuable medicinal herb.

The key here is not that God doesn't want the church to be holy, but that the task of making the church holy ultimately belongs to God's Spirit. St. Augustine thought that the presence of sinners in the church was a small price to pay for the great good of leaving the judgment of souls to God. For it is God, as our second reading states, who is "the one who searches hearts." In this way, the parable reminds us that in our dealings with those both outside and within the Church we must hold to what the first reading tells us: "those who are just must be kind."

✢ Consider/Discuss

- Are there people whom I think the church would be better off without? How does my attitude toward them measure up against God's mercy?
- Can we make judgments about the rightness or wrongness of people's actions without passing judgment on the people themselves?

✢ Responding to the Word

Lord of the harvest, help me to nurture what is good and holy day by day. May I live today as on the last day, removing what is unhealthy and unholy from my life. Amen.

July 27, 2014

SEVENTEENTH SUNDAY IN ORDINARY TIME

Today's Focus: Valuing What Is Truly Valuable

What do we value in life? Our daily living requires us to be aware of the worth and value of things, but the things of this world are not, conversely, what are truly valuable.

FIRST READING
1 Kings 3:5, 7–12

The LORD appeared to Solomon in a dream at night. God said, "Ask something of me and I will give it to you." Solomon answered: "O LORD, my God, you have made me, your servant, king to succeed my father David; but I am a mere youth, not knowing at all how to act. I serve you in the midst of the people whom you have chosen, a people so vast that it cannot be numbered or counted. Give your servant, therefore, an understanding heart to judge your people and to distinguish right from wrong. For who is able to govern this vast people of yours?"

The LORD was pleased that Solomon made this request. So God said to him: "Because you have asked for this—not for a long life for yourself, nor for riches, nor for the life of your enemies, but for understanding so that you may know what is right—I do as you requested. I give you a heart so wise and understanding that there has never been anyone like you up to now, and after you there will come no one to equal you."

PSALM RESPONSE
Psalm 119:97a

Lord, I love your commands.

SECOND READING
Romans 8:28–30

Brothers and sisters: We know that all things work for good for those who love God, who are called according to his purpose. For those he foreknew he also predestined to be conformed to the image of his Son, so that he might be the firstborn among many brothers and sisters. And those he predestined he also called; and those he called he also justified; and those he justified he also glorified.

In the shorter form of the reading, the passages in brackets are omitted.

GOSPEL
*Matthew
13:44–52
or 13:44–46*

Jesus said to his disciples: "The kingdom of heaven is like a treasure buried in a field, which a person finds and hides again, and out of joy goes and sells all that he has and buys that field. Again, the kingdom of heaven is like a merchant searching for fine pearls. When he finds a pearl of great price, he goes and sells all that he has and buys it. [Again, the kingdom of heaven is like a net thrown into the sea, which collects fish of every kind. When it is full they haul it ashore and sit down to put what is good into buckets. What is bad they throw away. Thus it will be at the end of the age. The angels will go out and separate the wicked from the righteous and throw them into the fiery furnace, where there will be wailing and grinding of teeth.

"Do you understand all these things?" They answered, "Yes." And he replied, "Then every scribe who has been instructed in the kingdom of heaven is like the head of a household who brings from his storeroom both the new and the old."]

❖ Understanding the Word

The First and Second book of Kings chronicle the rise and fall of kingship in Israel and Judah. In today's reading, Solomon is presented as the model of a good king. When invited by God to make a request, Solomon outlines the blessings he has already received. God granted Solomon the throne of his father, David, though he was neither the oldest son nor the most experienced. The kingdom is composed of a people too vast to be numbered. In light of these gifts, Solomon asks for the one thing that will enable him to hold onto both the kingdom and the people—an understanding heart so as to distinguish right from wrong.

The second reading from Paul's Letter to the Romans continues this theme of God's sovereignty and benevolence. In the ancient world, kings were thought to represent divine qualities. Paul engages the Old Testament idea that participating in the divine image is not solely the prerogative of the king, but is shared among God's chosen people. Believers share in the image of God's Son and so become the first of many brothers and sisters. God's foreknowledge and the predestination of believers affirm for the struggling Christians in Rome that they too are part of God's larger plan.

The Gospel recounts several parables that describe the kingdom of God. These are unique to Matthew, indicating that he had a separate source of information about Jesus unknown to Mark or Luke. The parable of the dragnet shares similar themes with the parable of the weeds in the wheat (Matthew 13:24–30). The decision about what is good or bad is left up to the angels at the end-time. Only then will there be divine punishment. The closing comment about a scribe trained for the kingdom is thought to be a biographical indication of the identity of Matthew. Some scholars posit that a Jewish Christian scribe "who can bring from his store both the new and the old" would explain Matthew's use of Old Testament scriptures and his interest in bridging Christianity's Jewish roots with its Gentile future.

What is the kingdom of God worth to you? Throughout our lives we engage, usually subconsciously, in cost-benefit analyses, trying to balance cost and risk on the one hand with the potential gains on the other. This might seem a somewhat cold-hearted approach to take toward faith, but Jesus' parables in today's Gospel seem to imply that if we reflect on the matter we ought to see that gaining the kingdom of heaven is worth any cost, worth any risk.

The great seventeenth-century mathematician and philosopher Blaise Pascal is famous for his "wager" regarding religious faith. He said that if we weigh the potential benefit of faith (gaining eternal life) against the cost (a life of religious devotion) and the risk (being wrong and there being no eternal life), it seems perfectly reasonable to have faith. This is not, of course, meant to be any sort of proof of the truth of religious faith. Rather, Pascal's point is the same one made in today's parables: the kingdom of heaven is something of such surpassing good that even the slightest chance of it being real should make us willing to surrender everything we have in order to gain it. Faith in an uncertainty is a small price to pay for the promise of eternal life.

But even we who are believers, who have made the risky choice for faith, sometimes undervalue the gift of God's kingdom. Unlike Solomon in our first reading, we seek a long life or wealth or power over others rather than the pearl of great price, which is the wisdom of God's kingdom. Reflecting, as Pascal did, on the infinite value of what God offers us in the kingdom ought to lead us to live wholeheartedly for God.

❖ *Consider/Discuss*

- What things do I value most? What am I willing to risk in order to have those things?
- Where does God fall in the order of priorities I have for my life?

❖ *Responding to the Word*

God of wisdom, help me see beyond the needs and realities of my day-to-day living to find what is truly of value, and to live as generously as you. Amen.

August 3, 2014

EIGHTEENTH SUNDAY IN ORDINARY TIME

Today's Focus: Do You Believe in Miracles?

It is sometimes difficult in our modern world to believe in—much less to get others to believe in—miracles. At the heart of miracles, however, is the heart of our faith: knowing the saving power of God.

FIRST READING
Isaiah 55:1–3

Thus says the LORD:
All you who are thirsty,
    come to the water!
You who have no money,
    come, receive grain and eat;
Come, without paying and without cost,
    drink wine and milk!
Why spend your money for what is not bread;
    your wages for what fails to satisfy?
Heed me, and you shall eat well,
    you shall delight in rich fare.
Come to me heedfully,
    listen, that you may have life.
I will renew with you the everlasting covenant,
    the benefits assured to David.

PSALM RESPONSE
Psalm 145:16

The hand of the Lord feeds us; he answers all our needs.

SECOND READING
Romans 8:35, 37–39

Brothers and sisters: What will separate us from the love of Christ? Will anguish, or distress, or persecution, or famine, or nakedness, or peril, or the sword? No, in all these things we conquer overwhelmingly through him who loved us. For I am convinced that neither death, nor life, nor angels, nor principalities, nor present things, nor future things, nor powers, nor height, nor depth, nor any other creature will be able to separate us from the love of God in Christ Jesus our Lord.

GOSPEL
Matthew
14:13–21
When Jesus heard of the death of John the Baptist, he withdrew in a boat to a deserted place by himself. The crowds heard of this and followed him on foot from their towns. When he disembarked and saw the vast crowd, his heart was moved with pity for them, and he cured their sick. When it was evening, the disciples approached him and said, "This is a deserted place and it is already late; dismiss the crowds so that they can go to the villages and buy food for themselves." Jesus said to them, "There is no need for them to go away; give them some food yourselves." But they said to him, "Five loaves and two fish are all we have here." Then he said, "Bring them here to me," and he ordered the crowds to sit down on the grass. Taking the five loaves and the two fish, and looking up to heaven, he said the blessing, broke the loaves, and gave them to the disciples, who in turn gave them to the crowds. They all ate and were satisfied, and they picked up the fragments left over—twelve wicker baskets full. Those who ate were about five thousand men, not counting women and children.

❖ Understanding the Word

Second Isaiah paints a picture of hope and restoration for a people still in exile. God will provide them with all they need. Regardless of money, they are invited to eat a rich fare and drink wine and milk. The festive banquet is available for those who heed God's word. They will have life, for God will renew the everlasting covenant made with David.

The second reading concludes Romans Chapter 8. Earlier Paul had acknowledged the difficult stance of believers who must live in the present age of suffering and sin, but are promised to a new age of glory. Those led by the Spirit are children of God, and that same Spirit intercedes of their behalf. Finally, Paul poses a rhetorical question: Who will separate us from the love of Christ? He lists various sufferings, culminating in death. Yet neither death nor life nor powers present or to come can separate believers from the love of God, which they have received in Christ Jesus.

All four Gospels recount the miraculous feeding of the multitudes (Matthew 14:13–21; Mark 7:32–44; Luke 9:10–17; John 6:1–13), but only Matthew mentions that the event occurs after Jesus has heard of John the Baptist's death and has withdrawn to a deserted place. One would expect that Jesus, who was seeking solitude, would have been perturbed by the appearance of the crowd. But Matthew records that upon seeing the throng, "his heart was moved with pity for them" (Matthew 14:14). Some translations say: "he had compassion on them." Both translations fail to grasp the physical aspects of the Greek word *splagchnizomai*, which means literally to have one's guts moved. It isn't Jesus' heart that is touched, but his innards. Compassion is a physical reaction to the plight of the other. His compassionate response is to heal the sick, but as evening comes, he extends his compassion to feeding them as well.

The Gospel miracles are sometimes difficult for us modern people to believe in (of course, scripture indicates that they were difficult for people in Jesus' day as well). So we attempt to find ways to make them fit more easily into our world-view, to say that they are not really miracles, but rather inspiring stories that teach a moral lesson.

One sometimes hears the stories of the feeding of the multitudes found in the Gospels explained in terms of a "miracle of sharing." That is, the seemingly miraculous event is explained with the claim that the people in the crowd actually had brought food with them, but were unwilling to share it with others. When they saw the five loaves and two fish being shared so generously, they were inspired to share their own food and by means of this "miracle" there was plenty of food for everybody.

This would be an inspiring story of what human beings are capable of, but it is not the story that the Gospels recount. The focus of the stories of the feeding of the crowds is not on what human beings are capable of, but on what God is capable of. The story is not about our generosity, but about God's. The story is about how God in Christ can do for us what we are incapable of doing for ourselves, no matter how inspired we might feel. As the first reading reminds us, in the end only God can quench our thirst and satisfy our hunger. This is echoed in the second reading as well: it is the love of God given to us in Christ that allows us to "conquer overwhelmingly" the challenges that face us in life and in death. This is the miracle and mystery to which all the other miracles point, and which we accept in faith.

❖ *Consider/Discuss*

- What makes a miracle difficult to believe in? Have I ever seen something that I considered a miracle?
- What are my spiritual hungers? How does God feed them?

❖ *Responding to the Word*

Almighty God, I know you continue to work marvels and wonders in our world today, for you alone have the power to save. Amen.

August 10, 2014

NINETEENTH SUNDAY IN ORDINARY TIME

Today's Focus: A True Leap of Faith

When Peter leapt out of the boat at Christ's calling, it was a literal leap of faith. As we seek to be closer to Christ, we may be called upon to make a similar leap.

FIRST READING
1 Kings 19:9a, 11–13a

At the mountain of God, Horeb, Elijah came to a cave where he took shelter. Then the LORD said to him, "Go outside and stand on the mountain before the LORD; the LORD will be passing by." A strong and heavy wind was rending the mountains and crushing rocks before the LORD—but the LORD was not in the wind. After the wind there was an earthquake—but the LORD was not in the earthquake. After the earthquake there was fire—but the LORD was not in the fire. After the fire there was a tiny whispering sound. When he heard this, Elijah hid his face in his cloak and went and stood at the entrance of the cave.

PSALM RESPONSE
Psalm 85:8

Lord, let us see your kindness, and grant us your salvation.

SECOND READING
Romans 9:1–5

Brothers and sisters: I speak the truth in Christ, I do not lie; my conscience joins with the Holy Spirit in bearing me witness that I have great sorrow and constant anguish in my heart. For I could wish that I myself were accursed and cut off from Christ for the sake of my own people, my kindred according to the flesh. They are Israelites; theirs the adoption, the glory, the covenants, the giving of the law, the worship, and the promises; theirs the patriarchs, and from them, according to the flesh, is the Christ, who is over all, God blessed forever. Amen.

GOSPEL
Matthew
14:22–33

After he had fed the people, Jesus made the disciples get into a boat and precede him to the other side, while he dismissed the crowds. After doing so, he went up on the mountain by himself to pray. When it was evening he was there alone. Meanwhile the boat, already a few miles offshore, was being tossed about by the waves, for the wind was against it. During the fourth watch of the night, he came toward them walking on the sea. When the disciples saw him walking on the sea they were terrified. "It is a ghost," they said, and they cried out in fear. At once Jesus spoke to them, "Take courage, it is I; do not be afraid." Peter said to him in reply, "Lord, if it is you, command me to come to you on the water." He said, "Come." Peter got out of the boat and began to walk on the water toward Jesus. But when he saw how strong the wind was he became frightened; and, beginning to sink, he cried out, "Lord, save me!" Immediately Jesus stretched out his hand and caught Peter, and said to him, "O you of little faith, why did you doubt?" After they got into the boat, the wind died down. Those who were in the boat did him homage, saying, "Truly, you are the Son of God."

❖ Understanding the Word

Elijah the Tishbite had the unlucky fate of being a prophet of Israel's God. In the previous chapter, he had challenged the prophets of Ba'al, the Canaanite storm god (1 Kings 18). A drought had descended on the land, and each prophetic camp was to demonstrate its supremacy by having its deity bring rain. After the unsuccessful attempt by the prophets of Ba'al, Elijah prayed to God and rain fell, ending the drought. Elijah then slaughtered the prophets, inciting the wrath of Queen Jezebel, the wife of King Ahab. In today's reading, Elijah has fled to the mountain of Horeb (known as Sinai in some texts). He discovers that despite the powerful actions that God has wrought through him, the presence of God is most keenly felt in a whisper.

The second reading is a continuation of Paul's Letter to the Romans. Addressed to a mostly Gentile community, Paul answers questions about the role and fate of Israel in God's divine plan. The refusal of Israel to accept Jesus as the Christ was a constant sorrow for the apostle. So strong was his heartbreak that in today's reading he would suffer separation from Christ if it would bring Israel to true righteousness, which comes not from works of the law but from faith in God.

In today's Gospel, Jesus is able to find time for prayer, which had been interrupted by the crowds (Matthew 14:14). Oddly, the disciples have gone off in the boat without him. When he sees the boat being tossed by the sea, he walks toward it on the water. Into Mark's version, Matthew inserts the story of Peter's attempt to walk on the water. Jesus' question to Peter, "Why did you doubt?" would have resonated with the community of Matthew, which saw Peter as its founding leader. The community could take heart that though Peter struggled, he could respond with the others in the boat, "Truly, you are the Son of God" (Matthew 14:33). So too could they surmount their own doubt, hearing Jesus' words to the disciples as if addressed to them: "Take courage, it is I; do not be afraid" (Matthew 14:27).

157

✤ Reflecting on the Word

It is striking how confident Peter is as he hops out of that boat. What was he thinking? Was he thinking that walking on water must be easy since Jesus did it so effortlessly? Was he thinking that this would impress Jesus? Most likely he wasn't thinking much at all, but simply acting in his typically impulsive manner. We see throughout the Gospels that Peter's overriding impulse is to be where Jesus is. This is one of the things that makes his denial of Jesus after his arrest so shocking: Peter wanted more than anything else to be with Jesus.

This story also suggests that wanting to be where Jesus is can sometimes put you in a pretty perilous place. No matter how much confidence we may have when we step out in faith, we can find ourselves in deep water, with the wind howling around us and nothing but an abyss below our feet. We can find ourselves fill with fear at what might befall us. We might even begin to regret our impulsive decision.

Like Peter, when we find ourselves in such a situation, we must call upon Jesus: "Lord, save me." We must remember why it is that we wanted to be with Jesus in the first place: he is the one who has the power to grasp our outstretched hand, no matter what our situation, and pull us up when we are sinking. The choice to be with Jesus is always the right choice, no matter how perilous it might seem at the time.

✤ Consider/Discuss

- What is a situation in which I have found myself in "deep water" and felt the need to cry out, "Lord, save me"?
- What perils do I face in my daily life because of my decision to follow Jesus?

✤ Responding to the Word

Lord, save me, seek me, search me—so I desire more and more each day to know your love for me, and to be with you forever. Amen.

August 15, 2014

ASSUMPTION OF
THE BLESSED VIRGIN MARY

Today's Focus: Fully Saved—Body and Soul

God does not save or redeem partially, but fully. And so, like the Blessed Virgin Mary, we will one day be resurrected in both body and spirit.

FIRST READING
Revelation 11:19a; 12:1–6a, 10ab

God's temple in heaven was opened, and the ark of his covenant could be seen in the temple.

A great sign appeared in the sky, a woman clothed with the sun, with the moon under her feet, and on her head a crown of twelve stars. She was with child and wailed aloud in pain as she labored to give birth. Then another sign appeared in the sky; it was a huge red dragon, with seven heads and ten horns, and on its heads were seven diadems. Its tail swept away a third of the stars in the sky and hurled them down to the earth. Then the dragon stood before the woman about to give birth, to devour her child when she gave birth. She gave birth to a son, a male child, destined to rule all the nations with an iron rod. Her child was caught up to God and his throne. The woman herself fled into the desert where she had a place prepared by God.

Then I heard a loud voice in heaven say:
"Now have salvation and power come,
    and the Kingdom of our God
    and the authority of his Anointed One."

PSALM RESPONSE
Psalm 45:10bc

The queen stands at your right hand, arrayed in gold.

SECOND READING
1 Corinthians 15:20–27

Brothers and sisters: Christ has been raised from the dead, the firstfruits of those who have fallen asleep. For since death came through man, the resurrection of the dead came also through man. For just as in Adam all die, so too in Christ shall all be brought to life, but each one in proper order: Christ the firstfruits; then, at his coming, those who belong to Christ; then comes the end, when he hands over the Kingdom to his God and Father, when he has destroyed every sovereignty and every authority and power. For he must reign until he has put all his enemies under his feet. The last enemy to be destroyed is death, for "he subjected everything under his feet."

GOSPEL
Luke 1:39–56

Mary set out and traveled to the hill country in haste to a town of Judah, where she entered the house of Zechariah and greeted Elizabeth. When Elizabeth heard Mary's greeting, the infant leaped in her womb, and Elizabeth, filled with the Holy Spirit, cried out in a loud voice and said, "Blessed are you among women, and blessed is the fruit of your womb. And how does this happen to me, that the mother of my Lord should come to me? For at the moment the sound of your greeting reached my ears, the infant in my womb leaped for joy. Blessed are you who believed that what was spoken to you by the Lord would be fulfilled."

And Mary said:

"My soul proclaims the greatness of the Lord;
   my spirit rejoices in God my Savior
   for he has looked upon his lowly servant.
From this day all generations will call me blessed:
   the Almighty has done great things for me
   and holy is his Name.
He has mercy on those who fear him
   in every generation.
He has shown the strength of his arm,
   and has scattered the proud in their conceit.
He has cast down the mighty from their thrones,
   and has lifted up the lowly.
He has filled the hungry with good things,
   and the rich he has sent away empty.
He has come to the help of his servant Israel
   for he has remembered his promise of mercy,
   the promise he made to our fathers,
   to Abraham and his children for ever."

Mary remained with her about three months and then returned to her home.

❖ *Understanding the Word*

The book of Revelation is a late-first-century work composed by John, the seer, while he was imprisoned on the island of Patmos. Filled with symbols and images, it is the only fully apocalyptic work—completely devoted to a description of the end of time—in the New Testament. Today's reading speaks of God's appearance (theophany) as symbolized by the visible ark of the covenant. The dramatic imagery of a woman giving birth has often been thought to symbolize Mary the mother of Jesus. However, as scholars note, the woman was likely intended to be an image of the church in trial, caught between the end of the evil age and God's reign. The twelve stars are reminiscent of the twelve tribes of Israel: this church is the heir to the covenant. A dragon in ancient myths represents the powers against God, and red indicates death. In Revelation, the seven-headed dragon is also the symbol of the satanic empire (17:3). After giving birth, the woman flees into the desert, a place where God has traditionally cared for the Chosen People.

Paul shares a similar worldview with the author of Revelation. The orderly end of history will conclude with God's triumph and the last enemy to be destroyed will be death. This belief, called apocalypticism, anticipated the end of the current age, which was under the dominion of evil, and the emergence of a new age of God's reign. The resurrection of Jesus demonstrated that this new age had dawned and was in the process of fulfillment. Adam represents humanity enslaved by sin, and Christ is the firstfruits who redeems humanity.

The Gospel reading presents the story of the visitation of Mary and Elizabeth. In response to Elizabeth's greeting of blessing, Mary sings a song of praise to God, the Magnificat. The canticle foreshadows themes that Luke will develop throughout the Gospel. The lowly will be raised and the mighty cast down, as Luke records the parable of the humble tax collector and haughty Pharisee (Luke 18:9–14). The hungry are fed (Luke 9:10–17) and the rich are sent away empty (Luke 18:18–25). God's promise of mercy is extended to Abraham and his children forever (Luke 16:19–31; 19:1–9).

❖ Reflecting on the Word

On this solemnity, the Church affirms that the Blessed Virgin Mary has been taken, body and soul, into "heavenly glory." This is a statement more about God's promises to humanity being realized in Mary than it is about cosmic geography. St. Augustine wrote, "We ascend to heaven if we think of God who has put ascending steps in the heart" (*Exposition Psalm* 123). To be in heavenly glory is not to be located at some particular spot above the earth, but to have entered fully into the mystery of God.

What is true of Mary now will be true of all the saved in the Kingdom of God. We too shall be fully united to God, not only in our souls, but also in our risen bodies. Of course, the nature of this risen body is mysterious. In the second reading, Paul uses an agricultural metaphor of the risen Christ as the "firstfruits" of the crop being harvested. Later, Paul extends the metaphor to speak of our mortal bodies as seeds that are planted, from which our risen bodies will grow. Just as we cannot picture the full-grown plant based on what we know of the seed, so too it is difficult for us to imagine our risen bodies in God's kingdom based on what we know of our bodies now.

The key point is that all that God creates—both the spiritual and the material—is subject to redemption. We see this in the resurrection of Jesus and we see it in the bodily assumption of Mary into heavenly glory. Mary is blessed because she "believed that what was spoken to you by the Lord would be fulfilled," and in the Assumption we celebrate that fulfillment. In this way, Mary stands as a sign of hope to us of the scope of God's redeeming activity, extending not simply to souls, but to our material bodies themselves.

161

- How might I think of heaven in some way other than a place that is located above my head?
- How does our belief that God will redeem both our souls and our bodies affect how I treat my body now?

❖ Responding to the Word

Creator of all, you made me as I am, both my body and my spirit. Let me live each day as a temple of your Spirit, knowing that one day you will bring me completely to live with you on high. Amen.

August 17, 2014

TWENTIETH SUNDAY IN ORDINARY TIME

Today's Focus: Insiders and Outsiders

Too often we allow the things that differentiate us as individuals or groups to become barriers that exclude and alienate. Jesus shows us how to overcome those barriers.

FIRST READING
Isaiah 56:1, 6–7

Thus says the LORD:
Observe what is right, do what is just;
    for my salvation is about to come,
    my justice, about to be revealed.

The foreigners who join themselves to the LORD,
    ministering to him,
loving the name of the LORD,
    and becoming his servants—
all who keep the sabbath free from profanation
    and hold to my covenant,
them I will bring to my holy mountain
    and make joyful in my house of prayer;
their burnt offerings and sacrifices
    will be acceptable on my altar,
for my house shall be called
    a house of prayer for all peoples.

PSALM RESPONSE
Psalm 67:4

O God, let all the nations praise you!

SECOND READING
Romans 11: 13–15, 29–32

Brothers and sisters: I am speaking to you Gentiles. Inasmuch as I am the apostle to the Gentiles, I glory in my ministry in order to make my race jealous and thus save some of them. For if their rejection is the reconciliation of the world, what will their acceptance be but life from the dead?

For the gifts and the call of God are irrevocable. Just as you once disobeyed God but have now received mercy because of their disobedience, so they have now disobeyed in order that, by virtue of the mercy shown to you, they too may now receive mercy. For God delivered all to disobedience, that he might have mercy upon all.

GOSPEL
Matthew
15:21–28

At that time, Jesus withdrew to the region of Tyre and Sidon. And behold, a Canaanite woman of that district came and called out, "Have pity on me, Lord, Son of David! My daughter is tormented by a demon." But Jesus did not say a word in answer to her. Jesus' disciples came and asked him, "Send her away, for she keeps calling out after us." He said in reply, "I was sent only to the lost sheep of the house of Israel." But the woman came and did Jesus homage, saying, "Lord, help me." He said in reply, "It is not right to take the food of the children and throw it to the dogs." She said, "Please, Lord, for even the dogs eat the scraps that fall from the table of their masters." Then Jesus said to her in reply, "O woman, great is your faith! Let it be done for you as you wish." And the woman's daughter was healed from that hour.

❖ Understanding the Word

Today's first reading comes from the third section of the book of Isaiah (56–66), composed by an anonymous prophet who writes of the anticipated blessings for the returned exiles. Through this prophet, God proclaims a plan of salvation and justice that is expansive. This universal invitation, mentioned by Second Isaiah in Isaiah 49:6, is not without conditions. Those who wish to join the covenant community of Israel must keep the Sabbath, without profaning it, and hold to God's covenant (Isaiah 56:6). Then the foreigner will be welcome in the house of God, and even be able to offer sacrifice. Thus the temple of the Lord will be called "a house of prayer for all peoples" (Isaiah 56:7).

The theme of inclusion is also evident in Paul's Letter to the Romans. As Isaiah had announced, God has opened the covenant to the Gentiles. The rejection of Christ by Israel has led to the reconciliation of the world. Yet Israel's fate is not sealed. God's gifts are irrevocable. As the Gentiles have found mercy with God, so too will Israel.

The Gospel continues the theme of the foreigner coming to faith. Altering Mark's story of the Syro-Phoenician woman (Mark 7:24–30), Matthew depicts the story of a faithful Canaanite (Israel's archenemies). Since the Canaanite mother acknowledges Jesus as "Son of David," she is likely not surprised when Jesus responds, "I was sent only to the lost sheep of the House of Israel . . . It is not right to take the food of the children and throw it to the dogs" (Matthew 15:24, 26). Nonetheless, the Canaanite woman persists, reminding him that even dogs eat the crumbs from the master's table (Matthew 15:27). Jesus applauds the Canaanite, "O woman, great is your faith!" (Matthew 15:28). The Gospel reading is a narrative confirmation of the universal invitation of God. The foreigner who joins herself to the Lord (Isaiah 56:6) has received God's mercy (Romans 11:32).

164

✥ Reflecting on the Word

It seems to be a fundamental feature of human communities that, to one degree or another, we divide the world into "us" and "them," insiders and outsiders. Our sense of belonging to any entity larger than us seems to require making such a distinction. We distinguish between family members and non-family members, those who are citizens and those who are aliens, those who belong to the Church and those who do not. In some ways, this is simply what it means to belong, and it need not imply any negative judgment by "us" against "them." After all, we hardly fault people for not being members of our family. But the insider-outsider distinction can all too easily lapse into a friend-enemy distinction, at which point it becomes harmful and dangerous, as we perceive the outsider as a threat.

In today's Gospel an outsider approaches Jesus: a Canaanite (i.e. non-Jewish) woman asks Jesus to heal her daughter. At first, Jesus observes the ancient distinction between Jew and Gentile, noting that his mission is to the Israelites. He even insultingly compares the woman to a dog, casting the insider-outsider distinction in sharp relief. In doing so, he awakens in the woman that which can overcome all of our human distinctions—faith. The woman brushes aside the implied insult and acknowledges her dependence on God. Jesus praises her faith and her daughter is healed.

The good news that Jesus brings does not erase all of the distinctions that we find in our world. But it introduces a new principle—faith in the God who desires "to have mercy on all"—that unites us across all our human divisions. It is now faith in God's goodness and mercy, not any ethnic or national identity, that makes one an "insider" in God's kingdom.

✥ Consider/Discuss

- What instances can I think of in the world today where the insider-outsider distinction has become a friend-enemy distinction?
- What does it mean to call the Church a "community of faith"?

✥ Responding to the Word

Lord of life, grant me the vision to honor the differences among peoples by breaking down boundaries and barriers, so your love and mercy may fill the earth. Amen.

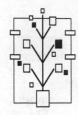

August 24, 2014

TWENTY-FIRST SUNDAY IN ORDINARY TIME

Today's Focus: Building on Rock

Jesus very wisely chose, when he was looking ahead to the continuation of his mission, to build on a rock: Peter. Rocks may have cracks and flaws, but they are strong and stable and enduring.

FIRST READING
Isaiah 22:19–23

Thus says the Lord to Shebna, master of the palace:
"I will thrust you from your office
  and pull you down from your station.
On that day I will summon my servant
  Eliakim, son of Hilkiah;
I will clothe him with your robe,
  and gird him with your sash,
  and give over to him your authority.
He shall be a father to the inhabitants of Jerusalem,
  and to the house of Judah.
I will place the key of the House of David on Eliakim's shoulder;
  when he opens, no one shall shut
  when he shuts, no one shall open.
I will fix him like a peg in a sure spot,
  to be a place of honor for his family."

PSALM RESPONSE
Psalm 138:8bc

Lord, your love is eternal; do not forsake the work of your hands.

SECOND READING
Romans 11:33–36

Oh, the depth of the riches and wisdom and knowledge of God!
How inscrutable are his judgments and how unsearchable his ways!
  For who has known the mind of the Lord
    or who has been his counselor?
  Or who has given the Lord anything
    that he may be repaid?
For from him and through him and for him are all things. To him be glory forever. Amen.

GOSPEL
Matthew
16:13–20

Jesus went into the region of Caesarea Philippi and he asked his disciples, "Who do people say that the Son of Man is?" They replied, "Some say John the Baptist, others Elijah, still others Jeremiah or one of the prophets." He said to them, "But who do you say that I am?" Simon Peter said in reply, "You are the Christ, the Son of the living God." Jesus said to him in reply, "Blessed are you, Simon son of Jonah. For flesh and blood has not revealed this to you, but my heavenly Father. And so I say to you, you are Peter, and upon this rock I will build my church, and the gates of the netherworld shall not prevail against it. I will give you the keys to the kingdom of heaven. Whatever you bind on earth shall be bound in heaven; and whatever you loose on earth shall be loosed in heaven." Then he strictly ordered his disciples to tell no one that he was the Christ.

❖ Understanding the Word

Chapters 1–39 of the book of Isaiah record the prophecies and oracles of a court prophet known as Isaiah of Jerusalem. For forty or fifty years, Isaiah called the leaders and people of Judah to rely on God's promises rather than their own human designs. The backdrop of today's reading is King Hezekiah's revolt against the Assyrian overlords in 701 BCE. As 2 Kings 18 recounts, Shebna, the scribe and master of the palace, had been part of the embassy to the envoys of Sennacherib, the king of Assyria. God chastises Shebna, who glories in his chariots and disgraces the king's house (Isaiah 11:18). In punishment, Shebna will not be buried in the tomb he has so carefully made for himself. Rather, God will toss him away like a ball to die. The symbol of power—the key of the House of David—will be given instead to a more worthy servant, Eliakim. In Matthew's Gospel, it is Peter who will be given the keys of authority, keys to the Kingdom of Heaven.

Paul's Letter to the Romans echoes the acknowledgment of Job, who, after enduring hardship, comes to learn that God's gifts are beyond our repayment (Job 41:3). But Paul's expression is not rooted in the experience of suffering, but of joy. The Gentiles have come to faith through the mercy of God (Romans 11:13–15). This unlikely occurrence is indeed evidence of God's unsearchable ways.

The Gospel reading demonstrates the inscrutability of God's judgments. It is not to a notable Pharisee, educated scribe, or pious priest that Jesus trusts the keys of the kingdom of heaven. Rather, a fisherman from Galilee, known to doubt (Matthew 14:31), is called "Rock" and becomes the foundation of the church. But as the first reading recorded, God vests with power and authority only those worthy of the task. The term translated as "church" comes from the Greek *ekklesia*, which means an assembly, and is a synonym for synagogue. Matthew's community may have been excluded from worship in the synagogue because of their confession of Jesus as the Messiah. Thus, the Jewish Christians gather in a new synagogue, which they call "church." Peter stands as the foundation of this new assembly, "and the gates of the netherworld shall not prevail against it" (Matthew 16:18).

✤ Reflecting on the Word

Today's Gospel is one of the places Catholics look to understand the office of the pope, who is the successor of Peter. Following upon Peter's confession of faith in Jesus as Messiah, Jesus declares Peter to be the "rock" upon which the church shall be built. He is, like Eliakim in the first reading, "a peg in a sure spot," a fixed point of reference in the life of the Catholic community.

Non-Catholics, and even some Catholics, occasionally misunderstand Church teaching regarding the role of the pope. We believe that the pope is infallible in his role as head of the Church, meaning that under his leadership, as it says in the Gospel reading, "the gates of the netherworld shall not prevail against it." This does not mean that the pope is always correct in his views on matters that are not directly related to faith and morals. The pope can be mistaken about the weather or the stock market, or even sometimes issues of Church governance. The pope also does not necessarily have special insight into God's will; what our second reading says applies to popes as much as to any other member of the Church: "who has known the mind of the Lord or who has been his counselor?"

At the same time, while we should not overstate Catholic beliefs about the pope, we also should not understate them. The papacy is a great gift to the Church, uniting Catholics with each other around the world and down through history. In his teaching, the pope continues to fulfill the office of "rock" that Jesus conferred on Peter, providing stability to the faith of the Church so that we can journey with confidence on our way to God's kingdom.

✤ Consider/Discuss

- How can popes set good examples for the members of the Church? How can they set bad examples?
- How does Jesus' promise that the gates of the netherworld will not prevail against the church give me confidence in living my life as a Christian?

✤ Responding to the Word

You have chosen me to follow you, Lord Jesus. May I prove to be strong and steadfast, like Peter, a rock upon which your Church may continue to grow.

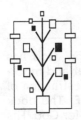

August 31, 2014

TWENTY-SECOND SUNDAY IN ORDINARY TIME

Today's Focus: Foundation or Obstacle?

Peter, the rock, turns into an obstruction to Jesus' message today. Like rock, he was strong, but sometimes difficult for the message of Jesus to penetrate.

FIRST READING
Jeremiah 20:7–9

You duped me, O LORD, and I let myself be duped;
  you were too strong for me, and you triumphed.
All the day I am an object of laughter;
  everyone mocks me.

Whenever I speak, I must cry out,
  violence and outrage is my message;
the word of the LORD has brought me
  derision and reproach all the day.

I say to myself, I will not mention him,
  I will speak in his name no more.
But then it becomes like fire burning in my heart,
  imprisoned in my bones;
I grow weary holding it in, I cannot endure it.

PSALM RESPONSE
Psalm 63:2b

My soul is thirsting for you, O Lord my God.

SECOND READING
Romans 12:1–2

I urge you, brothers and sisters, by the mercies of God, to offer your bodies as a living sacrifice, holy and pleasing to God, your spiritual worship. Do not conform yourselves to this age but be transformed by the renewal of your mind, that you may discern what is the will of God, what is good and pleasing and perfect.

GOSPEL
Matthew 16:21–27

Jesus began to show his disciples that he must go to Jerusalem and suffer greatly from the elders, the chief priests, and the scribes, and be killed and on the third day be raised. Then Peter took Jesus aside and began to rebuke him, "God forbid, Lord! No such thing shall ever happen to you." He turned and said to Peter, "Get behind me, Satan! You are an obstacle to me. You are thinking not as God does, but as human beings do."

Then Jesus said to his disciples, "Whoever wishes to come after me must deny himself, take up his cross, and follow me. For whoever wishes to save his life will lose it, but whoever loses his life for my sake will find it. What profit would there be for one to gain the whole world and forfeit his life? Or what can one give in exchange for his life? For the Son of Man will come with his angels in his Father's glory, and then he will repay all according to his conduct."

169

In today's first reading, Jeremiah laments his prophetic vocation. God has tricked him and Jeremiah allowed it. Now he is an object of laughter and mockery. Jeremiah preached to the people of Judah shortly before the destruction of Jerusalem at the hands of the Babylonians in the sixth century BCE. The book of the prophet Jeremiah reveals the costs of being a spokesperson for God. His enemies—the very people to whom he is sent to prophesy—dig a pit in which to snare him (Jeremiah 18:20). He is thrown into a cistern and left for dead (Jeremiah 38:16). God forbade him to marry and have a family (Jeremiah 16:2). The repeated rebukes and derisions lead Jeremiah to regret the day he was born (Jeremiah 20:17–18). Nonetheless, the prophet admits, "Your words were my joy, the happiness of my heart" (Jeremiah 15:16).

Christians are to offer themselves as a living sacrifice, urges Paul in the second reading. In the Jewish tradition, the priest offered grain, incense, or animals as sacrifices in the temple. But Christians themselves are to become the offering, holy and pleasing to God. Paul encourages the mostly Gentile community of Rome to use their head, so to speak. They are to discern God's desire, and they are to avoid the trappings and temptations of the current age. As the letter continues, Paul warns against exalted thinking and encourages everyone to think soberly, according to the measure of faith given them by God (Romans 12:3).

In the first of three prophecies (Matthew 16:21–23; 17:22–23; 20:17–19), Jesus predicts what awaits him in Jerusalem in today's Gospel passage. As Jeremiah suffered on account of God's word, so too will Jesus at the hands of the religious authorities. Peter, upon whom Jesus had just recently bestowed authority (Matthew 16:18), rebukes him. Jesus' response is sharp. Peter is Satan and a stumbling block. The Greek word translated as "stumbling block" is *skandalon*, from which we get the word "scandal." Peter scandalizes Jesus by his attempt to prevent the plan of God. In response to Peter's misunderstanding, Jesus explains the expectations of discipleship. Disciples must take up their cross and follow Jesus, even unto death. But upon the return of the Son of Man, each will be repaid according to his or her conduct.

Let's get this straight—

#1 Mission of JC M to God { Atone
Q to God { Reprobation
{ Apologize

Peter already

#2 Disciples

Last week we read of the greatness of Peter's confession of faith and Jesus's declaration that he is the rock on which the church is built. Today, in a scene that immediately follows upon last week's, Peter's faith wavers in the face of Jesus' prediction of his imminent suffering, death, and resurrection. Peter the rock goes from being a sure foundation for the church to being an obstacle, a stumbling block. He has not yet learned the lesson that the events of Good Friday and Easter will teach him: the only way to gain your life is to loose it for the sake of Jesus.

The German Protestant theologian Dietrich Bonhoeffer, who was executed by the Nazis near the end of World War II, wrote in his classic work *Discipleship*, "Every call of Jesus is a call to death." He means by this that, like the disciples who followed Jesus during his earthly ministry, we too are called to deny ourselves and to take up our crosses. As St. Paul exhorted the Christians at Rome, we are to offer our bodies, our lives, and our loves as a "living sacrifice" to God. We are not to conform ourselves to the trends and fashions of our day, but we are to be transformed into the image of Jesus. We are to die to our old self so that we can live the risen life of Jesus.

It is only if we do this that we can become, like Peter, a rock that forms part of the living temple of God's people, and not be a stone of stumbling, an obstacle in the path of those who follow Jesus on the way of his cross.

✦ *Consider/Discuss*

- How do I serve as a stone of stumbling, an obstacle, in the lives of other people?
- What does Jesus' call to take up his cross, his call to give up our lives for his sake, mean for me in my life? What sort of death is he calling me to undergo?

✦ *Responding to the Word*

Help me to be a rock of faith and not an obstacle to your gospel, Lord Jesus Christ. Help me to be open to your word, so I may follow you faithfully. Amen.

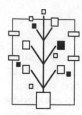

September 7, 2014

TWENTY-THIRD SUNDAY IN ORDINARY TIME

Today's Focus: Prophets and Judges

Though few of us think of ourselves as prophets or judges in the biblical sense, the life of the disciple is one that sometimes calls on us to speak out, and to evaluate what is happening in the world around us.

FIRST READING
Ezekiel 33:7–9

Thus says the LORD: You, son of man, I have appointed watchman for the house of Israel; when you hear me say anything, you shall warn them for me. If I tell the wicked, "O wicked one, you shall surely die," and you do not speak out to dissuade the wicked from his way, the wicked shall die for his guilt, but I will hold you responsible for his death. But if you warn the wicked, trying to turn him from his way, and he refuses to turn from his way, he shall die for his guilt, but you shall save yourself.

PSALM RESPONSE
Psalm 95:8

If today you hear his voice, harden not your hearts.

SECOND READING
Romans 13:8–10

Brothers and sisters: Owe nothing to anyone, except to love one another; for the one who loves another has fulfilled the law. The commandments, "You shall not commit adultery; you shall not kill; you shall not steal; you shall not covet," and whatever other commandment there may be, are summed up in this saying, namely, "You shall love your neighbor as yourself." Love does no evil to the neighbor; hence, love is the fulfillment of the law.

GOSPEL
Matthew 18:15–20

Jesus said to his disciples: "If your brother sins against you, go and tell him his fault between you and him alone. If he listens to you, you have won over your brother. If he does not listen, take one or two others along with you, so that 'every fact may be established on the testimony of two or three witnesses.' If he refuses to listen to them, tell the church. If he refuses to listen even to the church, then treat him as you would a Gentile or a tax collector. Amen, I say to you, whatever you bind on earth shall be bound in heaven, and whatever you loose on earth shall be loosed in heaven. Again, amen, I say to you, if two of you agree on earth about anything for which they are to pray, it shall be granted to them by my heavenly Father. For where two or three are gathered together in my name, there am I in the midst of them."

The lot of the prophet is not a pleasant one. Ezekiel is appointed guardian over the House of Israel. He is to be God's mouthpiece, announcing exactly what God wishes. If he fails to do so, Ezekiel himself will be responsible for what becomes of the people of God. Ezekiel's prophetic powers come upon him as he and many of the Israelites are in exile in Babylon. In this oracle, he proclaims on behalf of God that God takes no pleasure in the death of the wicked. God would much prefer that all turn from evil and do what is just and right. But in order for repentance to occur, the prophet must first announce a warning about the dire consequences of sin. As is seen in all three of today's readings, authority is a responsibility not to be taken lightly.

Chapter 13 in Paul's Letter to the Romans addresses how the Roman faithful are to respond to authority—both civil and divine. Ultimately, no one has power or authority unless God has granted it to him or her. In response to legitimate authority, believers are to fulfill the law. As Paul notes, the one who loves his neighbor has fulfilled the law.

The Gospel reading also speaks of love of neighbor, but Matthew's text is directed to the neighbor who is a member of the church. Jesus outlines how one should approach a brother or sister who has wronged them. The first step is least invasive and allows the offender an opportunity to repent without public embarrassment. If the offender does not listen, others are called to witness to the offense. Finally, the church (Matthew's preferred term for his community of believers) is called in. If the offender does not listen, he or she is to be cast out. While this last step sounds harsh, it actually demotes the offender to the status of tax collector or Gentile. Since whenever two or three believers gather in his name Jesus is effectively in their presence, the responsibilities of the members of the church are not to be taken lightly.

❖ *Reflecting on the Word*

It is an almost unquestionable principle among many people today that it is bad to be judgmental. After all, doesn't Jesus say, "Judge not, lest you be judged"? But today's scriptures imply that holding people accountable for their actions is not only something that God commands us to do, but it is also one of the ways in which we show love to our neighbors. When we see someone doing something wrong, it is an act of kindness to turn him or her from that course of action.

Important here is the distinction between judging a person and judging an action. Only God can judge a person because only God can see into the heart and know the intention with which someone acts. But, as Paul reminds us in the second reading, God has also shown us the sort of actions that befit a truly loving person, the sort of actions that lead us toward God rather than away from God. While we cannot judge how a person stands in the eyes of God, we are called to make judgments all the time about our own actions and the actions of others. If we see people acting to a way that is unloving, we are obligated to point this out, for their own good as well as for the good of those around them.

We should ask ourselves whether our hesitation to judge another person's actions grows out of genuine humility and acceptance or out of a desire simply not to be perceived as a scold. Few of us relish the role of keeper of public morality. But when we see someone engaged in behavior that is harmful to themselves or others, it is our role to speak out honestly and with love.

❖ Consider/Discuss

- How can I be sure that my reluctance to pass judgment on others' actions doesn't grow out of fear of rejection or unpopularity?

- When I make a negative judgment regarding another's actions, how can I communicate at the same time a genuine love and concern for that person?

❖ Responding to the Word

Loving God, give us your Spirit of gentleness and wisdom, so that we may know what is truly good and make it known to others with fearlessness and love, through Christ our Lord.

September 14, 2014

EXALTATION OF THE HOLY CROSS

Today's Focus: Being Raised Up

Christians sometimes forget that for Christ to be raised from the dead he had to be raised on a cross; sometimes we look only at the cross and don't recall the Resurrection. We must always keep both ways of being raised up in mind.

FIRST READING
Numbers 21:4b–9

With their patience worn out by the journey, the people complained against God and Moses, "Why have you brought us up from Egypt to die in this desert, where there is no food or water? We are disgusted with this wretched food!"

In punishment the LORD sent among the people saraph serpents, which bit the people so that many of them died. Then the people came to Moses and said, "We have sinned in complaining against the LORD and you. Pray the LORD to take the serpents from us." So Moses prayed for the people, and the LORD said to Moses, "Make a saraph and mount it on a pole, and if any who have been bitten look at it, they will live." Moses accordingly made a bronze serpent and mounted it on a pole, and whenever anyone who had been bitten by a serpent looked at the bronze serpent, he lived.

PSALM RESPONSE
Psalm 78:7b

Do not forget the works of the Lord!

SECOND READING
Philippians 2:6–11

Brothers and sisters:
Christ Jesus, though he was in the form of God,
   did not regard equality with God something to be grasped.
Rather, he emptied himself,
taking the form of a slave,
coming in human likeness;
and found human in appearance,
he humbled himself,
becoming obedient to the point of death,
even death on a cross.
Because of this, God greatly exalted him
   and bestowed on him the name
   which is above every name,
   that at the name of Jesus
   every knee should bend,
   of those in heaven and on earth and under the earth,
   and every tongue confess that
   Jesus Christ is Lord,

GOSPEL to the glory of God the Father.

Jesus said to Nicodemus: "No one has gone up to heaven except the one who has come down from heaven, the Son of Man. And just as Moses lifted up the serpent in the desert, so must the Son of Man be lifted up, so that everyone who believes in him may have eternal life."

For God so loved the world that he gave his only Son, so that everyone who believes in him might not perish but might have eternal life. For God did not send his Son into the world to condemn the world, but that the world might be saved through him.

❖ Understanding the Word

The first reading is taken from the book of Numbers, the fourth book of the Bible. The book describes the Israelites' journey through the wilderness from Mount Sinai to the Promised Land. This passage evidences a pattern of rebellion-punishment-intercession-forgiveness, which is found throughout the book (11:1–3; 12:2–16; 17:6–15). A new generation remains as rebellious as their parents, complaining against God and Moses. They protest about the lack of food and water: "We are disgusted with this wretched food!" (v. 5). God punishes the people by sending serpents to bite them. Confessing their sins, they beg Moses to intercede for them again. The source of their healing (the bronze serpent) is ironically symbolic of what caused their pain. The serpent symbolized life, since it was believed to be able to regenerate itself.

In Paul's Letter to the Philippians, the apostle likely is quoting an early Christian hymn that recounted Christ's willingness to enter into human form. Christ's obedience—unlike the grumbling Israelites in the wilderness—is to be a reminder to the Philippians to behave like Christ in all their actions.

The Pharisee Nicodemus comes to Jesus at night, acknowledging that Jesus is a teacher sent by God. But Nicodemus fails to recognize who Jesus truly is. In today's reading from the Gospel of John, Jesus attempts to enlighten Nicodemus, describing himself as the one who has come down from heaven, the Son of Man. The evangelist expects his readers to remember the grumbling Israelites who complained against Moses. But unlike the scene in the wilderness, the punishment will be borne by Jesus. As the bronze serpent brought healing to those who looked upon it, so the Son of Man, when lifted up, will bring eternal life to those who believe. The pattern of rebellion-punishment-intercession-forgiveness is ended once and for all. As Jesus explains to Nicodemus, "For God so loved the world that he gave his only Son" (v. 16), not to condemn the world but to save it.

❖ Reflecting to the Word

The story goes that as the ship *Titanic* sank into the North Sea the ship's band played the hymn "Nearer, My God, to Thee," the first verse of which is:

Nearer, my God, to Thee, nearer to Thee!

E'en though it be a cross that raiseth me,
Still all my song shall be, nearer, my God, to Thee.

While some have questioned the truth of this account, the appeal of the story remains, because the bravery of the musicians who continued to play to lift the hearts of the passengers reminds us of how suffering and disaster, rather than beating us down and defeating us, can become the means by which we are lifted up to God.

This feast is called the "Exaltation of the Holy Cross" because it celebrates the cross as the occasion of Jesus' being lifted up to God to be a sign of the world's salvation. In some paradoxical way, it is in his humiliation that Jesus most clearly shows us the nature of divine love. In coming to know and believe in this love, we are healed and given eternal life. Just as the sight of the bronze serpent saved the Israelites from the venom of the seraph, so too our coming to "see" Jesus in faith heals us of the deadly poison of sin.

What we see in Jesus we see also in our own lives. In a way that we cannot always understand, the crosses that we encounter in our lives lift us nearer to God, provided that we embrace them in the faith that Jesus has transformed the meaning of suffering. If in the midst of suffering and disaster we can look to the one who was raised up on the cross for our salvation, we will not perish but have eternal life.

✣ Consider/Discuss

- When I look at an image of the crucified Jesus, how does it speak to me of God's love and healing?
- Are there experiences in my life when I have felt that distress or suffering have ultimately drawn me closer to God?

✣ Responding to the Word

Lord Jesus, on the cross you were lifted up as a sign of God's love. Let that love heal us from the poison of sin so that we might live our lives for your glory.

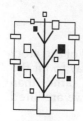

September 21, 2014

TWENTY-FIFTH SUNDAY IN ORDINARY TIME

Today's Focus: The Evil Eye, the Generous Heart

Sometimes our merciful, generous God acts graciously toward others, but we look upon this with jealousy, not joy or gratitude. To see as God sees is to behold the divine at work in the world, and respond in a similar merciful and generous way.

FIRST READING
Isaiah 55:6–9

Seek the LORD while he may be found,
    call him while he is near.
Let the scoundrel forsake his way,
    and the wicked his thoughts;
let him turn to the LORD for mercy;
    to our God, who is generous in forgiving.
For my thoughts are not your thoughts,
    nor are your ways my ways, says the LORD.
As high as the heavens are above the earth,
    so high are my ways above your ways
    and my thoughts above your thoughts.

PSALM RESPONSE
Psalm 145:18a

The Lord is near to all who call upon him.

SECOND READING
Philippians 1:20c–24, 27a

Brothers and sisters: Christ will be magnified in my body, whether by life or by death. For to me life is Christ, and death is gain. If I go on living in the flesh, that means fruitful labor for me. And I do not know which I shall choose. I am caught between the two. I long to depart this life and be with Christ, for that is far better. Yet that I remain in the flesh is more necessary for your benefit.

GOSPEL
Matthew
20:1–16a

Only, conduct yourselves in a way worthy of the gospel of Christ.

Jesus told his disciples this parable: "The kingdom of heaven is like a landowner who went out at dawn to hire laborers for his vineyard. After agreeing with them for the usual daily wage, he sent them into his vineyard. Going out about nine o'clock, the landowner saw others standing idle in the marketplace, and he said to them, 'You too go into my vineyard, and I will give you what is just.' So they went off. And he went out again around noon, and around three o'clock, and did likewise. Going out about five o'clock, the landowner found others standing around, and said to them, 'Why do you stand here idle all day?' They answered, 'Because no one has hired us.' He said to them, 'You too go into my vineyard.' When it was evening the owner of the vineyard said to his foreman, 'Summon the laborers and give them their pay, beginning with the last and ending with the first.' When those who had started about five o'clock came, each received the usual daily wage. So when the first came, they thought that they would receive more, but each of them also got the usual wage. And on receiving it they grumbled against the landowner, saying, 'These last ones worked only one hour, and you have made them equal to us, who bore the day's burden and the heat.' He said to one of them in reply, 'My friend, I am not cheating you. Did you not agree with me for the usual daily wage? Take what is yours and go. What if I wish to give this last one the same as you? Or am I not free to do as I wish with my own money? Are you envious because I am generous?' Thus, the last will be first, and the first will be last."

❖❖ *Understanding the Word*

Isaiah 55 is the concluding chapter from the prophet known as Second Isaiah. Beginning in Chapter 40, this anonymous prophet preaches to the exiles in Babylon, reminding them of God's faithfulness and, in turn, their responsibility. In today's reading, the prophet encourages the exiles to seek God where God is to be found—in the midst of their suffering. Though God's thoughts are beyond human comprehension, God's actions are not. God is merciful and generous in forgiving.

Paul writes to his beloved community at Philippi, poignantly describing his dilemma. He is imprisoned for preaching the gospel, and yet he rejoices, confident in the Philippians' prayers and the help of the Spirit (v. 19). This sense of joy is rooted in his understanding of baptism. One is baptized into Christ's death in order to share in eternal life. If Paul should die, he will be reunited with Christ. If he lives, he can serve Christ by remaining in his ministry among the Philippians. He chooses life and reminds the community that they too are to behave in ways worthy of the gospel of Christ.

In the Gospel reading, Jesus recounts a parable drawn from the Galilean countryside where day laborers struggled to eke out a living. Parables are effective because they rely on commonplace events with which the hearers are familiar. But then there's an unexpected twist, which upsets expectations and challenges the listeners to respond. Jesus describes the good fortune of the last laborers invited to the field. In the settling of accounts, these workers receive the same amount as those who worked the whole day. The daily wage given would have been just enough for the worker and his family to survive until the next day. The landowner is not only generous (paying for services he did not receive), but also compassionate, recognizing that the last have the same needs as the first. Within the setting of Matthew's Gospel, this parable serves to remind Matthew's community that God's justice and generosity are not based on human expectations. As the reading from Isaiah rightly noted, God's ways are beyond our comprehension.

✤ Reflecting on the Word

In many of the cultures of the Mediterranean world, there is a folk belief in what is called "the evil eye." This is the belief that if you have some sort of good fortune and someone looks upon you jealously—i.e. with the evil eye—then you will be cursed. This belief is reflected in today's Gospel reading, buried within the translation. Where it says, "Are you envious because I am generous?" the original Greek actually says, "Is your eye evil because I am good?" This reflects the idea that the eye that looks upon another person's good fortune with envy can bring misfortune upon that person.

In fact, in Matthew's Gospel Jesus mentions the evil eye twice. In addition to today's Gospel reading, Jesus says in the Sermon on the Mount, "The eye is the lamp of the body. So, if your eye is healthy, your whole body will be full of light; but if your eye is unhealthy, your whole body will be full of darkness." Jesus contrasts having an evil eye with having a "single" eye, which means, more or less, the same thing as being "single minded" or, to use another phrase from the Sermon on the Mount, being "pure of heart." It means having your life focused on God and not on what others get that you don't have. If you live your life focused on God—if you are "single-eyed"—then you will be filled with light. But if you are evil-eyed—if you live your life resenting the good fortune of others—then you will be filled with darkness.

For Jesus, the evil eye, contrary to folk belief, does no harm to the person who has good fortune, but rather to the one who is envious. When we, like the workers in today's Gospel who came early, resent the good fortune of others, it does no harm to them. We are the ones who are harmed. We are the ones who are filled with darkness, who lose our focus and so experience a kind of blowback of our own envy and find ourselves being made miserable by the happiness of another.

- Have I felt jealousy at the good fortune of others? How have I been able to overcome those feelings of jealousy?
- Is it fair that God should save those who turn to God at the end of their lives, when others have served God faithfully throughout their lives?

✤ *Responding to the Word*

Generous God, help us to look on others with the same kindness with which you look upon us, so that we may rejoice in the salvation of all people, through Christ our Lord.

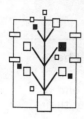

September 28, 2014

TWENTY-SIXTH SUNDAY IN ORDINARY TIME

Today's Focus: Doing, Not Merely Saying

Walking the walk if we're going to talk the talk is common jargon these days. Though we don't believe we are saved by the works we do, we do believe that if we truly have faith, it will show forth in our actions.

FIRST READING
Ezekiel 18:25–28

Thus says the LORD: You say, "The LORD's way is not fair!" Hear now, house of Israel: Is it my way that is unfair, or rather, are not your ways unfair? When someone virtuous turns away from virtue to commit iniquity, and dies, it is because of the iniquity he committed that he must die. But if he turns from the wickedness he has committed, and does what is right and just, he shall preserve his life; since he has turned away from all the sins that he has committed, he shall surely live, he shall not die.

PSALM RESPONSE
Psalm 25:6a

Remember your mercies, O Lord.

In the shorter form of the reading, the passage in brackets is omitted.

SECOND READING
Philippians 2:1–11 or 2:1–5

Brothers and sisters: If there is any encouragement in Christ, any solace in love, any participation in the Spirit, any compassion and mercy, complete my joy by being of the same mind, with the same love, united in heart, thinking one thing. Do nothing out of selfishness or out of vainglory; rather, humbly regard others as more important than yourselves, each looking out not for his own interests, but also for those of others.

Have in you the same attitude
    that is also in Christ Jesus,
        [Who, though he was in the form of God,
        did not regard equality with God
        something to be grasped.
    Rather, he emptied himself,
        taking the form of a slave,
        coming in human likeness;
        and found human in appearance,
        he humbled himself,
        becoming obedient to the point of death,
        even death on a cross.

Because of this, God greatly exalted him
and bestowed on him the name
which is above every name,
that at the name of Jesus
every knee should bend,
of those in heaven and on earth and under the earth,
and every tongue confess that
Jesus Christ is Lord,
to the glory of God the Father.]

GOSPEL
Matthew
21:28–32

Jesus said to the chief priests and elders of the people: "What is your opinion? A man had two sons. He came to the first and said, 'Son, go out and work in the vineyard today.' He said in reply, 'I will not,' but afterwards changed his mind and went. The man came to the other son and gave the same order. He said in reply, 'Yes, sir,' but did not go. Which of the two did his father's will?" They answered, "The first." Jesus said to them, "Amen, I say to you, tax collectors and prostitutes are entering the kingdom of God before you. When John came to you in the way of righteousness, you did not believe him; but tax collectors and prostitutes did. Yet even when you saw that, you did not later change your minds and believe him."

❖ Understanding the Word

Ezekiel responds to a prevalent theology among the Babylonian exiles—that God was punishing them for the sins of others (Exodus 20:5; Deuteronomy 5:9). Speaking through the prophet, God announces, "Only the one who sins shall die" (v. 20). And more remarkably, if the wicked one turns away from sin and lives justly according to God's laws, that one will not be punished (v. 21). But If a just persons turns to wickedness, that one will die. The people react, claiming that the Lord is unfair, upsetting their theological perspective and making them individually responsible for their own salvation.

The second reading opens with Paul's litany of Christian attitudes: encouragement in Christ, solace in love, participation in the Spirit, compassion and mercy. If the Philippians possess these, then being of one mind and heart, they will complete Paul's joy. But lest they become haughty (as happened among the Corinthian believers), Paul warns against selfishness and vainglory. Humility is the watchdog of vanity. As an example of the appropriate attitude, Paul quotes an early Christian hymn, which describes Jesus' ultimate humility.

In the Gospel reading, Jesus is in the temple area defending himself against the chief priests and scribes who question his authority. In a parable unique to Matthew's Gospel, Jesus introduces two sons who say one thing and do another. When asked by their father to work in the vineyard, the first son replies, "I will not," but later relents and goes to the field. The second son responds oppositely. Jesus asks his interrogators, which son did the father's will? They answer that the first did. In its original context, a parable is not ordinarily explained. The readers are left to puzzle out the answer for themselves. When an explanation is given, it is likely from the hand of the evangelist shaping his sources for a particular end.

183

Matthew's community may have recently been ousted from worshiping in the synagogue, so he has Jesus explain the parable, establishing the tax collectors and prostitutes as the worthy son, while the religious leaders are the disobedient one.

❖ Reflecting on the Word

While we believe that we are saved by God's grace through faith and not by our good works, today's Gospel underscores for us the fact that true faith is a matter of doing and not just of saying. This is something that Jesus' parable of the two sons makes clear to his hearers, the chief priest and elders. What seems less clear to them is Jesus's suggestion that they might be the ones who profess obedience to God with their lips and deny it by their actions, and that those whom they look down upon, the tax collectors and prostitutes, might in fact have a more exalted place in God's kingdom than they do.

Being a Christian, as our second reading reminds us, is a matter of having the attitude that Jesus showed in humbling himself on the cross. This was perhaps the error of the chief priests and the elders to whom Jesus addressed his parable. We do not make ourselves worthy in God's eyes by pompous declarations of all that we will do for God. Instead, it is in laying our lives before God in humble openness that we let God raise us up.

Perhaps the tax collectors and prostitutes of whom Jesus speaks in today's Gospel have an exalted place in God's kingdom because they know that they cannot rely on anything other than God's mercy for their salvation. Knowing themselves to be sinners, they in their humility count themselves among the least of God's people, and in so doing they are lifted up by God.

❖ Consider/Discuss

- Who are the people whom I look down upon—my "tax collectors and prostitutes"—and consider unworthy of God's kingdom?
- What would it look like in my life for me to follow Paul's instruction to the Philippians not to look out for my own interests, but to look out for the interests of others? What concrete changes would this make in my life?

❖ Responding to the Word

Lord Jesus, you poured out your life on the cross as an offering to God and an example of humility for us to follow. Give us the grace to follow that example in word and deed through our love of others.

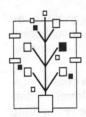

October 5, 2014

TWENTY-SEVENTH SUNDAY IN ORDINARY TIME

Today's Focus: Renters, Not Owners

It's easy to make the mistake of thinking that the many gifts and blessings we've received from God still remain, in a sense, God's and not ours. We are made stewards and caregivers, expected to use what we've been given in a wise, God-like fashion.

FIRST READING
Isaiah 5:1–7

Let me now sing of my friend,
    my friend's song concerning his vineyard.
My friend had a vineyard
    on a fertile hillside;
he spaded it, cleared it of stones,
    and planted the choicest vines;
within it he built a watchtower,
    and hewed out a wine press.
Then he looked for the crop of grapes,
    but what it yielded was wild grapes.

Now, inhabitants of Jerusalem and people of Judah,
    judge between me and my vineyard:
What more was there to do for my vineyard
    that I had not done?
Why, when I looked for the crop of grapes,
    did it bring forth wild grapes?
Now, I will let you know
    what I mean to do with my vineyard:
take away its hedge, give it to grazing,
    break through its wall, let it be trampled!
Yes, I will make it a ruin:
    it shall not be pruned or hoed,
    but overgrown with thorns and briers;
I will command the clouds
    not to send rain upon it.
The vineyard of the LORD of hosts is the house of Israel,
    and the people of Judah are his cherished plant;
he looked for judgment, but see, bloodshed!
    for justice, but hark, the outcry!

PSALM RESPONSE
Isaiah 5:7a

The vineyard of the Lord is the house of Israel.

SECOND READING
Philippians 4:6–9

Brothers and sisters: Have no anxiety at all, but in everything, by prayer and petition, with thanksgiving, make your requests known to God. Then the peace of God that surpasses all understanding will guard your hearts and minds in Christ Jesus.

Finally, brothers and sisters, whatever is true, whatever is honorable, whatever is just, whatever is pure, whatever is lovely, whatever is gracious, if there is any excellence and if there is anything worthy of praise, think about these things. Keep on doing what you have learned and received and heard and seen in me. Then the God of peace will be with you.

GOSPEL
Matthew 21:33–43

Jesus said to the chief priests and the elders of the people: "Hear another parable. There was a landowner who planted a vineyard, put a hedge around it, dug a wine press in it, and built a tower. Then he leased it to tenants and went on a journey. When vintage time drew near, he sent his servants to the tenants to obtain his produce. But the tenants seized the servants and one they beat, another they killed, and a third they stoned. Again he sent other servants, more numerous than the first ones, but they treated them in the same way. Finally, he sent his son to them, thinking, 'They will respect my son.' But when the tenants saw the son, they said to one another, 'This is the heir. Come, let us kill him and acquire his inheritance.' They seized him, threw him out of the vineyard, and killed him. What will the owner of the vineyard do to those tenants when he comes?" They answered him, "He will put those wretched men to a wretched death and lease his vineyard to other tenants who will give him the produce at the proper times." Jesus said to them, "Did you never read in the Scriptures:

The stone that the builders rejected
has become the cornerstone;
by the Lord has this been done,
and it is wonderful in our eyes?

Therefore, I say to you, the kingdom of God will be taken away from you and given to a people that will produce its fruit."

❖❖ *Understanding the Word*

The first reading from Isaiah consists of an allegory, which can be interpreted on several levels. The literal sense addresses an agricultural scene, in which loving care is given to a vineyard, only to produce worthless fruit. Since the passage is introduced as a love song to a friend, it could be read as an allegory of marital infidelity, similar to Hosea Chapter 2. Finally, the verses understood in the historical context address the sins of the Northern Kingdom (Israel) and the Southern Kingdom (Judah). A vineyard is a symbol for wealth, but this wealth has not produced justice (v. 7).

The second reading reminds the Philippian faithful to have no anxiety, offering two paths to peace. Believers should confidently make requests to God (v. 6–7), and they are to continue to do what they have learned, received, heard, and seen in Paul (v. 9). Paul closes his letter to the Philippians with an exhortation, reminiscent of Stoic philosophy. The believers are to adhere to the virtues of truth, honor, justice, purity, loveliness, grace, and excellence.

The Gospel reading picks up the theme of the vineyard found in Isaiah, but it is not the produce that is rotten, but the tenants. Addressing the religious leadership of Jerusalem, Jesus presents three parables in response to their criticism of him—the parable of the two sons (Matthew 21:23–32), the parable of the wicked tenants (Matthew 21:33–43) and the parable of the wedding feast (Matthew 22:1–14). These parables serve as a response to the criticism from and an indictment of the religious leadership. In today's parable, Jesus describes an absentee landowner who attempts to collect his rent on three occasions, and each time the tenants beat, stone, and kill the servants sent. Finally, the landowner sends his son, expecting that the son will be respected. Instead the tenants kill the son, assuming that they will then inherit the vineyard. The vine is often a symbol for Israel (Hosea 10:1; Jeremiah 2:21; Ezekiel 15:1–8; Isaiah 5:1–7). But here it isn't the vine that is unproductive, but the caretakers. Jesus asks what the landowner should do to the tenants. The religious leaders respond, unaware that they are condemning themselves: "He will put those wretched men to a wretched death" (Matthew 21: 41). The chief priests and Pharisees recognize that Jesus is addressing them and want to arrest him (Matthew 21:45–46).

History

✥ Reflecting on the Word

The parable in today's Gospel is a little odd. The actions of the tenants don't really make a whole lot of sense. Do they really think that if they kill the son of the vineyard's owner they will become heirs to the property in his place? This is not the way that inheritance usually works. The tenants do not seem to be very realistic about the owner's response to their actions and may even be suffering some form of madness.

And yet, there is something familiar about the senseless actions of the tenants. Do not we humans sometimes act as if by rejecting God we will inherit the world? Do we not reject the message of Jesus in the insane hope of being able to live by our own rules? The idea that a violent rejection of God can turn us from servants into masters is perhaps more common than we might think.

But the fact remains that we are tenants in a vineyard that belongs to God. All of the fruit that we bear in this life belongs to God, because ultimately it comes from God, who is the source of all good gifts. If we, as God's servants, give up the delusion of being our own masters and hold fast to what is true and honorable, lovely and gracious, then we will discover that God is not an angry taskmaster calling us to account, but the God of peace who, Paul tells us in the second reading, will guard our hearts and minds in Christ Jesus.

- How have I tried to live as my own master, rather than as one who lives to serve God?
- Do I see God as a God of peace who guards me, or as a God who is constantly making demands on me?

❖ *Responding to the Word*

O God, all that we are and all that we have comes from you. Help us to serve you in love, and so inherit the reward of being your friends, through Christ our Lord.

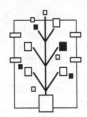

October 12, 2014

TWENTY-EIGHTH SUNDAY IN ORDINARY TIME

Today's Focus: A Filling Feast

There's a good deal of food talk in today's readings. In Israel, feasting was part of the agrarian cycle of planting, tending, and harvesting, keeping the people ever mindful of their dependence upon God. We still rely on God for our earthly and heavenly feasts.

FIRST READING
Isaiah 25:6–10a

On this mountain the LORD of hosts
    will provide for all peoples
a feast of rich food and choice wines,
    juicy, rich food and pure, choice wines.
On this mountain he will destroy
    the veil that veils all peoples,
the web that is woven over all nations;
    he will destroy death forever.
The Lord GOD will wipe away
    the tears from every face;
the reproach of his people he will remove
    from the whole earth; for the LORD has spoken.
    On that day it will be said:
"Behold our God, to whom we looked to save us!
    This is the LORD for whom we looked;
    let us rejoice and be glad that he has saved us!"
For the hand of the LORD will rest on this mountain.

PSALM RESPONSE
Psalm 23:6cd

I shall live in the house of the Lord all the days of my life.

SECOND READING
Philippians 4:12–14, 19–20

Brothers and sisters: I know how to live in humble circumstances; I know also how to live with abundance. In every circumstance and in all things I have learned the secret of being well fed and of going hungry, of living in abundance and of being in need. I can do all things in him who strengthens me. Still, it was kind of you to share in my distress.

My God will fully supply whatever you need, in accord with his glorious riches in Christ Jesus. To our God and Father, glory forever and ever. Amen.

GOSPEL
Matthew 22:1–14 or 22:1–10

Jesus again in reply spoke to the chief priests and elders of the people in parables, saying, "The kingdom of heaven may be likened to a king who gave a wedding feast for his son. He dispatched his servants to summon the invited guests to the feast, but they refused to come. A second time he sent other servants, saying, 'Tell those invited: "Behold, I have prepared my banquet, my calves and fattened cattle are killed, and everything is ready; come to the feast." ' Some ignored the invitation and went away, one to his farm, another to his business. The rest laid hold of his servants, mistreated them, and killed them. The king was enraged and sent his troops, destroyed those murderers, and burned their city. Then he said to his servants, 'The feast is ready, but those who were invited were not worthy to come. Go out, therefore, into the main roads and invite to the feast whomever you find.' The servants went out into the streets and gathered all they found, bad and good alike, and the hall was filled with guests. [But when the king came in to meet the guests, he saw a man there not dressed in a wedding garment. The king said to him, 'My friend, how is it that you came in here without a wedding garment?' But he was reduced to silence. Then the king said to his attendants, 'Bind his hands and feet, and cast him into the darkness outside, where there will be wailing and grinding of teeth.' Many are invited, but few are chosen."]

❖ *Understanding the Word*

The reading from Isaiah comes from a section of First Isaiah known as the Apocalypse of Isaiah (24–27), though these chapters lack some of the traits one would expect in a true apocalyptic piece. It does envision a future time when a city of chaos is destroyed by God, and the mountain (presumably Zion, Jerusalem's mountain) will be the site of God's salvific action. To celebrate God's victory over the tyrants, a feast of rich food and pure, choice wines (v. 6) will be provided not only for Israel, but for all people. On this mountain of Jerusalem, God will destroy death, and the reproach of God's people will be removed (v. 8). The prophet envisions a future of hope, filled with sumptuous food and drink, the absence of death, and the rejuvenation of God's people. Though found within the work of Isaiah of Jerusalem (Chapters 1–39), the Apocalypse likely comes from the oracles of a later Isaianic prophet, who was writing during the Exile.

The second reading comes from the conclusion of Paul's Letter to the Philippians, in which Paul is thanking the community for their financial support. As he stated in 1 Corinthians 9, Paul has the right to financial support as an apostle, but he doesn't take it. However, when it is freely offered, he is grateful.

The Gospel introduces a scene similar to Isaiah's banquet, only here the invited guests refuse to attend. Within the setting of Matthew's Gospel, this is the third parable Jesus has told to the religious leadership who question his authority. Matthew's allegorical aspects seem clear. Those invited reflect the people of Israel. Some simply return to their way of life (farm and business, v. 5), but others attack the servants and kill them (v. 6). Since the chosen guests refused to attend, others are brought into the banquet. Understood within the historical context of Matthew's community, these are the Jewish Christians who believed that Jesus was the Messiah. However, entrance into the banquet is not without restrictions. One must be properly attired. As Jesus announced, repentance is required in order to enter the kingdom of heaven (Matthew 4:17). Just because one believes that Jesus is the Messiah does not guarantee a place at the table.

✤ Reflecting on the Word

Jesus' parable in today's Gospel draws into itself the imagery of the great feast at the end of time that God, as the first reading tells us, "will provide for all peoples," a feast of "rich food and choice wines, juicy, rich food and pure, choice wines." At this feast, "The Lord GOD will wipe away the tears from every face." It is this feast that fulfills the promise in the second reading that "God will fully supply whatever you need, in accord with his glorious riches in Christ Jesus." The joy of a feast becomes an image of the joyous event of the union of our life with God's life, when God will consummate human history, wipe away all its tears, and fill every cup to overflowing.

In the Eucharist that we celebrate every Sunday we share already in that feast. We come, week after week, to have our lives joined to the life of God, to have our tears wiped away, to have our cups filled to overflowing. We have been called, like the guests in the parable, to the wedding supper of the Lamb who has taken away our sins. But the parable is also a warning not to take lightly so great a call. Though the actions of the king in the parable seem extreme, burning down the cities of those who reject the invitation and throwing out those who arrive underdressed, the very exaggeration of those actions drives home the point that this is a call to the feast of life itself; to decline that invitation is to reject the gift of life that is offered. The invitation ought neither be ignored nor accepted lightly; we are to adorn our souls with the wedding garment of love, a garment that, as St. Gregory the Great put it, is woven of two strands of wool: love of God and love of neighbor (Homily 37).

How we respond to God's invitation is a matter of life and death, and our weekly presence at the wedding feast of the Lamb is an obligation that we should joyfully fulfill: the obligation to let our lives be joined to God's, to let our tears be wiped away, to let our cup be filled to overflowing.

✤ Consider/Discuss

- How important is it to respond to God's invitation to gather weekly at the banquet of the Eucharist?
- The Church understands the Eucharist to be both a feast and a sacrifice. Is one of these more significant than the other in my own understanding of Eucharist? How might I develop a more complete understanding of the Eucharist?

✤ Responding to the Word

Lord Jesus, you invite us to the banquet of your love. Help us to respond to that invitation with our hearts adorned with love of God and neighbor.

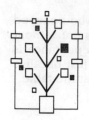

October 19, 2014

TWENTY-NINTH SUNDAY IN ORDINARY TIME

Today's Focus: Religion and Politics

Unlike conventional wisdom, today's readings take on the often tricky relationship between these two topics. God uses a pagan ruler as mashiach (messiah), and Jesus denies a ruler's divinity while remaining a faithful citizen. It can be done!

FIRST READING
Isaiah 45:1, 4–6

Thus says the LORD to his anointed, Cyrus,
　whose right hand I grasp,
subduing nations before him,
　and making kings run in his service,
opening doors before him
　and leaving the gates unbarred:
For the sake of Jacob, my servant,
　of Israel, my chosen one,
I have called you by your name,
　giving you a title, though you knew me not.
I am the LORD and there is no other,
　there is no God besides me.
It is I who arm you, though you know me not,
　so that toward the rising and the setting of the sun
　people may know that there is none besides me.
I am the LORD, there is no other.

PSALM RESPONSE
Psalm 96:7b

Give the Lord glory and honor.

SECOND READING
1 Thessalonians 1:1–5b

Paul, Silvanus, and Timothy to the church of the Thessalonians in God the Father and the Lord Jesus Christ: grace to you and peace. We give thanks to God always for all of you, remembering you in our prayers, unceasingly calling to mind your work of faith and labor of love and endurance in hope of our Lord Jesus Christ, before our God and Father, knowing, brothers and sisters loved by God, how you were chosen. For our gospel did not come to you in word alone, but also in power and in the Holy Spirit and with much conviction.

192

GOSPEL
Matthew
22:15–21

The Pharisees went off and plotted how they might entrap Jesus in speech. They sent their disciples to him, with the Herodians, saying, "Teacher, we know that you are a truthful man and that you teach the way of God in accordance with the truth. And you are not concerned with anyone's opinion, for you do not regard a person's status. Tell us, then, what is your opinion: Is it lawful to pay the census tax to Caesar or not?" Knowing their malice, Jesus said, "Why are you testing me, you hypocrites? Show me the coin that pays the census tax." Then they handed him the Roman coin. He said to them, "Whose image is this and whose inscription?" They replied, "Caesar's." At that he said to them, "Then repay to Caesar what belongs to Caesar and to God what belongs to God."

✤ Understanding the Word

Second Isaiah, the anonymous prophet of the Exile, recognizes the Persian ruler Cyrus as God's servant who becomes Israel's redeemer. The term "anointed"—*mashiach* in the Hebrew—is also translated "Messiah." Ordinarily in Israel, kings (1 Samuel 16:13), prophets (1 Kings 19:16), and priests (Exodus 28:41) were anointed. But Cyrus is given the title, since he acts as an agent of God, though he "knows him not" (v. 4–5). Cyrus is not simply another rising star on the horizon of history; his actions are directed by God for the sake of Jacob and Israel (v. 4).

The First Letter to the Thessalonians is the oldest extant Pauline epistle, written while Paul was in Corinth around 52–53 CE (common era). Addressed to the community in Thessalonica, Paul tries to assuage their fears about the delay of the *parousia* (Jesus' second coming). Paul is joined by Silvanus and Timothy as co-writers. These three had also proclaimed the gospel among the Corinthians (2 Corinthians 1:19). In the thanksgiving section of the letter, which is read today, the three compliment the community for their work of faith, labor of love, and endurance in hope (v. 3). Likely here and in 1 Thessalonians 5:8, we find the earliest mention of these Christian virtues.

Upon Jesus' arrival in the temple area, he had been questioned by the religious authorities, represented by the chief priests and elders (Matthew 21:23). In today's reading, the Pharisees send their disciples and some Herodians to entrap Jesus. The topic is the question of paying taxes to Caesar, a requirement for every man, woman, and adult slave. Pharisees were laymen whose locus of power was the synagogue. They likely opposed paying taxes to a foreign power. Herodians were members of a political party that supported Herod Antipas, a Roman appointee. Where the temple leaders had grilled Jesus about his religious authority, these adversaries question his political orientation. By responding with a theological answer, Jesus avoids choosing sides. The disciples of the Pharisees and the Herodians are duly amazed (v. 22).

The story of Jesus and the Roman coin is sometimes used to argue that Christians should not worry about how their religious duties and their political duties might conflict; one can repay to Caesar the things that are Caesar's without any worry that this might take away from the things that we ought to give to God.

But matters are not really that simple because the division between the secular and the sacred is often a blurry one. The coin that was given to Jesus would likely have had an inscription on it—*divi filius*—that ascribed divinity to Caesar himself. This is why Jesus did not have one on his person: to carry such a coin would have been to be complicit in idolatry; it would have implied that he accepted not just Caesar's political authority but also his claim to be a divine being. In other words, as part and parcel of his political authority, Caesar claimed a status and an allegiance from his subjects that rightly belonged to God alone. So while Jesus commands us to give to political rulers what is their due, the whole context of the story implies that political leaders might expect more from us than they rightfully should, demanding an absolute loyalty that rightly belongs only to God.

The first reading shows us that God can use political rulers, even an unbeliever like the Persian king Cyrus, to fulfill the divine will in the world. But we ought not to presume that such rulers always fulfill God's will, or that the loyalty that they ask of us is something that we automatically give. We are to be discerning about the possible conflicts between our political loyalties and our ultimate loyalty, which is to God.

❖ Consider/Discuss

- Do modern political leaders ever demand things of me that I should rightly give only to God?
- How do I take my political responsibilities seriously while still giving my primary loyalty to God?

❖ Responding to the Word

God of the nations, give us a due respect for earthly rulers, but an even greater respect for the law you have planted in our hearts and revealed most fully in your Son, Jesus.

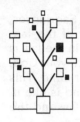

October 26, 2014

THIRTIETH SUNDAY IN ORDINARY TIME

Today's Focus: The Command to Love

Obeying the Ten Commandments gets a lot of notice in current media; less so, the command to love as God in Christ has loved us. That commandment often leads us to live and work for the lowly and marginalized in our world.

FIRST READING
Exodus 22:20–26

Thus says the LORD: "You shall not molest or oppress an alien, for you were once aliens yourselves in the land of Egypt. You shall not wrong any widow or orphan. If ever you wrong them and they cry out to me, I will surely hear their cry. My wrath will flare up, and I will kill you with the sword; then your own wives will be widows, and your children orphans.

"If you lend money to one of your poor neighbors among my people, you shall not act like an extortioner toward him by demanding interest from him. If you take your neighbor's cloak as a pledge, you shall return it to him before sunset; for this cloak of his is the only covering he has for his body. What else has he to sleep in? If he cries out to me, I will hear him; for I am compassionate."

PSALM RESPONSE
Psalm 18:2

I love you, Lord, my strength.

SECOND READING
1 Thessalonians 1:5c–10

Brothers and sisters: You know what sort of people we were among you for your sake. And you became imitators of us and of the Lord, receiving the word in great affliction, with joy from the Holy Spirit, so that you became a model for all the believers in Macedonia and in Achaia. For from you the word of the Lord has sounded forth not only in Macedonia and in Achaia, but in every place your faith in God has gone forth, so that we have no need to say anything. For they themselves openly declare about us what sort of reception we had among you, and how you turned to God from idols to serve the living and true God and to await his Son from heaven, whom he raised from the dead, Jesus, who delivers us from the coming wrath.

GOSPEL
Matthew 22:34–40

When the Pharisees heard that Jesus had silenced the Sadducees, they gathered together, and one of them, a scholar of the law, tested him by asking, "Teacher, which commandment in the law is the greatest?" He said to him, "You shall love the Lord, your God, with all your heart, with all your soul, and with all your mind. This is the greatest and the first commandment. The second is like it: You shall love your neighbor as yourself. The whole law and the prophets depend on these two commandments."

❖ Understanding the Word

Today's first reading comes from the section of the book of Exodus that introduces God's covenant with Israel (Exodus 19–24). Once the people have been purified (Exodus 19), the Ten Commandments are presented (Exodus 20:1–21). A further discussion of individual laws outlines how the people are to live (Exodus 21:22 — 23:33). Finally, the community solemnly assents to the laws of the covenant (Exon 24). Today's passage focuses on the legally helpless—the widow, orphan, alien—and the impoverished. The covenant of God requires that Israel respond with compassion, because God has shown them compassion.

The second reading continues Paul's Letter to the Thessalonians. Paul praises the believers because they have become imitators of Paul and of the Lord, models for those in Macedonia and Achaia. What they imitate and model is their willingness to undergo affliction for the sake of their belief (v. 6). Formerly pagans (v. 9), they now serve the true God, awaiting Jesus' return. Paul's letters reveal some of the personal costs early Christians had to endure for their new faith. Pagan rituals and traditions imbued every aspect of personal and public life. To turn to the living God meant turning one's back on the old ones, and those who worshiped them.

Matthew 21:23 — 22:45 is a series of controversy stories and parables. Jesus is beset by adversaries in the temple area who seek to discredit him and eventually plot his death. Immediately before today's reading, the Sadducees had challenged Jesus about the existence of resurrection from the dead (22:23–33). The Pharisees, who had previously co-opted the Herodians (22:16), now join in support of the Sadducees (22:34). Matthew recounts that despite their own philosophical and religious differences, several groups within Judaism find common ground in their distrust of Jesus. In today's passage, when asked which commandment is the greatest, Jesus replies as would be expected of a faithful Jew, citing the words of Deuteronomy 6:5. He then adds a second, "love your neighbor," from Leviticus 19:18. The combination of these two commandments may have already been recognized in first-century Judaism. Here in the Gospel of Matthew, they demonstrate that despite what his adversaries believe, Jesus is a faithful Jew, confirming what he had said earlier: "Do not think that I have come to abolish the law or the prophets. I have come not to abolish but to fulfill" (5:17).

Today's Gospel points to the centrality of love in our Christian understanding of God and of how we are to live in God's presence. Indeed, St. Thomas Aquinas wrote, "Nothing shows the truth of the gospel better than the love of those who believe" (*Commentary on John* 17.5). It is love that has the power to convince others of the truth of the message that Christians bear. But love can do this only if it is genuine, since we know that there are many counterfeit forms of love abroad in our world. So how do we know that our love is the kind of love that truly reveals God?

Our first reading gives one clue. Godly love is always deeply concerned about the weak, the defenseless, the marginalized—those whom the Old Testament refers to as the *anawim* or "little ones." These include the foreigner living among us, the widow, the orphan, and the poor, all of whom are the object of God's passionate concern. So if our love is to be a godly love, it must be a love that acts in such a way that the needs of these little ones are of paramount importance.

Our second reading gives another clue. Paul speaks of how the Thessalonians "became imitators of us and of the Lord" both in their affliction and in their joy, and so "became a model for all the believers." In other words, love that is genuine takes the suffering, joyful love of Christ and the saints as its model. Godly love not only cares for the vulnerable, but does so both at personal cost and joyfully.

The task of discerning the path of genuine love is challenging, but in teaching us the importance of defending the defenseless and in providing us models of love to imitate, God helps us to stay on that path.

❖ Consider/Discuss

- Who are the "little ones" in today's society? Who should be the special object of my concern?
- Who in my life has served as a model of genuine love that I have sought to imitate?

❖ Responding to the Word

God of love, help us to search out the path that truly leads to you by following the examples of love that you have given to us, above all the example of your Son, our Lord, Jesus.

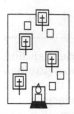

November 2, 2014

THE COMMEMORATION OF ALL THE FAITHFUL DEPARTED (ALL SOULS)

Today's Focus: An Unusual Friend

We believe that God created all things, even though all things must die. Into this pattern we bring our belief in God's triumph over death in the resurrection of Christ. For those who follow Christ, death can become a friend, not a foe.

FIRST READING
Isaiah 25:6–9

On this mountain the LORD of hosts
　will provide for all peoples.
On this mountain he will destroy
　the veil that veils all peoples,
　the web that is woven over all nations;
　he will destroy death forever.
The Lord GOD will wipe away
　the tears from every face;
　the reproach of his people he will remove
　from the whole earth; for the LORD has spoken.
　On that day it will be said:
"Behold our God, to whom we looked to save us!
　This is the LORD for whom we looked;
　let us rejoice and be glad that he has saved us!"

PSALM RESPONSE
Psalm 23:1

The Lord is my shepherd; there is nothing I shall want.

SECOND READING
1 Thessalonians 4:13–18

We do not want you to be unaware, brothers and sisters, about those who have fallen asleep, so that you may not grieve like the rest, who have no hope. For if we believe that Jesus died and rose, so too will God, through Jesus, bring with him those who have fallen asleep. Indeed, we tell you this, on the word of the Lord, that we who are alive, who are left until the coming of the Lord, will surely not precede those who have fallen asleep. For the Lord himself, with a word of command, with the voice of an archangel and with the trumpet of God, will come down from heaven, and the dead in Christ will rise first. Then we who are alive, who are left, will be caught up together with them in the clouds to meet the Lord in the air. Thus we shall always be with the Lord. Therefore, console one another with these words.

GOSPEL
Matthew 5:1–12

When Jesus saw the crowds, he went up the mountain, and after he had sat down, his disciples came to him. He began to teach them, saying:
　"Blessed are the poor in spirit,
　　for theirs is the kingdom of heaven.

Blessed are they who mourn,
  for they will be comforted.
Blessed are the meek,
  for they will inherit the land.
Blessed are they who hunger and thirst for righteousness,
  for they will be satisfied.
Blessed are the merciful,
  for they will be shown mercy.
Blessed are the clean of heart,
  for they will see God.
Blessed are the peacemakers,
  for they will be called children of God.
Blessed are they who are persecuted for the sake of
  righteousness,
  for theirs is the kingdom of heaven.
Blessed are you when they insult you and persecute you and utter
every kind of evil against you falsely because of me. Rejoice and
be glad, for your reward will be great in heaven."

❖ Understanding the Word

The prophet Isaiah paints a picture of God's triumph over the ultimate enemy, death. On the mountain of the Lord (Zion in the city of Jerusalem), God will provide not only for the Chosen People but for all people. God is portrayed as a hero vanquishing death, but also as a compassionate parent, wiping away tears. This image of salvation and solace provided comfort and encouragement to the exiles who awaited their deliverance.

The second reading from Paul's Letter to the Thessalonians addresses a concern that we continue to hold today. What happens to our beloved dead? Paul had preached that Jesus' resurrection from the dead signaled the beginning of God's reign. At any moment Jesus was to return and welcome all believers into this kingdom. As time passed, Jesus had not yet returned, many faithful died, and believers began to doubt their own commitment. Paul answers their worries with a description of those final moments when all will be raised in Christ.

The Beatitudes from Matthew's Gospel remind believers that the reign of God is yet to be fully realized. With the exception of the poor in spirit, the others who are blessed will receive their reward in the future. Those who mourn will be comforted. Those who are meek will inherit the land. The reign of God that Jesus preached was initiated by his death and resurrection. Its completion awaits the *parousia*, Jesus' return. Nonetheless, believers are to rejoice and be glad, trusting that their reward awaits them. Jesus and his followers and subsequently the early Christians believed in an apocalyptic eschatology—that this current world of injustice and impiety would be replaced by God's justice and holiness. Jesus' resurrection from the dead stood as a proof of the dawning of this new age. The Beatitudes will be fulfilled when all believers are resurrected from the dead and God's reign will be complete

On the one hand, death seems to be a natural part of life. Every living organism that we know of undergoes death. It seems to be built into biological life. At the same time, we human beings rebel against death as something profoundly unnatural; we seem to have a deep-seated sense that death violates a profound truth about the meaning of our existence. It is a power that oppresses us; the first reading calls it "the veil that veils all peoples." And yet we also believe that it is for us a necessary part of the journey toward eternal life; the late Cardinal Joseph Bernardin of Chicago, facing terminal cancer, spoke of the need to see death as a "friend."

Perhaps the key to reconciling all our conflicting feelings regarding death is our faith that God and God's love are stronger than death. According to St. Paul in the second reading, God will raise the dead in the same way that God created everything from nothing: "with a word of command." It is our faith that the God who in the Gospel reading promises a reward that is great in heaven is powerful enough to bring that about.

And yet, despite our faith, we still mourn those who have died. Perhaps this is only natural, since they have passed from our sight and we no longer relate to them as we once did. In the Gospel reading, Jesus does not tell mourners to stop mourning immediately; rather, he promises that they shall one day be comforted. Yet while we mourn, we do not mourn as those without hope. On this day we celebrate the fact that we are still united with the dead within the embrace of God's love.

❖   Consider/Discuss

- When has death seemed like an enemy to me? When has it seemed like a friend?
- Does my faith give me a sense of connection with my loved ones who have died?

❖   Responding to the Word

God of life, all peoples are in your hands. Hold gently those who have died, and bring them to the perfection of your kingdom, in Jesus name.

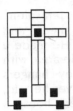

November 9, 2014

DEDICATION OF THE LATERAN BASILICA IN ROME

Today's Focus: No Place Like Home

We celebrate the feast of our "mother church" today. It is a day to recall that we are the living stones of which the Church is built; that we are temples of the Spirit; that our zeal for God's dwelling among us must consume us!

FIRST READING
Ezekiel 47:1–2, 8–9, 12

The angel brought me back to the entrance of the temple, and I saw water flowing out from beneath the threshold of the temple toward the east, for the façade of the temple was toward the east; the water flowed down from the southern side of the temple, south of the altar. He led me outside by the north gate, and around to the outer gate facing the east, where I saw water trickling from the southern side. He said to me, "This water flows into the eastern district down upon the Arabah, and empties into the sea, the salt waters, which it makes fresh. Wherever the river flows, every sort of living creature that can multiply shall live, and there shall be abundant fish, for wherever this water comes the sea shall be made fresh. Along both banks of the river, fruit trees of every kind shall grow; their leaves shall not fade, nor their fruit fail. Every month they shall bear fresh fruit, for they shall be watered by the flow from the sanctuary. Their fruit shall serve for food, and their leaves for medicine."

PSALM RESPONSE
Psalm 46:5

The waters of the river gladen the city of God, the holy dwelling of the Most High.

SECOND READING
1 Corinthians 3:9c–11, 16–17

Brothers and sisters: You are God's building. According to the grace of God given to me, like a wise master builder I laid a foundation, and another is building upon it. But each one must be careful how he builds upon it, for no one can lay a foundation other than the one that is there, namely, Jesus Christ.

Do you not know that you are the temple of God, and that the Spirit of God dwells in you? If anyone destroys God's temple, God will destroy that person; for the temple of God, which you are, is holy.

GOSPEL
John 2:13–22
Since the Passover of the Jews was near, Jesus went up to Jerusalem. He found in the temple area those who sold oxen, sheep, and doves, as well as the money changers seated there. He made a whip out of cords and drove them all out of the temple area, with the sheep and oxen, and spilled the coins of the money changers and overturned their tables, and to those who sold doves he said, "Take these out of here, and stop making my Father's house a marketplace." His disciples recalled the words of Scripture, *Zeal for your house will consume me*. At this the Jews answered and said to him, "What sign can you show us for doing this?" Jesus answered and said to them, "Destroy this temple and in three days I will raise it up." The Jews said, "This temple has been under construction for forty-six years, and you will raise it up in three days?" But he was speaking about the temple of his body. Therefore, when he was raised from the dead, his disciples remembered that he had said this, and they came to believe the Scripture and the word Jesus had spoken.

✛ Understanding the Word

In exile in Babylon, the prophet Ezekiel is given a vision of hope. In an earlier vision, he had witnessed God's presence departing the temple in Jerusalem (10:18). In Chapters 40–48, Ezekiel describes a new temple, built in a new city. The city is named "The LORD is there" (48:35). In today's passage, Ezekiel witnesses a life-giving river flowing out of the threshold of the temple toward the arid east. As the river flows, it brings life—freshening the salt waters of the Dead Sea, and causing living creatures to multiply and thrive. Fruit trees blossom and bear fruit; their leaves will be used for medicine. Ezekiel's vision shows the new Israel as a source of life for others. Ezekiel's prophecies, like the river he witnessed, brought life to a people still in exile.

Paul's Letter to the Corinthians picks up a familiar image and transforms it. Familiar with the temples and public buildings of the city, Paul explains to the Corinthian believers that they too are edifices, built upon the foundation of Jesus Christ. They are temples because the Spirit of God dwells within them. The former pagan Corinthians would undoubtedly think of the myriad temples found in their cities, while the Jewish believers would have in mind the temple in Jerusalem. Paul often used common metaphors (feeding babies, 1 Corinthians 3:2; athletic races and boxing, 1 Corinthians 9:26) to explain faith in Christ.

Unlike the Synoptic Gospels (Matthew, Mark, and Luke), John places the incident in the temple at the beginning of Jesus' public ministry. Jesus had just demonstrated his first sign—the changing of water into wine at Cana. He now travels to Jerusalem for the Passover. In John, seven signs demonstrate to believers who Jesus is. In today's reading, the Jewish leaders ask him what sign he can show for his actions. "Destroy this temple and in three days I will raise it up." The Christian believers would recognize in this statement Jesus' resurrection from the dead, but the Jewish leaders understood the statement literally and heard this as a threat against the temple.

The Basilica of St. John Lateran was given to the church by the Emperor Constantine shortly after he legalized Christianity in the early fourth century. It was dedicated as a place of Christian worship on November 9, 324 CE. It, and not St. Peter's Basilica, as many people think, is the cathedral of the city of Rome and thus the home church of the bishop of Rome—that is, the pope.

It might seem strange to celebrate the anniversary of the dedication of some-body else's church building. But this feast reminds us that our communion with the Church of Rome and her bishop, the pope, is one of the things that unites us in the Catholic Church. In the baptistery of the church of St. John Lateran, where the Christians of Rome have been baptized since the fourth century, there is an ancient inscription that reads: "There is no barrier between those who are reborn and made one by the one font, the one Spirit, and the one faith. . ." The Church asks us to join in this celebration because those who have worshiped at St. John Lateran, from the Emperor Constantine in the fourth century to the humblest Roman worker worshiping there on this day, are our brothers and sisters in the Holy Spirit.

This feast reminds us that part of our faith is that the Church is the temple in which God's Spirit dwells. The celebration of this feast is a challenge to love our fellow Catholics as those who, along with us, are the stones that are being built into that living temple. The stones of this temple are bound together by a love that we live not just inwardly, but also in the outward forms — church buildings, institutions, ecclesiastical offices — that make visible our bonds of unity. It is this unity that we are called to celebrate this day.

✥   *Consider/Discuss*

- When I hear the word "church," do I think first of a building or of a community of people?
- Is there a religious structure that has been particularly significant in my life?

✥   *Responding to the Word*

Lord Jesus, your body is a temple built with living stones. Make your Church a faithful witness to your love in the world by being a worthy dwelling place for your Spirit.

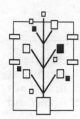

November 16, 2014

THIRTY-THIRD SUNDAY IN ORDINARY TIME

Today's Focus: The Talent Show

Our gifts and talents have been bestowed on us by God; as stewards of those gifts, we show God's love and life to the world. As we watch and wait for Christ's return in glory, we should be prudent stewards of what God has given.

FIRST READING
Proverbs 31:10–13, 19–20, 30–31

When one finds a worthy wife,
    her value is far beyond pearls.
Her husband, entrusting his heart to her,
    has an unfailing prize.
She brings him good, and not evil,
    all the days of her life.
She obtains wool and flax
    and works with loving hands.
She puts her hands to the distaff,
    and her fingers ply the spindle.
She reaches out her hands to the poor,
    and extends her arms to the needy.
Charm is deceptive and beauty fleeting;
    the woman who fears the LORD is to be praised.
Give her a reward for her labors,
    and let her works praise her at the city gates.

PSALM RESPONSE
Psalm 128:1a

Blessed are those who fear the Lord.

SECOND READING
1 Thessalonians 5:1–6

Concerning times and seasons, brothers and sisters, you have no need for anything to be written to you. For you yourselves know very well that the day of the Lord will come like a thief at night. When people are saying, "Peace and security," then sudden disaster comes upon them, like labor pains upon a pregnant woman, and they will not escape.

But you, brothers and sisters, are not in darkness, for that day to overtake you like a thief. For all of you are children of the light and children of the day. We are not of the night or of darkness. Therefore, let us not sleep as the rest do, but let us stay alert and sober.

GOSPEL
*Matthew
25:14–30
or 25:14–15,
19–21*

Jesus told his disciples this parable: "A man going on a journey called in his servants and entrusted his possessions to them. To one he gave five talents; to another, two; to a third, one—to each according to his ability. Then he went away. [Immediately the one who received five talents went and traded with them, and made another five. Likewise, the one who received two made another two. But the man who received one went off and dug a hole in the ground and buried his master's money.]

After a long time the master of those servants came back and settled accounts with them. The one who had received five talents came forward bringing the additional five. He said, 'Master, you gave me five talents. See, I have made five more.' His master said to him, 'Well done, my good and faithful servant. Since you were faithful in small matters, I will give you great responsibilities. Come, share your master's joy.' [Then the one who had received two talents also came forward and said, 'Master, you gave me two talents. See, I have made two more.' His master said to him, 'Well done, my good and faithful servant. Since you were faithful in small matters, I will give you great responsibilities. Come, share your master's joy.' Then the one who had received the one talent came forward and said, 'Master, I knew you were a demanding person, harvesting where you did not plant and gathering where you did not scatter; so out of fear I went off and buried your talent in the ground. Here it is back.' His master said to him in reply, 'You wicked, lazy servant! So you knew that I harvest where I did not plant and gather where I did not scatter? Should you not then have put my money in the bank so that I could have got it back with interest on my return? Now then! Take the talent from him and give it to the one with ten. For to everyone who has, more will be given and he will grow rich; but from the one who has not, even what he has will be taken away. And throw this useless servant into the darkness outside, where there will be wailing and grinding of teeth.' "]

❖ Understanding the Word

In the first nine chapters of the book of Proverbs, Wisdom is personified as a woman who goes into the streets to invite all to seek her (Proverbs 8:3). Chapters 10–31 contain a compilation of adages and wise sayings thought to guide one to a successful life. The book closes with today's first reading, often titled "the ideal wife" or "the virtuous woman." Where Wisdom is pounding the pavement, seeking adherents, the virtuous woman is found at home, tending to the needs of the household. Though composed within a patriarchal society, this book demonstrates that wisdom and success are available to all, regardless of their gender.

The concern to which Paul responds in his First Letter to the Thessalonians is best understood in light of eschatology, or concern about the end-times. Paul and the early Christians believed that Jesus' return was imminent. That eschatological urgency drove the apostles and preachers to spread the word of repentance far and near. When Jesus returned he would judge the living and the dead and their actions would decide their fate. But a generation of believers was now dying, and Jesus had not returned. The Thessalonians rightly asked Paul "when," to which he responds "when you least expect"— "like a thief in the night." The eschatological urgency leads to an eschatological anxiety that should shape the actions of believers.

The Gospel reading is known as the parable of the talents, in which a householder goes on a journey, entrusting his servants with his property. It shares with the preceding parable of the wise and foolish maidens (Matthew 25:1–13) an eschatological tone. While the householder is absent, the servants are to remain at their tasks, ready for his return. The main focus of this parable is the judgment scene. Two servants invested their talents and were rewarded. The third feared the homeowner and buried his. For his improper behavior, he is punished. Originally a talent was a sum of money. This parable is the source of the English term "talent," which came to refer to one's ability. Like the invited guest at the wedding feast who was not properly attired (Matthew 22:11) and the foolish maidens who failed to bring a surplus of oil, the Christian is expected to stay "sober and alert," ready for Christ's return and prepared for his judgment.

❖ Reflecting on the Word

In keeping with the focus on the Last Judgment that prevails at the end of the Church year, St. Paul reminds us in the second reading that the "day of the Lord"—the day of Christ's return—will come just when we least expect it and are confidently predicting a new era of peace and security. And Matthew's Gospel gives us a parable about a master who returns and expects a good return on the investments made by his servants.

One of the paradoxes of the Christian life is that even though it is only through God's grace that we are saved, God still holds us accountable for our actions. The "talents" that God puts into our hands are to be used by us, and those who make good use of them, like the woman in the first reading, are to be praised. Those who timidly hide their talents, like the servant in the Gospel parable, will lose that which they seek to preserve.

We ought not let the fear of loss keep us from acting boldly for God's cause. It is precisely because God's grace and mercy are the source of our salvation that we can run the risk of using our talents without knowing for sure what the outcome will be. Grace liberates us and enables us to take a chance on living our lives wholly for God, so that when the day of the Lord comes we may welcome it with joy.

- When has my faith led me to take a risk that I would not otherwise have taken?
- If the final judgment of the world were to happen tomorrow, would I be ready? What would I need to change in my life in order to be ready?

❖ *Responding to the Word*

Make us ready, O God, for the coming of your Son, Jesus, so that we might be filled with joy when we behold him face to face.

November 23, 2014

OUR LORD JESUS CHRIST, KING OF THE UNIVERSE

Today's Focus: The Shepherd-King

It has been said that Christians have easily made God more like earthly rulers, and haven't been as comfortable demanding that earthly rulers be more God-like in their mercy, justice, and care for the least of the world.

FIRST READING
Ezekiel 34: 11–12, 15–17

Thus says the Lord GOD: I myself will look after and tend my sheep. As a shepherd tends his flock when he finds himself among his scattered sheep, so will I tend my sheep. I will rescue them from every place where they were scattered when it was cloudy and dark. I myself will pasture my sheep; I myself will give them rest, says the Lord GOD. The lost I will seek out, the strayed I will bring back, the injured I will bind up, the sick I will heal, but the sleek and the strong I will destroy, shepherding them rightly.

As for you, my sheep, says the Lord GOD, I will judge between one sheep and another, between rams and goats.

PSALM RESPONSE
Psalm 23:1

The Lord is my shepherd; there is nothing I shall want.

SECOND READING
1 Corinthians 15:20–26, 28

Brothers and sisters: Christ has been raised from the dead, the firstfruits of those who have fallen asleep. For since death came through man, the resurrection of the dead came also through man. For just as in Adam all die, so too in Christ shall all be brought to life, but each one in proper order: Christ the firstfruits; then, at his coming, those who belong to Christ; then comes the end, when he hands over the kingdom to his God and Father, when he has destroyed every sovereignty and every authority and power. For he must reign until he has put all his enemies under his feet. The last enemy to be destroyed is death. When everything is subjected to him, then the Son himself will also be subjected to the one who subjected everything to him, so that God may be all in all.

GOSPEL
Matthew 25:31–46

Jesus said to his disciples: "When the Son of Man comes in his glory, and all the angels with him, he will sit upon his glorious throne, and all the nations will be assembled before him. And he will separate them one from another, as a shepherd separates the sheep from the goats. He will place the sheep on his right and the goats on his left. Then the king will say to those on his right, 'Come, you who are blessed by my Father. Inherit the kingdom prepared for you from the foundation of the world. For I was hungry and you gave me food, I was thirsty and you gave me drink, a stranger and you welcomed me, naked and you clothed me, ill and you cared for me, in prison and you visited me.' Then the righteous will answer him and say, 'Lord, when did we see you hungry and feed you, or thirsty and give you drink? When did we see you a stranger and welcome you, or naked and clothe you? When did we see you ill or in prison, and visit you?' And the king will say to them in reply, 'Amen, I say to you, whatever you did for one of the least brothers of mine, you did for me.' Then he will say to those on his left, 'Depart from me, you accursed, into the eternal fire prepared for the devil and his angels. For I was hungry and you gave me no food, I was thirsty and you gave me no drink, a stranger and you gave me no welcome, naked and you gave me no clothing, ill and in prison, and you did not care for me.' Then they will answer and say, 'Lord, when did we see you hungry or thirsty or a stranger or naked or ill or in prison, and not minister to your needs?' He will answer them, 'Amen, I say to you, what you did not do for one of these least ones, you did not do for me.' And these will go off to eternal punishment, but the righteous to eternal life."

❖ Understanding the Word

The readings for this Sunday have a strong eschatological emphasis. As the liturgical year comes to a close, we are reminded that we continue to await Jesus' return and the final judgment.

Through the prophet Ezekiel God is portrayed as a shepherd, tending and rescuing the sheep who have scattered. God is frequently presented as the good shepherd (Genesis 48:15; Psalm 23; Jeremiah 31:10; Mark 6:34; John 10:1–18), who intervenes to save his sheep. God must shepherd the people because those who were appointed to the task have failed (Ezekiel 34:1–10). This passage is part of a series of encouragements to the exiles after the fall of Jerusalem (587 BCE).

In the reading from First Corinthians, Paul outlines the process by which Christ's death is salvific for believers. Since death came through one person, so too can one person, namely Christ, bring life. Christ is the firstfruits of the manifestation of God's kingdom. When he returns, he will gather those who belong to him. The end of the evil age will be signaled by the destruction of every power and authority. The final enemy to be defeated will be death.

The last unique parable in the Gospel of Matthew is the story of the sheep and the goats (25:31–46), though some scholars argue that this is more an apocalyptic prediction than a parable. It concludes Jesus' eschatological discourse to his disciples, the final of five teaching blocks in Matthew's Gospel. The parable envisions a mixed herd of sheep and goats, a common sight in the Middle East even today. Since goats required warmth at night and sheep preferred the open air, flocks would be separated in the evening. In the parable, the sheep are given the privileged position on the right of the shepherd, since they had greater value. This story encapsulates early Christian apocalyptic understanding. The Son of Man sits as judge over all the nations, who will be evaluated based on their treatment of the least brothers and sisters of the Lord. Those who cared for the least will receive their reward, while those who didn't will have everlasting punishment. The "least" may refer to the poor in general or to a specific group. More recently scholars have suggested that the term could refer to Christian missionaries who suffered for their preaching of the gospel.

❖❖ Reflecting on the Word

The Church year ends with a celebration of the universal kingship of Jesus. While today kings have for most of us a quaint, folkloric quality, in the ancient world they were a force to be reckoned with. The ideal king was of a powerful defender of his people, a mighty warrior, while a bad king was one who exploited his people for his own gain. Today's readings, however, use the imagery of a shepherd, which runs counter to ancient ideas of both bad kings and good ones. God as our shepherd-king is neither a warrior nor an exploiter, but rather one who guards his flock and seeks out those who are straying.

This image of God as shepherd is in one sense a very tender one. But the first reading reminds us that the shepherd also has the role of judging "between one sheep and another, between rams and goats." The theme of judgment that was prominent in last week's readings carries through to this Sunday. But the story told in the Gospel reading puts that judgment in its proper perspective. The shepherd-king judges on the basis of how closely we have modeled ourselves on God's own way of acting. Have we guarded the members of God's flock and sought out the lost by feeding the hungry and giving drink to the thirsty, welcoming the stranger and clothing the naked? How we conducted ourselves in a way that would identify us as members of God's flock, or have we acted like those bad kings who exploit those put into their care for their own gain?

- Since both kings and shepherds are somewhat alien to our cultural experience, what image would I use to describe God's authority in my life?
- What opportunities do I have to engage in activities like clothing the naked, feeding the hungry and so forth? Have I made good use of those opportunities?

❖ Responding to the Word

Lord Jesus, our shepherd and guide, look over the flock that you have gathered. Protect us from all danger and lead us safely home.

A Dominican of Sinsinawa, Laurie Brink, O.P., Ph.D., is an Associate Professor of New Testament Studies at Catholic Theological Union. She also serves as an associate editor for *The Bible Today*. Sr. Brink has recorded two lecture series (*Acts of the Apostles* and *Philippians*) for Now You Know Media and authored several articles on biblical topics. She is currently researching and writing a book on the biblical foundations of friendship. Having worked as a senior staff member for the Combined Caesarea Expeditions, Brink attempts to integrate archaeological research and biblical exegesis. An example of this commitment is her monograph, *In This Place: Reflections on the Land of the Gospels for the Liturgical Cycle* (Wipf & Stock, 2008), co-authored with Marianne Race, C.S.J.

Frederick Bauerschmidt is Professor of Theology at Loyola University Maryland and, since 2007, a deacon of the Archdiocese of Baltimore, assigned to Corpus Christi Parish. He has a master's degree from Yale Divinity School and a Ph.D. from Duke University. He is the author of numerous articles and book, including *Why the Mystics Matter Now*, *Holy Teaching: Introducing the Summa Theologiae of St. Thomas Aquinas*, and *Thomas Aquinas: Faith, Reason, and Following Christ*. He is also a regular contributor to the blog *Pray Tell* (www.praytellblog.com). He is married with three almost-grown children.

Notes

Notes

216